The Decoration of Houses

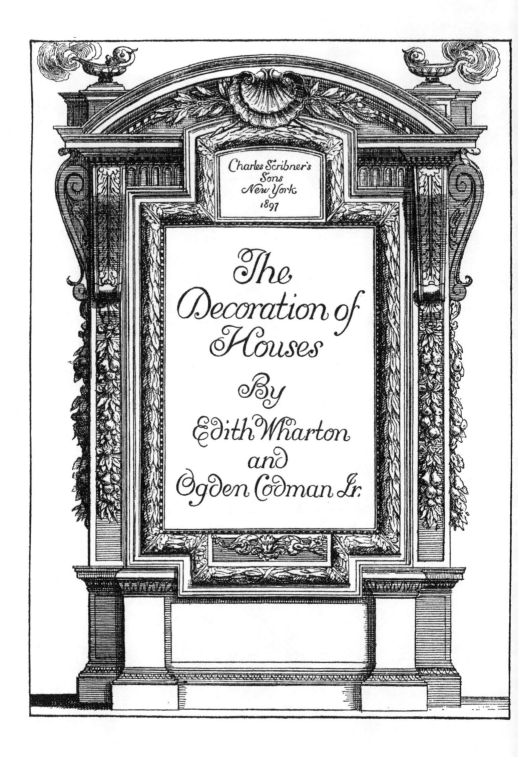

Charles Scribner's
Sons
New York
1897

The
Decoration of
Houses

By

Edith Wharton
and
Ogden Codman Jr.

THE
DECORATION
of HOUSES

Edith Wharton
AND Ogden Codman Jr.

Edited and with an Introduction by
Emily J. Orlando

Additional notes and translations from the French by
Joel D. Goldfield

Syracuse University Press

Copyright © 2024 by Syracuse University Press
Syracuse, New York 13244-5290

All Rights Reserved

First Edition 2024

24 25 26 27 28 29   6 5 4 3 2 1

∞ The paper used in this publication meets the minimum requirements
of the American National Standard for Information Sciences—Permanence
of Paper for Printed Library Materials, ANSI Z39.48-1992.

For a listing of books published and distributed by Syracuse University Press,
visit https://press.syr.edu.

ISBN: 9780815604730 (paperback)
9780815657224 (e-book)

Library of Congress Cataloging-in-Publication Data

Names: Wharton, Edith, 1862-1937, author. | Orlando, Emily J. (Emily Josephine), 1969–
editor, writer of introduction. | Codman, Ogden, author.
Title: The decoration of houses / Edith Wharton and Ogden Codman, Jr. ;
edited and with an introduction by Emily J. Orlando ; additional notes
and translations from the French by Joel Goldfield.
Description: First edition. | Syracuse, New York : Syracuse University Press, 2024. |
Includes bibliographical references and index.
Identifiers: LCCN 2024012239 (print) | LCCN 2024012240 (ebook) |
ISBN 9780815604730 (paperback) | ISBN 9780815657224 (ebook)
Subjects: LCSH: Interior decoration. | BISAC: ARCHITECTURE / History /
Modern (late 19th Century to 1945) | HOUSE & HOME / Decorating & Furnishings
Classification: LCC NK2110 .W5 2024 (print) | LCC NK2110 (ebook) |
DDC 747—dc23/eng/20240719
LC record available at https://lccn.loc.gov/2024012239
LC ebook record available at https://lccn.loc.gov/2024012240

Manufactured in the United States of America

Une forme doit être belle en elle-méme et on
ne doit jamais compter sur le décor appliqué pour
en sauver les imperfections.[1]
       —Henri Mayeux,
         La Composition Décorative

---

1. "A shape must be beautiful in itself, and we must never rely on decoration to correct imperfections." A guiding principle for *The Decoration of Houses*. Henri Mayeux (1845–1929), a French architect, published *La Composition Décorative*, a manual of decorative composition comprised mostly of engravings, in 1885 (Mayeux 1888).

Contents

Illustrations

Plates

Acknowledgments

It is my pleasure to thank the many authors, architects, and advisors who gave their time and support to the construction of this new edition of *The Decoration of Houses*. I must first thank Edith Wharton and Ogden Codman Jr. for collaborating on a masterpiece that has stood the test of time. I am grateful to Carol Singley, Donna Campbell, and Frederick Wegener for suggesting I work on this book and for detailed feedback on my earliest writings on it. I owe a great debt of thanks to the Humanities Institute (HI) of the College of Arts and Sciences at Fairfield University for meaningfully supporting this project from its beginnings. My HI colleagues Ron Davidson, Sara Brill, Shannon Kelley, Kris Sealey, Maryann Carolan, and Patricia Behre generously lent their kind eyes and ears in support of this volume. Superstar English majors Angela Sammarone, Elizabeth (Ellie) Conklin, Colleen Vann, Katherine (Kerry) Kircher, Lillian (Lily) Snyder, and most recently Lauren Behrens offered inspired research and eagle-eyed editorial assistance. The book would not have come together without their help.

I must especially thank Dr. Joel D. Goldfield for his expert assistance with the translations from French and for his precision, kindness, good cheer, and collegiality.

For sustaining and inspiring my work, I thank the many friends that Edith Wharton has brought into my life. Special mention must be made of my generous colleagues in the Edith Wharton Society, especially Dale Bauer, Rita Bode, Shannon Brennan, Donna Campbell, Melanie Dawson, Myrto Drizou, Johanna X. K. Garvey, Meredith Goldsmith, Irene Goldman-Price, Jennifer Haytock, Katherine Joslin,

Jill Kress Karn, Sharon Kim, Paul Ohler, Julie Olin-Ammentorp, Laura Rattray, Elaine Showalter, Susan Tomlinson, Gary Totten, and Shafquat Towheed. Very special thanks for brilliant feedback on the introduction are due to Jaime Osterman Alves, Paul Ohler, Julie Olin-Ammentorp, Nels Pearson, Laura Rattray, and Gary Totten. For impeccable editorial assistance in the preparation of the manuscript, including the bibliography, I must thank Lauren Behrens. Thanks are also due to Peggy Solic, Laura K. Fish, Jessica LeTourneur Bax, and the two anonymous external reviewers for their excellent suggestions and unwavering support; the edition is a thousand times better for their help.

For kind assistance with images and archives pertaining to Edith Wharton and Ogden Codman Jr., I must also thank the staff at Yale University's Beinecke Library; Indiana University's Lilly Library; Lorna Condon, senior curator of the Historic New England Library and Archives; Nick Hudson, Anne Schuyler, and Susan Wissler at The Mount; and the Watkins-Loomis Agency, which oversees the estate of Edith Wharton.

As this is a book about homes, it is relevant to mention that I can't imagine one better than Fairfield University. At every turn I meet with colleagues whose teaching, research, and creative work inspires my own. The university has supported me with sabbatical leaves, research grants, and, more recently, the 2022 Senior Summer Research Fellowship. I owe an extraordinary debt of thanks to the family of Cathy E. Minehan and the late E. Gerald Corrigan, Fairfield University class of 1963, for the Endowed Chair in the Humanities and Social Sciences, which it has been my honor to hold since the fall of 2018. Since my arrival in 2007, the university has provided a community of kindred spirits in the shape of faculty, staff, administration, and students that has made every part of me better and happier for being here. I am especially grateful to Provost Christine Siegel and my colleagues in the Provost Office and Dean Richard Greenwald and the Office of the Dean of the College of Arts and Sciences.

Thanks also are due to my sister Lisa Orlando for unswerving love and support and particularly for lending me Shari Benstock's biography of Edith Wharton the year I started graduate school. I am exceedingly grateful to Julie Gillis for the blessing of her friendship and wise counsel.

Edith Wharton, a lifelong believer that canines complete a home, would understand my debt of thanks to Levi, Molly, and Carlo for dogged loyalty and good cheer.

This annotated edition of *The Decoration of Houses* is lovingly dedicated to a number of humans who have helped make possible what could easily have been thought impossible: my parents Anita Marie Orlando (1927–2014) and Frank Paul Orlando (1925–2003), the Vesper George–schooled artist and interior designer and the Harvard-trained "Boston architect," who taught me to exhaust the possibilities of my living spaces, who took me to museums when I was a girl, and who would've appreciated Wharton and Codman's commitment to proportion and symmetry in architectural design and nodded in agreement at their claim that "to teach a child to appreciate any form of beauty is to develop his intelligence, and thereby to enlarge his capacity for wholesome enjoyment"; to Professors Denise T. Askin, Danielle Blais, and Gary Bouchard at Saint Anselm College, whose models of personal and professional excellence continue to inspire; to Marilee Lindemann, who has invigorated and championed my work on Wharton from the start, to Robert S. (Bob) Levine, career-long adviser and generous friend, and to all University of Maryland and Fairfield University mentors and friends who shaped me personally and professionally; lastly, to my beloved husband Nels Pearson, with whom it has been the greatest pleasure of my life to decorate a happy house and enjoy numerous pilgrimages to the homes that Edith made.

—Emily J. Orlando

"That Rare Harmony of Feeling"

An Introduction to The Decoration of Houses
by Edith Wharton and Ogden Codman Jr.

EMILY J. ORLANDO

Everything about her seemed to contribute to that rare harmony
of feeling which levied a tax on every sense. The large coolness
of the room, its fine traditional air of spacious living. . . . ; the
very scent of the late violets in a glass on the writing-table; the
rosy-mauve masses of hydrangea in tubs along the terrace; the
fall, now and then, of a leaf through the still air—all, somehow,
were mingled in the suffusion of well-being . . .
> —Edith Wharton, *Sanctuary*

To a torn heart uncomforted by human nearness a room may
open almost human arms, and the being to whom no four
walls mean more than any others, is, at such hours, expatriate
everywhere.
> —Edith Wharton, *The House of Mirth*

We workers among the refugees are trying, first and foremost, to
help a homesick people . . . The present hope of France and Belgium
is in its children . . . The results have been better than we could
have hoped; and those who saw the arrival of the piteous waifs a
few months ago would scarcely recognize them in the round and
rosy children playing in the gardens of our Houses.
> —Edith Wharton, Preface to *The Book
> of the Homeless (Le Livre des Sans-Foyer)*

The opening moments of Edith Wharton's 1913 novel *The Custom of the Country* engage two themes central to the writer's life and work: the effects of spatial design on the human experience and the quest to find and make one's home. Wharton depicts the newly moneyed, socially tone-deaf Undine Spragg of Apex—whose initials flag her as decidedly American—lounging in the Stentorian, a New York hotel named, evidently, for its loud, raucous guests. The "highly-varnished" Spragg rooms feature "heavy gilt armchairs," gaudy bric-à-brac, and "salmon-pink" walls on which hang portraits of Marie-Antoinette and the princesse de Lamballe—aristocrats whose excesses, centuries earlier, ushered them to the guillotine (Wharton 2006, 3). The overdone décor of the Spragg rooms echoes the "wilderness of pink damask" of the nouveau riche, hotel-leasing Norma Hatch of Wharton's 1905 narrative, *The House of Mirth* (Wharton 2018, 238). It is particularly the "invading," indiscriminate class depicted in her New York fiction that Wharton sought to enlighten with her first book of prose, *The Decoration of Houses* (1897) (Wharton 2006, 45), the design treatise that hoped to remedy "the general decline of taste which marked the middle of the [nineteenth] century" (Wharton and Codman 1897, 82). The Spraggs, the Hatches, and the Wellington Brys, who host a series of tableaux vivants to attract the right set to their home, represent the "new people" described at the start of Wharton's Pulitzer Prize–winning novel *The Age of Innocence* (1920), those for whom "conspicuousness passed for distinction and the society column had become the roll of fame" (Wharton 2018, 186). Like Undine Spragg, Edith Wharton understood that "the future belonged to the showy and the promiscuous" (Wharton 2006, 117). Theirs is the "gilded age of decoration" (Wharton and Codman 1897, 196) indicted in *The Decoration of Houses*, which, in this century, has been called "the most important decorating book ever written" and the "pioneering guide" to which "[a]ll modern design books owe their existence" (Jayne 2018, 7; Owens 2013).[1]

---

1. For an overview of the book's influence on both sides of the Atlantic, see Bayley 1997, xxi; Coles 1997, xxiii–xxiv; Metcalf 1988, ix; Wilson 1988, 157–58; Gere 1989, 333.

1. Publicity photograph by Joseph Gaylord Gessford of Edith Wharton for Scribner's, at her desk at The Mount, 1905. Courtesy of Princeton University Firestone Library and The Mount.

The force behind this highly influential book, Edith Newbold Jones Wharton (1862–1937), was one of the most popular, critically acclaimed, and handsomely paid American writers of her time. Wharton was the first woman awarded the Pulitzer Prize for fiction, an honorary doctorate from Yale University, and full membership in the American Academy of Arts and Letters. In 1920, the year she published her prizewinning *The Age of Innocence* on the heels of a well-received travel volume on Morocco, the *New York Times* hailed her "one of the foremost contemporary writers of English prose."[2] With a life bracketed by the American Civil War and the rise of Nazi Germany, Wharton saw astonishing social and cultural change in her native country and abroad. As she concedes in her memoir, *A Backward Glance* (1934), she was "born into a world in which telephones, motors, electric light, central heating (except by hot-air furnaces), X-rays, cinemas, radium, aeroplanes and wireless telegraphy were not only unknown but still mostly unforeseen" (Wharton 1934, 6–7). The happy consequence of having been compelled by her parents' finances to relocate as a child to Europe was to relish, "for the rest of [her] life, that background of beauty and old-established order" (Wharton 1934, 44). Her early nomadic existence, and later exposure to the global disorder brought on by World War I—which she describes, in *French Ways and Their Meaning* (1919), as "a house on fire" (xvii)—informed her lifelong desire to create simpler, less cluttered domestic spaces whose rooms, to borrow an image from *The House of Mirth*, might "open almost human arms" and inspire in their occupants the "rare harmony of feeling" and "suffusion of well-being" described in her novella *Sanctuary*.

The very titles of her books—*Sanctuary*, *The House of Mirth*, *The Book of the Homeless*—affirm the extent to which home-building and writing are inextricably tied for Edith Wharton. This is a writer who regularly described her publications in architectural terms (rather than

---

2. October 1920 review of *In Morocco and The Age of Innocence* (reprinted in Hindley 2018, 17).

as offspring, as some authors have done). In a 1907 letter to Robert Grant, Wharton expresses thanks for a favorable response to her "construction of the book," admits she considers her characters *"building-material,"* and insists that she "conceive[s her] subjects . . . rather more architectonically or dramatically than most women" (Lewis and Lewis 1988, 124). This trope would remain with her. The fund-raising anthology, *The Book of the Homeless (Le Livre des Sans-Foyer)*, which, as an expatriate living in France, she compiled and edited in 1916 in support of a *"homesick people,"* is compared to a house constructed by an impressive roster of "builders," on whose "walls" "delightful pictures hang" (italics hers). Showcasing many of the era's most formidable thinkers and artists (e.g., Joseph Conrad, Thomas Hardy, Henry James, Pierre-August Renoir, John Singer Sargent, W. B. Yeats), the tome emerges as a "gallant piece of architecture" at whose "threshold" she "effaces" herself and invites us to "walk in" (xxiv–xxv).

It is a wonderful synchronicity that Edith Wharton was distinguishing herself, in the 1890s, as a homeowner at the time she was finding her place as a writer. While in 1905 she would become recognized as a consummate master of fiction with the appearance of the critically and commercially successful *The House of Mirth*, *The Decoration of Houses* had already put Wharton on the map as an authority on domestic aesthetics at the turn into the twentieth century. Indeed, the confidence she drew from the success of *The Decoration of Houses* must have helped her design and furnish *The House of Mirth*. In the stretch of time between the two books, Wharton published widely, to great acclaim, across a number of genres.[3] Wharton's establishment of herself as an expert on aesthetics and the art of fiction, with a special command of Italian art and culture, is particularly impressive given

---

3. Between the publication of *The Decoration of Houses* in 1897 and the release of *The House of Mirth* in 1905, Wharton published *The Greater Inclination* (1899), a short story collection; *The Touchstone* (1900), a novella; *Crucial Instances* (1901), a story collection; *The Valley of Decision* (1902), a historical novel; *The Descent of Man and Other Stories* (1904); *Italian Villas and Their Gardens* (1904), a treatise on garden design; and *Italian Backgrounds* (1905), a work of travel writing.

that she did so, as Laura Rattray has shown, in a publishing climate that frequently sought to undermine, silence, second guess, and/or pigeonhole her for being a woman (Rattray 2020, 6). To wit, an advertisement for the British publication of *The Decoration of Houses* sold it as a collaboration between "American Lady Artist" and "Architect" (Codman Family Papers 1906, box 116). The description probably did not surprise Wharton. After all, in *The Age of Innocence*, which returns to the 1870s of her youth, Wharton would write that the women of Newland Archer's family "consider[ed] architecture and painting as subjects for men, and chiefly for learned persons who read Ruskin" (2003, 22). Wharton, who was by any measure a learned person who found in Ruskin a formative influence, would complicate this model with her own career as a professional writer.

A shrewd social critic, a cosmopolitan in every sense, and the foremost American woman of letters of her time, Edith Wharton now rightfully occupies her place as a major figure in the literary canon. As I have recently noted elsewhere, "since the 'dazzling resurrection' in the 1990s of the writer's reputation, Edith Wharton studies has evolved from a largely US-based project grounded in feminist literary criticism to an increasingly global, multidisciplinary enterprise" (Orlando 2023, 1).[4] The past four decades have witnessed a renaissance in Wharton studies such that it is no longer a legitimate practice, if ever it was, to read Wharton as an imitation of her fellow cosmopolitan and dear friend Henry James—a comparison that made her cringe.[5] Writ-

4. As evidence of Wharton's international appeal, the *Edith Wharton Review*, the official journal of the Edith Wharton Society, is now published in Canada, the president of the Wharton Society is based in Norway, and major Wharton scholars can be found in England, France, Italy, Germany, and Scotland.

5. Wharton resisted the comparison, writing, as early as 1904, "The continued cry that I am an echo of Mr. James (whose books of the last ten years I can't read, much as I delight in the man) . . . makes me feel rather hopeless" (Lewis and Lewis 1988, 91). In April 1899, for instance, John Barry suggested in *Literary World* that Wharton was merely replicating James's worst literary faults (Tuttleton, Lauer, and Murray 1992, x). She was even accused, in the August 1899 issue of *Critic*, of plagiarizing James (Tuttleton, Lauer, and Murray 1992, x). Grant Overton summed it

ing at a breathtaking pace, for the forty years following the publication of *The Decoration of Houses*, "Wharton published at least one book almost every year of her life. (She has, altogether, forty-eight titles to her name)" (Lee 2007, 8) and she did so in all major literary genres: fiction (novels; novellas; short stories, including ghost stories), poetry, and drama. Equally proficient in nonfiction, with books and articles on travel, war, literary criticism, art history, interior design, war, and gardens, along with memoir, she chronicled European and American culture and her travel writings took her as far from the New York of her youth as northern Africa. Edith Wharton is more frequently taught, studied, and discussed in print and on social media across the continents than ever before.

The diverse range of contemporary voices declaring Edith Wharton a formative influence or favorite writer suggests the author's lasting appeal beyond the academy, across generations, party lines, and demographics. That roster includes Roxane Gay (*Bad Feminist*), Colm Tóibín (*Brooklyn*), Hernan Diaz (*Trust*), Brandon Taylor (*Real Life*), Ta-Nehisi Coates (*Between the World and Me*), Lisa Lucas (Knopf Doubleday), Peggy Noonan (Pulitzer Prize–winning columnist), Jennifer Egan (Pulitzer Prize–winning novelist), Elif Batuman (*The Idiot*), Claire Messud (*The Emperor's Children*), Ali Benjamin (*The Smash-Up*), Vendela Vida (*We Run the Tides*), Kristin Hannah (*The Four Winds*), Laura Bush (former First Lady of the United States), Tori Amos (singer-songwriter), Lena Dunham (*Girls*), Mindy Kaling (*The Mindy Project*), and the creative minds behind the television series *Sex and the City*, *Gossip Girl*, *Downton Abbey*, and *The Gilded Age* (currently filming season 3). In recent months Wharton has enjoyed coverage not only in the *New Yorker*, the *Atlantic*, the *New York Times*, the *Nation*, and *Vogue*,

---

up nicely in 1923: "Who, after reading the correspondence of Henry James, published since his death, believes any longer that Mrs Wharton ever owed anything to that man's patronage so nicely tinctured with snobbery?" (Overton 1923, 345). And yet the comparison haunted her literary debut in the 1890s and lingered until the late twentieth century. Even the plaque identifying her Paris residence at 53 rue de Varenne presents Wharton in the context of James.

which have long sustained an interest in her, but also the *Paris Review*, the *Los Angeles Review of Books*, the *Wall Street Journal*, the *Guardian*, the *Times Literary Supplement*, the website Jezebel, and *Entertainment Weekly*. For its second virtual book club meeting, which focused on *The Custom of the Country*, the *New York Times T-Magazine* drew over four thousand participants from around the world. As this book goes to print, Apple TV+ (Orlando 2023a),[6] riding the Wharton wave, is streaming what is now the second television adaptation of the writer's final, unfinished novel, *The Buccaneers*. Publishers are producing, at a heightened pace, new editions of the major and lesser known Wharton titles. Put another way, Edith Wharton has secured a permanent home in popular culture as well as in the canon of literature.

Of course, Edith Wharton's upbringing as a member of the New York aristocracy provided an unlikely passport to what she called "the Land of Letters" (1934, 119). She was born Edith Newbold Jones, into the fashionable family associated with the phrase "keeping up with the Joneses," an expression encouraging the acquisitiveness against which *The Decoration of Houses* would preach.[7] One can only "keep up," after all, if one has the finer things the moment they are available for purchase. With a pedigree that ensured access to Mrs. Astor's New York Four Hundred,[8] Edith's vocation, like that of Lily Bart in *The House of Mirth*, who is cultivated to "diffus[e] elegance as a flower sheds

---

6. The same platform that until recently was to host Oscar-winning filmmaker Sofia Coppola's eagerly anticipated adaptation of *The Custom of the Country*.

7. *The Decoration of Houses* discourages "the feminine tendency to want things because other people have them, rather than to have things because they are wanted" (17). While Undine Spragg is a case in point, Wharton's fiction suggests this tendency also manifests in men, as seen in the examples of Simon Rosedale in *The House of Mirth* and Elmer Moffatt in *The Custom of the Country*.

8. "The grandest of Wharton's distant relatives was Caroline Schermerhorn, a first cousin of her father's, who became Mrs. William B. Astor—*the* Mrs. Astor, the queen of New York society, maintaining its moral standards and respectability against the influx of new money, supported by her social disciple and master of ceremonies Ward McAllister, who coined the term 'the Four Hundred' to describe the number of people who could fit into her ballroom" (Lee 2007, 33–34).

perfume" (Wharton 2018, 87), would have been to marry well and serve her husband as a decorative hostess—surely not an intellectual peer committed to the life of the mind. While she made a socially acceptable marriage to the affable, older, and less intellectual Bostonian Teddy Wharton, divorcing after a trying twenty-eight years of marriage, Wharton managed to forge an identity as an accomplished writer and authority on aesthetics. At least three things made this possible. First, her exposure, at a young age, to her father's library, where she immersed herself in the writings of Anna Brownell Jameson, Franz Kugler, Walter Pater, Sir Joshua Reynolds, Joseph Gwilt, John Ruskin, and James Fergusson, whose *History of Architecture* "shed on [her] misty haunting sense of the beauty of old buildings the light of historical and technical precision" (Wharton 1934, 91), along with her lifelong love of learning, which she continually fed.[9] Second, her close friendships with art critics and collectors Vernon Lee (née Violet Paget), Charles Eliot Norton, Bernard Berenson, Kenneth Clark, Egerton Winthrop, and Royal Cortissoz, and third, her annual pilgrimages to France, Italy, Germany, and Spain. These influences, complementing the instruction at the hands of tutors and governesses, helped Wharton cultivate in herself what she calls, in *French Ways and Their Meaning*, "the gift of the seeing eye."[10]

Wharton's reverence for Italian art led to a major discovery, in the mid-1890s, which must have helped readers take seriously *The Decoration of Houses*. In her essay "A Tuscan Shrine" (1895), Wharton challenged the formidable Harvard art historian Bernard Berenson on an attribution. She correctly identified a group of life-size terracotta figures depicting the passion of Christ at the San Vivaldo Monastery near Florence. Berenson and others had ascribed the figures to

9. Wharton's December 30, 1895, letter to her beloved governess Anna Bahlmann speaks of her delight in receiving as a gift "the enchanting" and "delicious" book on European architecture by Adolphe Berty (1818–1867) (Goldman-Price 2012, 152).

10. Wharton seems to have been inspired by Thomas Carlyle's use of "the seeing eye" in his May 12, 1840, essay, "The Hero as Poet. Dante: Shakespeare."

the seventeenth-century sculptor Giovanni Gonnelli, but Wharton proved them to be the work of the earlier Renaissance artist Giovanni della Robbia. In *Italian Backgrounds*, Wharton describes this moment as "the rare sensation of an artistic discovery" (1998, 105). As Medina Lasansky has shown, "For someone whose career as a connoisseur of Italian art depended on assigning authorship and reattributing artworks, Wharton's claim to have discovered a new cache of *cinquecento* sculptures near Florence must have been extremely irksome ... Berenson never publicly acknowledged the significance of Wharton's claims, never referred to San Vivaldo in his private papers, and refrained from purchasing a set of the [authenticating] Alinari photographs of the chapels for his otherwise comprehensive *Fototeca* at I Tatti" (Lasansky 2016, 148).

While Berenson and his wife Mary would eventually enjoy a close friendship with Wharton, he did not appreciate being upstaged by a woman never formally trained. Nevertheless, Wharton's attribution is now accepted as authoritative.

The Decoration of Houses, which Wharton wrote with the Beaux-Arts architect and Boston-based interior designer Ogden Codman Jr. (1863–1951), argues for the limitless possibilities afforded by the appropriate design and décor of the home.

The opening chapter confidently asserts that "it is possible to produce great variety in the decoration of rooms without losing sight of the purpose for which they are intended" and that "the more closely this purpose is kept in view, and the more clearly it is expressed in all the details of each room, the more pleasing that room will be" (Wharton and Codman 1897, 16). *The Decoration of Houses* makes the case that aesthetically pleasing interiors emerge from sound decorating, emphasizing "those architectural features which are a part of the organism of every house, inside as well as out" (Wharton and Codman 1897, xix). Rooms, the authors argue, should be as beautiful as they are useful—an unpopular sentiment, as indicated by the number of over-crowded and ornately decorated late Victorian drawing rooms.

Anyone familiar with late nineteenth-century aesthetics will agree that Wharton and Codman's insistence on beauty and usefulness owes

2. Ogden Codman Jr., Bar Harbor, Maine, 1887. Codman Family Papers, folder 44; Copy negative 15666-B. Photograph by Thomas N. Codman. Courtesy of Historic New England.

something to William Morris (1834–96). Morris, leader of the Arts and Crafts Movement in late Victorian England and a sort of latter-day Pre-Raphaelite, famously implored his followers to "have nothing in your houses which you do not know to be useful or believe to be beautiful" (Triggs 2009, 78).[11] As Helena Chance has elucidated:

> Morris and his followers embraced the idea that good design and beauty could shape morality and play a key role in social reform. Their Arts and Crafts Movement promoted the ideal of honest construction in natural materials, and restraint in ornament—authentic forms based on vernacular styles, with their origins in the Middle Ages. The movement was influential in Europe, the United States, and further afield, and had an important impact on subsequent design theory and practice. However, Wharton and her fellow taste leaders, while in agreement with the Arts and Crafts doctrines of simplicity and authenticity, avowed classicism, not medievalism, as more appropriate to the national identity of a modern United States. (Chance 2012, 201)

While Wharton and Codman were emphatically opposed to wallpaper—for which Morris is perhaps most celebrated today—and they likely would not have sympathized with his socialism, they would have appreciated his disdain for the ugliness and tackiness on display at the Great Exhibition of 1851.

Wharton and Codman's turn-of-the-century design treatise insists that purpose, form, harmony, function, proportion, and order may all be honored without sacrificing visual pleasure—a governing principle echoed across Wharton's stories about the privileged as well as the unprivileged. An under-acknowledged detail about Edith Wharton, a writer better known for turning her mirror to the moneyed classes, is her career-long interest in the ways that domestic spaces can afford all persons a sense of place and belonging.

---

11. Morris's speech was delivered in 1880 and later published in *Hopes and Fears for Art: Five Lectures Delivered in Birmingham, London, and Nottingham, 1878–1881* (1882).

Wharton's keen sense of the home's sacredness would propel her to fight vociferously on behalf of those displaced by World War I. For the writer who rose to fame, in 1897, with a design manual addressed to the American leisure class would be the same who, two decades later, would oversee *The Book of the Homeless*, a collection of original writings in verse and prose along with paintings and drawings, whose table of contents reads like a who's who of early twentieth-century artists and intellectuals and whose proceeds were invested in the welfare of war-torn children and refugees. Wharton would write in her preface to *The Book of the Homeless*: "The present hope of France and Belgium is in its children, and in the hygienic education of those who have them in charge; . . . The results have been better than we could have hoped; and those who saw the arrival of the piteous waifs a few months ago would scarcely recognize them in the round and rosy children playing in the gardens of our Houses" (xxiv).

Wharton's humanitarian acts—for instance, the large houses in Normandy that she had refurbished for her Children of Flanders charity (e.g., Groslay), and her establishment of homes for tubercular soldiers and their families—for which in 1916 the French government would make her a Chevalier of the Legion of Honor, and the Belgian government, three years later, a Chevalier of the Order of Leopold, seem to have been driven by her awareness of the restorative properties of the home, illuminated in the example of the "round and rosy children playing in the gardens of our Houses." For Wharton, in her philanthropy and creative work, the care of the home is akin to the care of the soul.

Gaston Bachelard's *The Poetics of Space* (1958) enables us to see the extent to which Wharton's ideas on the relation between domestic space and lived experience have far-reaching implications across classes and across the Atlantic. Bachelard, a French philosopher who draws on many of Wharton's favorite writers (e.g., Honoré de Balzac, Marcel Proust), conceives of the house as one's "corner of the world": "It is our first universe, a real cosmos in every sense of the word. If we look at it intimately, the humblest dwelling has beauty" (Bachelard 2014, 26). Bachelard's remark ties nicely to Wharton's *The Book of the*

3. Rest house for tubercular children, American Hostels for Refugees. Arromanches, Normandy. Edith Wharton Collection. Courtesy of Yale Collection of American Literature, Beinecke Rare Book and Manuscript Library.

Homeless, whose frontispiece declares itself "sold for the benefit of the American Hostels for Refugees (with the Foyer Franco-Belge) and of the Children of Flanders Rescue Committee." Bachelard's use of the terms *refuge* and *redoubt* (a place of retreat meant to protect soldiers) underscores the home's protective capacities in a time of war:

> From having been a refuge, it has become a redoubt. The thatched cottage becomes a fortified castle for the recluse, who must learn to conquer fear within its walls . . . In a house that has become for the imagination the very heart of a cyclone, we have to go beyond the mere impressions of consolation that we should feel in any shelter . . . And so, faced with the bestial hostility of the storm and the hurricane, the house's virtues of protection and resistance are

transposed into human virtues. The house acquires the physical and moral energy of a human body. It braces itself to receive the downpour, it girds its loins. (Bachelard 2014, 66–67)

Bachelard's mid-century alignment of the house with a body—endowed with human virtues, a physical and moral energy, loins prepared for battle—poignantly echoes Wharton's description in *The House of Mirth* of what a sentimentally valuable home might do: "To a torn heart uncomforted by human nearness a room may open almost human arms, and the being to whom no four walls mean more than any others, is, at such hours, expatriate everywhere" (2018, 130).[12]

Wharton's Lily Bart, to her detriment, claims no meaningful connection to the "four walls" encircling her in her aunt's frigid, comfortless, Victorian home. Instead, she is, for all purposes, homeless, "expatriate everywhere"—a state that, for Wharton, literally expatriated but happily homed at the time she edits *The Book of the Homeless*, translates to the depths of despair.

Two years after the publication of *The Book of the Homeless*, Wharton would offer her prescription for the care of the soul in a letter to her now-close confidante Mary Berenson. World War I was still raging, and influenza was destroying lives in ways uncomfortably familiar to those who lived through the COVID-19 pandemic: "I believe I know the only cure, which is to make one's center of life inside of one's self, not selfishly or excludingly, but with a kind of unassailable serenity—to decorate one's inner house so richly that one is content there, glad to welcome anyone who wants to come and stay, but happy all the same when one is inevitably alone" (Lewis 1975, 413).

12. In a moment that powerfully resonates with Wharton's poetics of space, Bachelard invokes a story by the French writer Saint-Pol-Roux (1861–1940) called "Farewell to the Cottage" ("Adieux à la chaumière"), published in 1907 in the collection *Inner Enchantments* (Féeries intérieurs): "The minute they entered the cottage, it opened its heart and soul: 'At dawn, your freshly white-washed being opened its arms to us: the children felt that they had entered into the heart of a dove, and we loved the ladder—your stairway—right away'" (Bachelard 83).

The passage stands in sharp contrast to the early Wharton short story "The Fulness of Life" (1893, reprinted in Wharton 2001b), which imagines a woman's self as a home with public and private spaces: "I have sometimes thought that a woman's nature is like a great house full of rooms: there is the hall, through which everyone passes in going in and out; the drawing-room, where one receives formal visits . . . and in the innermost room, the holy of holies, the soul sits alone and waits for a footstep that never comes" (14).

Wharton's writings across the genres suggest a career-long investment in seeking a sanctuary for the (perhaps inevitably solitary) soul. Decorating one's inner and outer spaces is, for Wharton, the pathway to an "unassailable serenity." Her body of work continually suggests that the sanctuary one seeks lies within and is influenced by, and inextricably intertwined with, the spaces in which one lives and moves. The writer who would posit, in her 1901 story "The Angel at the Grave," that "each organism draws from its surroundings," would follow up her auspicious 1897 debut as a prose author with over forty volumes whose pages, over and again, attest to the influence architecture and design have on the human soul.

Building and Remodeling *The Decoration of Houses*

Although *The Decoration of Houses* is co-authored by the Boston architect and interior designer Ogden Codman Jr., the evidence points to Wharton as the primary author, and her fully developed, assured voice, paired with her knowledge across the disciplines, is heard on every page. Architectural historian Richard Guy Wilson makes the strongest case for crediting Wharton with the lion's share of the book: "Codman was not a writer and undoubtedly thought (as many non-writers—especially architects—do) that a book would be easy: he would tell Edith and she would write it down. Later they differed on who contributed what, with Ogden at one time claiming that it was his work and that Edith had simply polished up his sentences. Yet the unalphabetical arrangement of the authors' names on the published book and the surviving correspondence indicate that Edith not only wrote most of the book, but also contributed many of the ideas" (Wilson 1988, 148).

Wharton's irreverent wit and command of the English sentence permeates the prose. She is, after all, the writer who would declare in *The House of Mirth*—in a turn of phrase worthy of Oscar Wilde[13]—that "it is almost as stupid to let your clothes betray that you know you are ugly as to have them proclaim that you think you are beautiful." That epigram mirrors the following dictate from *The Decoration of Houses* on reconciling domestic ugliness: "There are but two ways of dealing with a room which is fundamentally ugly: one is to accept it, and the other is courageously to correct its ugliness. Half-way remedies are a waste of money and serve rather to call attention to the defects of the room than to conceal them" (Wharton and Codman 1897, 30).[14] Both declarations discourage directing the observer's gaze to that which aesthetically offends; doing so "only attracts attention to its ugliness" (95). Further, the third chapter of *The Decoration of Houses* draws an analogy between the craft of fiction and the art of house design, and here Wharton's authority as a literary artist is particularly palpable: "As in imaginative literature the author may present to his reader as possible anything that he has the talent to make the reader accept, so in decorative art the artist is justified in presenting to the eye whatever his skill can devise to satisfy its requirements" (38–39).

Wharton imagined the construct of a house as a site of immense possibility, as evidenced in her compelling ghost story "Afterward," whose heroine looks upon her newly acquired country home and

13. I have suggested elsewhere Oscar Wilde's 1882 American lectures on house decoration—which were widely reprinted in newspapers—as a possible source for *The Decoration of Houses*. See Orlando 2017a, 25–43.

14. The line also looks forward to a much-quoted maxim from Wharton's 1902 poem "Vesalius in Zante" and underscores the point that Wharton was the primary author: "There are two ways of spreading light; to be / The candle or the mirror that reflects it" (Goldman-Price 2012, 173). She uses a similar sentence construction in *French Ways and Their Meaning*: "There are two ways of judging a foreign people: at first sight, impressionistically, . . . ; or after residence among them" (1919, xviii).

contemplates the "endless possibilities still before her, such opportunities to bring out the latent graces of the old place" (1973, 61). In anticipation of Virginia Woolf, Wharton suggested that women, and especially those who write, must have "rooms of [one's] own" and that those rooms "ha[d] to be decorated" (Woolf 2008, 140–45).

The Decoration of Houses crystallizes what Wharton and Codman found to be troubling in American tastes at the turn into the twentieth century and its argument can be summarized in three main points. First, the authors insist that "proportion is the good breeding of architecture" (Wharton and Codman 1897, 31), claiming with a flourish that "the essence of a style lies not in its use of ornament, but in its handling of proportion" (11). In fact, the book's one use of the term *soul* occurs in a discussion of proportion: "In its effects [it is] as intangible as that all-pervading essence which the ancients called the soul" (31). The word *proportion* occurs forty-five times and, fittingly, appears as the book's final word. The sense of harmony and balance is, for Wharton, central also to the art of writing, and she praises Henry James's gothic tale *The Turn of the Screw* for its "perfect sense of proportion" (Wharton 1924, 75). Wharton and Codman advocate European principles of harmony and symmetry, many of which were borne of her time abroad and his having lived in France and traveled Italy, that would be important to Wharton's life and work. In both interior decoration and architecture, the authors assert, "a regard for symmetry, besides satisfying a legitimate artistic requirement, tends to make the average room not only easier to furnish, but more comfortable to live in" (Wharton and Codman 1897, 34). The book emphasizes proportion and design in furniture, ornament, walls, floors, ceilings, doors, and all aspects of domestic architecture. In privileging architectural proportion, Wharton and Codman were going against the contemporary grain which emphasized superficial application of ornament.[15] Although the authors were speaking to a late Victorian

15. The word *ornament* appears 112 times, almost always in a negative context. Wharton and Codman were particularly distrustful of the overly ornamental Victorian styles of their parents' generation. Chapter 7, "Ceilings and Floors," advises:

audience, their insistence on honoring proportion and limiting the application of ornament is timeless when one considers the awkwardness of, say, an oversized entryway on a modest home, a supersized gazebo in a diminutive yard, or a Cape-style home burdened by more holiday decorations than it can sensibly support.

The book's second key point is that by returning to the "best models" and traditions of the past, current house decoration can be elevated above its unfortunate status of confusion, decline, and vulgarity. Here Wharton and Codman echo the esteemed New York architect Charles Follen McKim, founder of McKim, Mead & White, whom Wharton considered "'the high-water-mark' of criticism in that line in America" (Wharton 1896 or 1897, quoted in Wilson 2012, 35). McKim, whose achievements by this time included the Boston Public Library (1887) and the Columbia University Library (1893), had noted in a correspondence with Wharton that "by conscientious study of the best examples of classic periods, including those of antiquity, it is possible to conceive a perfect result suggestive of a particular period . . . but inspired by the study of them all."[16] Third, Wharton and Codman suggest that those aspirational models can be found chiefly in the buildings erected in Italy after the early 1500s, and in France and England, once the full effect of the Italian influence set in.

Edith Wharton did not turn—as Isabella Stewart Gardner had done in Boston earlier in the nineteenth century—to the Italian palazzo for inspiration for her own majestic summer home in Lenox, Massachusetts, called The Mount. As Judith Fryer has observed, while Wharton clearly admired the Italian Renaissance, she looked to the palazzo's "successor, the English country house, specifically Belton

---

"Let the fundamental work be good in design and quality and the want of ornament will not be felt" (99).

16. Wilson notes that "the reply by McKim is a three-page typed 'memoranda' with 'to Mrs. Wharton' penciled in on the first page. Bound into his letter copybook; the surrounding letters are dated February 2 and 5, 1897. Library of Congress. McKim would have sent the original to Wharton, but it has not survived" (Wilson 2012, 36n61).

4. The Mount. Edith Wharton Collection. Courtesy of Yale Collection of American Literature, Beinecke Rare Book and Manuscript Library.

House in Lincolnshire (attributed to Sir Christopher Wren), as the cupola at the top of The Mount signals. Distributors of movement—doorways, passageways, stairways—in Edith Wharton's house would insure that human interaction was controlled, not random" (Fryer 1986, 69). In this way Wharton's The Mount, which she lovingly called in *A Backward Glance* her "first real home" (1934, 125) and which is the only house she built from the ground up, would honor the principles set forth in her design manual.

In its fidelity to architectural form, *The Decoration of Houses* practices the symmetry and continuity it preaches. The introduction lays the groundwork by offering a historical context for the evolution of taste in house decoration and design. The final chapter interrogates the problem of the contemporary moment—that is, overcluttered rooms

heavy on knickknacks and ostentatious design. The chapters com-
prising the heart of the book proceed like enfiladed drawing rooms,
divided into two major sections, the first half treating the chief components of a room (walls, doors, windows, fireplaces, ceilings, floors),
the second half studying the key types of rooms and their components
(entrance and vestibule, hall and stairs, drawing room, and so on).

Wharton's collaborator and, at times, kindred spirit, Ogden Codman Jr., had served as an advisor for the decoration and renovation of
Land's End, the newly married Edith and Teddy Wharton's summer
home in Newport, Rhode Island, purchased in 1893. Codman would
later design the interior of the Whartons's Park Avenue residence in
New York City. Letters exchanged between Wharton and Codman
in the mid- to late 1890s often are affectionate. They could both be
as particular as they could be kind. She adorably addresses him as
"Coddy" while he calls her "the cleverest and best friend I have ever
made" (Codman n.d., quoted in Dwight 2007, 18). A shared appreciation of architecture, interior design, travel (especially to Italy and
France), gardens, dogs, and gossip emerges. In her memoir, Wharton
explains how the two bonded over a mutual aesthetic sense: "Codman
shared my dislike of these sumptuary excesses, and thought as I did
that interior decoration should be simple and architectural" (1934, 107).

Although Codman consulted with Wharton on the early stages
of the design of The Mount, whose construction lasted from 1901 to
1902, he did not, ultimately, serve as its architect. As Eleanor Dwight
notes, "In the process of working with Codman on the design, the
two had a falling-out. Codman had raised his rates from fifteen to
twenty-five percent, and Teddy refused to pay this fee" (Dwight 1994,
20). The Whartons instead turned to Francis Laurens Vinton Hop-
pin, who apprenticed with McKim, Mead & White and had designed
the old police headquarters of New York City (Coles 1997, xxxi, n2).
When the Whartons later sought Codman's help with The Mount's
interiors, further discord ensued over his fees for the painted panels in
Edith's boudoir and the strain took a significant toll on the friendship.
Still, acquiring Land's End proved highly symbolic for Edith Wharton: it afforded her the requisite room(s) of her own and established

the relationship with the person with whom she would create her first book of prose and the only author with whom she would share a byline. The partnership, which spanned about a decade beginning in the early 1890s, would be as highly formative as it would be contentious.

In fact, because of the tensions in Wharton's collaboration with Codman, architects do not come across well in her writings. A case in point is Wharton's "The Valley of Childish Things, and Other Emblems" (1896), fables involving architects who, like Codman, are criticized for their inflated prices and egos. Wharton's novellas *Sanctuary* and *Summer* feature young male architects of questionable character. The turn-of-the-century conclusion of *The Age of Innocence* finds Newland Archer's son Dallas, employed by "the office of a rising New York architect," dashing to Versailles to gather inspiration for a Chicago millionaire's "Lakeside palace" (Wharton 2003, 206, 214, 209). As Laura Rattray has noted, the leading male protagonist of Wharton's unfinished play *Arch* shares Codman's profession (Rattray 2020, 141). A Boston architect plays a key role in "The Young Gentlemen" (1926). Further, thirty years after *The Decoration of Houses*, Wharton was working on a novel that was to feature an architect who sounds a lot like her descriptions of Codman: "Boastful, a little obtuse, and rather vain" (Wharton n.d., Yale Collection of American Literature).[17]

Nevertheless, Wharton and Codman's collaboration built a beautiful book. On its genesis, Wharton would later reflect that, given the aesthetic values she shared with Codman, they "drifted . . . [,] I hardly know how, toward the notion of putting them into a book" (1934, 107). "Drift" glosses a bit too lightly over what amounted to an exhausting and at times frustrating enterprise. Wharton seems to have begun working on the manuscript of *The Decoration of Houses* in the summer of 1896 (Evans 2012, 168). In a January 1897 letter to his mother, Codman reports that "we have now written about 100 pages" and concedes that "Mrs. Wharton is a great help . . . She takes my notes & puts them

---

17. For more on the tensions in Wharton and Codman's collaboration, which would result in a decades-long rift, see Orlando 2017b.

into literary form, & adds a good deal out of her own head."[18] Codman's description of the partnership fancies Wharton more secretary than co-author, a detail that confirms the writers conceived of their roles dramatically differently. The evidence indicates that the writing of the design treatise lasted more than a year. Wharton sent a draft to McKim, "probably in January 1897" (Wilson 2012, 34), a document that Irene Goldman-Price speculates was typed by her German governess and confidante Anna Bahlmann (Goldman-Price 2012, 172) and is the only known surviving draft of *The Decoration of Houses*. Favorably impressed, McKim suggested the authors rework the introduction (Wilson 2012, 34). Processing McKim's recommendations, Wharton wrote in a letter to Codman: "I think it would be well in some respects to remodel the Introduction . . . the other chapters he entirely agrees to, which is nice" (Wilson 2012, 34). Unpublished letters from Wharton to Codman make it clear that Wharton grew exasperated and discouraged by Codman's insufficient contributions to the project.[19] Wharton was, it seems, the force that brought the book to light.

Wharton originally had turned to Macmillan for the publication of *The Decoration of Houses* (Wharton 1934, 108). In early 1897, Wharton's sister-in-law put her in touch with George Platt Brett, the head of the American branch of Macmillan, who received the work favorably (Towheed 2007, 5). Yet Brett quibbled with the book's title and proposed renaming it *The Philosophy of House-decoration* (Wilson 1988, 149). There were other obstacles as well, and the letters between the co-authors suggest that Codman had offended Brett, who eventually turned down the project (Wilson 1988, 150).[20]

18. Ogden Codman Jr. to his mother Sarah Codman (quoted in Dwight 1994, 58).

19. Wharton's letters to Codman vocalize her frustration with his inability to produce the bibliography she had repeatedly asked him to compile for the book. Of particular note is a letter dated Thursday, June 1897, from Land's End, Newport, Rhode Island (Codman Family Papers, folder 1670).

20. On May 9, 1897, Wharton wrote to Codman: "Before we embark on any other experiments with the book, I am going to make it a condition that you leave the transaction entirely to me" (Codman Family Papers, folder 1670).

Ultimately, Wharton's good standing with Scribner .paved the way for publication. Wharton reached out to Edward L. Burlingame of the New York firm of Charles Scribner's Sons, whose magazine had published several of her stories and poems. Burlingame brought it to the attention of his colleague William Crary Brownell, who oversaw the book publishing department and who, with some hesitation about the book's ability to attract an audience, accepted the manuscript in July 1897 (Dwight 1994, 60) and imposed a September 1 deadline (Coles 1997, xxix–xxx). Walter Berry, perhaps Wharton's closest confidant, served as a literary consultant and advisor for what she humbly called the "lumpy pages" (Wharton 1934, 108) that evolved into *The Decoration of Houses*. In fact, William Vance has suggested that Berry, though unacknowledged in the book, "had to reshape the whole" (Vance 1995, 196n12). Scribner's published the book on December 3, 1897.

Readers familiar with Wharton's impeccable work ethic will not be surprised to learn that she immersed herself in all aspects of the production of *The Decoration of Houses*. Not only did she oversee the writing and editing, she also coordinated the less glamorous aspects of bookmaking, such as indexing, communicating with the publisher, and ensuring promotion and review (Dwight 2007, 19). She lined up reviewers and dissuaded the selection of others: Russell Sturgis, known for his distrust of classicism, was "not to touch it," Wharton admonished in a letter dated November 9, 1897, to Codman (Codman Family Papers, quoted in Wilson 2012, 35). Gary Totten has suggested that the book marked Wharton's first foray into the production and marketing of her writing (Totten 2012, 127). She also tracked down the illustrations, negotiated with editors and publishers, and selected the book designer, Daniel Berkeley Updike, a Boston Arts and Crafts printer who would also create the cover for *The Book of the Homeless*. Wharton insisted on fifty-six, not thirty-two, plates, and that the illustration size proposed by Brownell was too small (Lee 2007, 163). Additionally, she rejected the original title page: "I daresay I have already gone beyond the limits prescribed to a new author in the expression of opinion; but, since you send me the title page, I shall consider myself justified in criticizing it. To anyone who cares for old Italics, such lettering seems very inadequate" (Lee 2007, 163).

At every turn, Wharton managed the project and was aware that she could come across as fussy and, well, a bit too much: "Pardon my frankness—" she wrote at the close of a 1902 letter to Richard Watson Gilder of *Scribner's Monthly*, "but I always care very much for the make-up of my books" (Goldman-Price 2012, 74). Wharton's tireless interventions are responsible for building the book, and she gained valuable experience in directing and advancing her career as a professional writer (Benstock 1994, 84).

Reflecting, in *A Backward Glance*, on the book that yielded her first royalty check, Wharton reports that "the Scribners brought out a very small and tentative edition [of *The Decoration of Houses*], produced with great typographical care, probably thinking that the book was more likely to succeed as a gift book among my personal friends than as a practical manual. But the first edition was sold out at once; Batsford immediately asked for the book for England; and from that day to this it has gone on from edition to edition, and still, after nearly forty years, brings in an annual tribute to its astonished authors!" (1934, 110).

Those who envisioned *The Decoration of Houses* as a gift book grossly underestimated its potential. In a 1903 missive to Richard Watson Gilder, now of the *Century Magazine*, which would publish in serial form *Italian Villas and Their Gardens*, Wharton noted with satisfaction that "*The Decoration of Houses*, which began as a 'popular' book, and was rather looked down on by the profession, is now having a steady sale among architects, here and in England as well" (Wharton, June 10, 1903, quoted in Lee 2007, 135). Wharton sells herself short in saying the book was, only six years before, "looked down on by the profession," as the reviews discussed shortly suggest otherwise. Surely by the 1934 release of her memoir, *The Decoration of Houses* had proven its staying power. In 1937, Wharton and Codman, who had by 1905 fallen out over his fees for The Mount's design, were planning, at his suggestion, to collaborate on a more affordable edition of *The Decoration of Houses*. They seem to have resumed their acquaintance by the

1920s, at which point both resided in France. The new edition would have coincided with the book's fortieth anniversary. On June 1, 1937, soon after arriving at Codman's seventeenth-century chateau outside Paris, Wharton fell ill and was carried off in an ambulance. She never regained her health and expired on August 11. It is no small matter that her last recorded words, on August 7, were "I want to go home" (Lee 2007, 749). That detail, and the fact that in her final months of life Wharton was returning to *The Decoration of Houses*, suggests the central place the book, and the quest to find and make one's home, occupies in her legacy.

CRITICAL RECEPTION OF *THE DECORATION OF HOUSES*

Even from the first, critics warmly received *The Decoration of Houses*. In a review from December 1897, the *Nation* assessed it as "a handsome, interesting, and well-written book," notwithstanding its tendency to privilege beauty and revert to "quasi-classic styles and methods" (Tuttleton, Lauer, and Murray 1992, 3).[21] A reviewer for the *Critic* bemoaned the volume's illustrations of "magnificent places of temporary abode or festal use" instead of "the simpler residences and homes" that Wharton and Codman seek to instruct readers to decorate (January 8, 1898, 20; reprinted in Tuttleton, Lauer, and Murray 1992, 4), but conceded that "it is clear that much reading, much travel in Italy and France, and a good deal of independent thinking stand behind this pretty book" (Tuttleton, Lauer, and Murray 5). The presumably male reviewer, in assessing the book as "pretty," seems to see the volume as the kind of "gift book" from which Wharton and Codman successfully distinguished themselves by way of copious references to classical architecture, their evident command of art history, and their scientific treatment of house design. Edwin H. Blashfield, writing in *Book Buyer*, offers an effusively appreciative review celebrating the book's

---

21. Richard Guy Wilson suspects the *Nation* critic to have been Russell Sturgis, who opposed classicism and whom Wharton had expressly asked "not to touch it" (Wilson 2012, 40).

arrival at a most "opportune moment" (Tuttleton, Lauer, and Murray 1992, 5): "The book is a thoroughly welcome one and should be a very present help to the many who realize that the material environment of home life has a real influence, and who will be only too glad to find that this environment, if properly studied, can be understood, and that, although high art can be comprehended and great art possessed by few, any intelligent and well-to-do person may possess a good room or suite of rooms" (March 1898, 129–33, reprinted in Tuttleton, Lauer, and Murray 1992, 7).

Walter Berry, who, having assisted with revisions, was not exactly unbiased, perhaps best summarizes the book's cultural work in his review published in *Bookman*, noting that Wharton and Codman's volume compensates for the conspicuous shortage of books in the United States or United Kingdom that view "house decoration as a branch of architecture" (Tuttleton, Lauer, and Murray 1992, 8). In fact, Berry seeks to differentiate Wharton and Codman's book from "the many *Suggestions on Household Taste*, and the like, most of which have served only to aggravate the very defects which the present book is attempting to remedy" (10). One book targeted by Wharton and Codman for its shortcomings, in fact, is Charles Locke Eastlake's *Hints on Household Taste*. Echoing a criticism leveled in the fifth chapter of *The Decoration of Houses*, Berry notes that in Eastlake's book, "no mention whatever is made of doors, windows, and fireplaces" (9), even though "it was once thought that the effect of a room depended on the treatment of its wall-spaces and openings" (9). The reviewer for *Architect and Building News* criticized Wharton and Codman's wholesale dismissal of current American design but ultimately concluded that "on the whole, the volume is far ahead of anything of the kind we know of within the last half-century" (*Decoration of Houses* 1898, 28–29).

The Decoration of Houses sold well and was reprinted in London by B. T. Batsford in 1898 and in New York by Scribner's in 1902 and 1919 (Wilson 2012, 41). Wharton mailed copies to architects and critics from England who she thought would be in sympathy with the book (Wilson 2012, 41). She received warm responses from W. J. Loftie and Reginald Blomfield (Wilson 2012, 41). Loftie, in a January 3, 1898, letter to Wharton, commended the volume's critique of "excessive and unmeaning ornament." For his part, Blomfield hoped the book's influence would have a lasting impression on the United States and the United Kingdom. It certainly did.

AUDIENCE AND INFLUENCE OF *THE DECORATION OF HOUSES*

In his review of the volume for *Book Buyer*, Edwin H. Blashfield aptly pointed out that Wharton and Codman were targeting two reading audiences, both of them financially secure: "The moderately well-to-do and the wealthy": "To the former they show that any well-proportioned room is a handsome room if not deformed by the application of bad detail, bad color, or the introduction of ugly furniture" (Tuttleton, Lauer, and Murray 1992, 7). Blashfield suggested Wharton and Codman's message to the wealthier classes was to invest in good things such that their aesthetic choices will inform the less privileged (7). As Judith Fryer has shown, the emphasis, in *The Decoration of Houses*, on the "very distinctions between public and private, between the world and the house, mark the book, of course, as one for leisure-class consumption" (Fryer 1986, 113). Wharton and Codman were appealing to both segments of the upper class, in hopes of instructing them how to tastefully and sensibly decorate the home.

Based on a quick look at the illustrations, it would be easy to dismiss Wharton and Codman's tome as elitist, out of touch, and thus not useful to the typical contemporary reader interested in bettering their home. While it is true that their photographic models—images of Louis XVI's library at Versailles, a bathroom from Florence's Pitti Palace, for example—might appeal more to a reader from what in the twenty-first century would be considered the top one percent, Wharton and Codman's decorating advice resonates for the contemporary consumer interested in beautifying their domestic space on a sensible budget. Their advice, for instance, in the chapter titled "Rooms in General," on how to frugally furnish a room makes sense for the modern-day homeowner or studio apartment-renter:

When a room is to be furnished and decorated at the smallest possible cost, it must be remembered that the comfort of its occupants depends more on the nature of the furniture than of the wall-decorations or carpet. In a living-room of this kind it is best to tint the walls . . . keeping as much money as possible for the purchase of comfortable chairs and sofas and substantial tables. If little can be spent in buying furniture, . . . arm-chairs with denim cushions and solid tables with stained legs and covers of denim or corduroy will be more satisfactory than the "parlor suit" turned out in thousands by the manufacturer of cheap furniture, or the pseudo-Empire of the dealer in "high-grade goods." Plain bookcases may be made of deal, painted or stained; and a room treated in this way, with a uniform color on the wall, and plenty of lamps and books, is sure to be comfortable and can never be vulgar. (Wharton and Codman 1897, 25–26)

The authors note that, perhaps surprisingly, eighteenth-century France and England offered affordable models of "plain, inexpensive furniture of walnut, mahogany, or painted beechwood" (27). With a sigh they acknowledge that "were the modern public as fastidious, it would be easy to buy good furniture for a moderate price; but until people recognize the essential vulgarity of the pinchbeck article flooding our shops and overflowing upon our sidewalks, manufacturers will continue to offer such wares in preference to better but less showy designs" (27).

Wharton and Codman recognize a place for dimity and deal, materials that are relatively more affordable than marble or velvet and would never be mistaken for vulgar or showy. Wharton and Codman include in their audience "the householder who cannot afford to buy old pieces" (28) and give space to the challenges of decorating the smaller sized rooms in which twenty-first-century readers likely dwell. For instance, they attend to the importance of avoiding dark colors, which "have the disadvantage of making a room look small" (153). In decorating a room they advise that the color scale ascend gradually from a dark floor to a light ceiling—a tip still basic to twenty-first-century interior design. As a rule, Wharton and Codman suggest that the vulgar and the showy are to be sacrificed in the name of architectural integrity. This practice clearly speaks to the twenty-first-century decorator interested in clean lines and open, uncluttered spaces.

The Decoration of Houses effectively elevated American interior design to a legitimate professional activity. Indeed, Wharton would write that her hope was to advance "the more complex art of civilized living," something which, by the publication of her memoir in 1934, she suggested had fallen out of favor with the "emancipated," career-driven women of the 1920s and 1930s who facilitated what she bemoaned as "the extinction of the household arts"[22] (1934, 60). Wharton managed to repackage and validate those "household arts" while rescuing them from feminization and thus marginalization. The book, then, was revolutionary not only because it saved decoration from marginalization but also because it aligned it with the (presumably more serious and male-dominated) discipline of architecture. Laura Rattray has shown that while Wharton's "work in this field is not entirely original, . . . its scholarship and authority, under-pinned by immaculate research, elevated American public discourse on interior design and architecture to another level" (Rattray 2020, 12). Its design principles set a new standard for décor still followed today.

In *A Backward Glance*, Wharton observes that asking the "clever young Boston architect, Ogden Codman" to "alter and decorate the [Newport] house" was "a somewhat new departure, since the architects of that day looked down on house-decoration as a branch of

---

22. Here we see Wharton's much-discussed resistance to university-educated, career-focused women. As much as she would have resisted, as a staunch conservative, alignment with feminist politics, at least its early twentieth-century incarnation, recent scholarship has amply proven that Wharton's cultural work was decidedly feminist. For an excellent starting point, see Olin-Ammentorp 1988. Laura Rattray has more recently shown that "undoubtedly, Wharton could herself be sexist and did not always support other women—she was certainly no vocal advocate of women's suffrage even as she lived through the vital period of campaigning and constitutional change in much of Europe and the United States. But she was much more often a victim than a perpetrator of sexism, and persistently saw her work viewed and judged through a sexist lens" (Rattray 2020, 6).

dress-making, and left the field to the upholsterers, who crammed every room with curtains, lambrequins, jardinières of artificial plants, wobbly velvet-covered tables littered with silver gew-gaws, and festoons of lace on mantelpieces and dressing-tables" (1934, 106–7).

Wharton here describes the style informing her mother's Victorian drawing room, jammed with overstuffed furniture, bric-à-brac, gilded cabinets, old lace, painted fans, and busy wallpaper (see also posthumously published Wharton 1938, 361, 358). The introduction to *The Decoration of Houses* flags one of the book's chief purposes as discouraging the overreliance on the "upholsterer" habitually "called in to 'decorate' and furnish the rooms" (Wharton and Codman 1897, xx); Wharton and Codman consider the tendency to turn to the upholsterer in lieu of the architect a major cause of the "deficiency" of nineteenth-century house decoration, and the overstimulation of the senses resulting from the decoration of her mother's drawing room is one of the undesired consequences of the practice. Wharton's fundamental distrust of upholstery informs her description, in *The House of Mirth*, of "the world of the fashionable New York hotel": "A world over-heated, *over-upholstered*, and over-fitted with mechanical appliances for the gratification of fantastic requirements, while the comforts of a civilized life were as unattainable as in a desert. Through this atmosphere of torrid splendour moved wan beings *as richly upholstered as the furniture*, beings without definite pursuits or permanent relations, who drifted on a languid tide of curiosity from restaurant to concert-hall, from palm-garden to music-room, from "art exhibit" to dress-maker's opening" (2018, 235; emphasis added).

This is the newly moneyed class whose taste Wharton and Codman sought to inform, those who had been casualties of "an epidemic of supposed 'Marie-Antoinette' rooms break[ing] out over the whole country" (Wharton 1897, 27). The authors envisioned house decoration as a branch of architecture and while they do not suggest architect and interior designer should be the same person, they argue that the decorator must conceive of his or her function architecturally—that is, honoring the structural integrity of the room rather than simply adding ornament to it. Their book seeks to invest the reader with "that regard for harmony of parts which distinguishes interior architecture from mere decoration" (Wharton and Codman 1897, 172).

The Decoration of Houses is, of course, informed by shortsighted class assumptions. First, the insistence that "proportion" is tantamount to "good breeding" (Wharton and Codman 1897, 31) resonates with the patrician undertones associated with the leisure class that Wharton's New York fiction would indict. The book suggests (some) readers might be able to import a carved ceiling from Italy, acquire "properly made French windows," employ live-in servants, and enjoy the resources to not only own but decorate a ballroom, saloon, music room, or gallery. The absence of a chapter on the kitchen—the word only appears thrice—suggests the limited time a member of their class spent working in one. Their confidence in a kind of trickle-down aesthetics is evident when the authors suggest that the sort of reform they advocate must begin with "those whose means permit any experiments which their taste may suggest. When the rich man demands good architecture his neighbors will get it too" (xxi–xxii). The authors' classist ideas are also palpable when they declare, in a line partially cited by the *Book Buyer* critic, that "every good moulding, every carefully studied detail, exacted by those who can afford to indulge their taste, will in time find its way to the carpenter-built cottage" (xxii). In fact, the "rich men" and the less fiscally fortunate "neighbors" who populate *The House of Mirth* would prove these assertions to be less than accurate.

Yet within these class biases lies an important critique of commodity display and ostentatious wealth. Wharton and Codman bemoaned America's transition from "the golden age of architecture to the gilded age of decoration" (196). The word *vulgar*—used to describe the newly moneyed social-climbing outsiders Simon Rosedale of *The House of Mirth*, Elmer Moffatt of *The Custom of the Country*, and Julius Beaufort of *The Age of Innocence*—appears ten times in this book, where a variant of *ugly* surfaces twenty-eight times. In fact, an early draft of *The Decoration of Houses* laments the "hopeless quagmire of vulgarity and wrongness" into which nineteenth-century architecture and decoration had wandered.[23] Wharton and Codman sought to instill in their readers a more refined sense of good taste, and they illustrated their book with photographs from French, Italian, and British homes and furniture from the sixteenth to eighteenth centuries. The book instructed designers how to avoid the pitfalls of the "incongruous effects" they recognized in the conspicuous displays of wealth evident in contemporary hotels (such as the overdone Spragg rooms in *The Custom of the Country*), public buildings, and millionaires' homes (Chance 2012, 201).

Wharton and Codman were particularly critical of the conspicuous displays of wealth in the leisure-class mansions erected across the East Coast in the 1880s and 1890s—those residences boasting, like Julius Beaufort's of *The Age of Innocence*, "a ball-room lined with gold and marbles, in which the laws of rhythm and logic have been ignored" (Wharton 2003, 16). The conclusion of *The Decoration of Houses* takes to task those Gilded Age excesses, noting with confidence that the "supreme excellence is simplicity. Moderation, fitness, relevance—these are the qualities that give permanence to the work of the great architects" (Wharton and Codman 1897, 198).[24] Eleanor

---

23. Comparing draft to final copy, one notes a conspicuous softening of tone particularly as concerns the use of the word *vulgar*. For example, in the second paragraph of the original introductory chapter, the "hopeless quagmire of vulgarity and wrongness" into which nineteenth-century architecture and decoration had wandered, becomes, in the published version, "a labyrinth of dubious eclecticism" (Codman Family Papers n.d.).

24. Comparing Wharton's leisure-class narratives with those documenting the working classes further underscores her sense that money and taste do not go hand in hand. Wharton's short story "The Reckoning" (1904), depicting well-heeled New Yorkers, describes a day "radiant, metallic . . . one of those searching American days so calculated to reveal the shortcomings of our street-cleaning and the excesses of our architecture" (Lewis 1968, 432). Her *Bunner Sisters* (1916), on the other hand, describes two women in a very different 1870s New York, who, living in cramped back rooms, manage to set up a "pleasantly fixed," "cosy" home, though they "live very plainly" and have "very simple tastes" (183).

Dwight observes that "although they admired the Italians and their splendid villas and palaces, the authors deemed Italian architecture more appropriate for court functions and suggested the reader look to eighteenth-century France or England for models for the private house" (Dwight 1994, 54).

That particular directive may well have been aimed at the Vanderbilts, whom Wharton knew and to whom she introduced Ogden Codman Jr., and it helps explain her disdain for Isabella Stewart Gardner, who audaciously erected a copy of an Italian villa in the heart of Boston. The Vanderbilts were responsible, for example, for the Petit Chateau on the corner of Fifth Avenue and 52nd Street in New York, designed by Richard Morris Hunt in 1883 for William K. and Alva Vanderbilt, and for such august "cottages" as the Breakers, the Newport home of Cornelius Vanderbilt II and Alice Vanderbilt. In fact, on Wharton's recommendation, Codman oversaw the interior design of the second- and third-floor bedrooms of the Breakers, his refined, streamlined style contrasting starkly with the overdone décor of the first floor overseen by the Parisian firm of Jules Allard and Sons. In a letter to Codman, Wharton makes clear her conviction that the sort of wealth possessed by the Vanderbilts does not necessarily denote taste: "I wish the Vanderbilts didn't retard culture so very thoroughly. They are entrenched in a sort of *Thermopylae* of bad taste, from which apparently no force on earth can dislodge them" (May 1, 1897, quoted in Metcalf 1988, 149). That "bad taste" is on display in Wharton's description, in *The Custom of the Country*, of Peter Van Degen's Fifth Avenue mansion. The residence is a loosely veiled reference to the Petit Chateau: "A muddle of misapplied ornament over a thin steel shell was built up in Wall Street, the social trimmings were hastily added in Fifth Avenue; and the union between them was as monstrous and factitious, as unlike the gradual homogeneous growth which flowers into what other countries know as society, as that between the Blois gargoyles on Peter Van Degen's roof and the skeleton walls supporting them" (Wharton 2006, 45).

Wharton and Codman offered the book as a kind of corrective for the overly ornamental and perversely "monstrous" mansions of the

Editor's Introduction   ⌐   li

robber barons—what William Shakespeare might have anticipated in speaking of "the gilded monuments / of princes" which shall not "outlive [his] powerful rhyme" (Sonnet 55, lines 1–2). Indeed many of the original Gilded Age mansions were razed. Wharton and Codman also sought to counter the advice found in two exceedingly popular decorating guides they despised: the aforementioned *Hints on Household Taste in Furniture, Upholstery and Other Details* (1868) by Charles Locke Eastlake, a British architect and designer who established the style named for him, and *House Beautiful* (1877) by the American author and art critic Clarence Cook. They dismissed both tomes as sentimental, unscholarly, and unscientific, and with their book established rules for domestic law and order that are far more authoritative than the sort of "hints" provided in the earlier tracts.

In *A Backward Glance*, Wharton speaks to the book's usefulness when she reflects on the change in the American scene and how the principles advocated in *The Decoration of Houses* were drawn upon at the turn into the twentieth century:

> With the coming of the new millionaires the building of big houses had begun, in New York and in the country, bringing with it (though not always to those for whom the building was done) a keen interest in architecture, furniture and works of art in general . . . With the coming of Edward Robinson (formerly of the Boston Museum) as Director of the Metropolitan, and the growth of the Hewitt sisters' activities in organizing their Museum of Decorative Art at the Cooper Union, the doctrines first preached by "The Decoration of Houses" were beginning to find general expression; and in many houses there was already a new interest in letters as well as art. (Wharton 1934, 148)

Wharton would elaborate on her sense of this budding "interest in letters as well as art" in a rare speaking engagement in October 1897, addressed to an audience of Newport schoolteachers (Wharton 1897, 8). While lamenting her native country's failure to afford conditions conducive to "the development of taste," Wharton saw signs of hope: "People are beginning to understand the immense educational value of good architecture and art."[25] To her mind, immersing children in beauty was akin to shielding them from "ugliness—the ugliness of indifference, the ugliness of disorder, the ugliness of evil." Ugliness, she would note in her memoir, had "always vaguely frightened" her and she would write often of what she called "the intolerable ugliness of New York" (Wharton 1934, 28).[26] Her antidote to ugliness was to hang copies from the great masters in schoolrooms to cultivate in young persons an appreciation of beauty. Beautiful environments, Wharton argued, improve a person's quality of life, education, and character. "Who," she wondered, "can long be rough and slatternly and indifferent in a pretty, well-kept house?" As she saw it, "If a little of the prettiness and order is allowed to overflow into each room, each member of the family will come to regard himself as holding a share in the capital of beauty, and as vitally interested in preserving and increasing that capital." Wharton thus drew on the language of the stock market to describe the dividends of investing in fine art and design.

Wharton and Codman's book, then, which has never gone out of print, helped ignite in the late nineteenth-century reading public a new passion for art and design and a reverence for the "best models" of architecture, which they identified in the buildings erected in Italy after the beginning of the sixteenth century. As Alvin Holm has noted, "The marvel of *The Decoration of Houses* is that it marries the practitioner's or insider's view to the layman's or outsider's perspective" (1997, 276). That marriage would stand the test of time, for with

25. Wharton and Codman would use a similar sentence construction throughout *The Decoration of Houses*. They note that architects, decorators, and consumers are "beginning to" perceive, see, understand, and rediscover good art and architecture.

26. In an October 1897 letter to the *Newport Daily News*, Wharton would argue a point that would resonate across *The Decoration of Houses*, which she was then preparing for publication, about the democratizing influence of art and the fact that beautiful things are now more universally within reach, or at least within reach of her target audience: "Better bare walls in a schoolroom than bad art. But nowadays there is no excuse for either . . . The best is within reach; let us for ourselves and our children refuse anything less than the best" (1897, 8).

each new generation the book continues to attract and delight new friends and admirers.

"The Exotic Coquetry of Architecture": A *Decoration of Houses* for the Twenty-First Century

Edith Wharton is arguably the only American writer who taught herself architecture, interior design, art history, and garden planning. Architecture was so important to Wharton that she listed it, in her personal diary, as a "ruling passion," alongside justice, order, dogs, books, flowers, travel, and a good joke.[27]

The very notion of order was part of her personal mantra as evidenced in her private papers[28] and in the home she designed and named The Mount.[29] Wharton's respect for and command of visual culture and sound design, her insistence on eliminating "bric-à-brac" and cultivating one's garden, permeate just about every piece of writing she produced. We see it in the penurious but fastidious heroine of "Mrs. Manstey's View" (1891), Wharton's first published story, who "deeply

---

27. "My ruling passions: Justice—Order. Dogs. Books. Flowers. Architecture. Travel. A good joke—& perhaps that should have come first." From a list Edith Wharton made in 1906. Fragment reproduced with permission from the Lilly Library, Indiana University.

28. Wharton identified as "My Motto" the line "order the beauty even of Beauty is," drawn from "The Vision" by the seventeenth-century poet Thomas Traherne, in a private journal begun in the year 1924 called "Quaderno Dello Studente." She also chose it as the epigraph to her treatise *The Writing of Fiction* (1924) (Rattray 2009, 209).

29. As Judith Fryer has noted in her discussion of The Mount, "What emerges most clearly from this plan is a sense of *order*: the careful symmetry allows for no unexpected mingling of servants and masters, no penetration of guests into private quarters, no romantic hermitages in the gardens, but rather a kind of social interaction that is carefully planned, controlled, deliberate. The plan says: patterns of movement here express certain kinds of long-standing traditions; and at the same time this house is a projection of an idealized self, a retreat, a series of protective enclosures" (Fryer 1986, 73–74).

W. always said that ~~prob.~~ Success in life depended more on luck than was generally admitted. In the main I agree. but there are people who knock bad luck into good by just butting at it

_____

My ruling passions:
Justice & order.
Dogs.
Books.
Flowers
Architecture.
Travel —
a good joke — +
perhaps that should have come first

5. Ruling Passions. Courtesy of Lilly Library, Indiana University.

disapprov[es] of the mustard-colored curtains which . . . hung in the doctor's window opposite" her boarding-house room (4).[30] Mrs. Manstey's fierce commitment to and adoration of her view is not unlike her creator's, evident when we consider Wharton's (resplendent, hard-earned) vista from the terrace of her French Riviera property discussed below. The meticulous attention to domestic detail that marks Mrs. Manstey surfaces in the haunting Wharton poem from the same period, "The Dead Wife": "The door . . . I shall open no more," "the room I knew," "that one opal cup," a "Venice glass" (Wharton 1889–93, reprinted in Goldman-Price 2019, 254). In the chilling tale "Afterward," Wharton writes that "the house knew [where and why the protagonist's husband had vanished]—"the library in which she spent her long lonely evenings knew" (1973, 71). Wharton's body of work reveals a career-long fascination with what she provocatively called, in *The House of Mirth*, the "exotic coquetry of architecture" (2018, 158). She would employ similar terms to describe interior décor, playfully suggesting that "the most perilous coquetry may not be in a woman's way of arranging her dress but in her way of arranging her drawing-room" ("New Year's Day"). Henry James would affectionately suggest of Wharton that "no one fully knows our Edith who hasn't seen her in the act of creating a habitation for herself" (quoted in Lubbock 1947). Similarly, readers of Wharton's celebrated novels, and increasingly appreciated achievements in the short story, poetry, playwriting, travel writing, and memoir, can only become fully acquainted with her by turning to her contributions to the study of architecture and design.

30. The opening line of Wharton and Codman's chapter on "Windows" lends a new context to a reading of Wharton's first published short story, "Mrs. Manstey's View": "In the decorative treatment of a room the importance of openings can hardly be overestimated. Not only do they represent the three chief essentials of its comfort,—light, heat and means of access,—but they are the leading features in that combination of voids and masses that forms the basis of architectural harmony. In fact, it is chiefly because the decorative value of openings has ceased to be recognized that modern rooms so seldom produce a satisfactory and harmonious impression" (1897, 64).

This new edition of *The Decoration of Houses*, annotated for the first time to contextualize Wharton's richly allusive prose, seeks to enable readers to draw meaningful connections between the design ideas expressed in the 1897 book and Wharton's strategic use of spaces throughout her writings across genre and class. For instance, the well-heeled Newland Archer's refusal to relinquish his thrice-referenced "'sincere' Eastlake furniture"—a writing desk and bookcases—show him, in the Gilded Age milieu of *The Age of Innocence*, to be more old-fashioned than he would care to admit.[31] A loosely veiled Vanderbilt's "Newport villa" with its expensive lawn, marble hall, and underused library in the short story "The Line of Least Resistance" (1900) tells us all we need to know about him. The "unusually forlorn and stunted" facade of the impecunious Ethan Frome's house unsubtly reflects the emotionally and physically bereft state of the eponymous protagonist (Wharton 1911, 8). The Connecticut home of Sara Clayburn, described in Wharton's posthumously published story "All Souls'" (1937), calls to mind Wharton's own sensibly designed residences and her relation to them: "The house . . . was open, airy, high-ceilinged, with electricity, central heating and all the modern appliances; and its mistress was—well, very much like her house" (1973, 152); although Mrs. Clayburn's home underwent renovation, "the architect had respected the character of the old house, and the enlargement made it more comfortable without lessening its simplicity" (253–54). The "horribly poor but very expensive" Lily Bart's sense that she might

---

31. Judith Fryer insightfully confirms the criticism implied by Wharton's scare quotes: "She [Wharton] had only scorn for the eclectic house whose rooms represented a variety of styles and for the modern room with its lack of balance and its confusion between the essential and the inessential. She took Eastlake to task for focusing on furniture and ornament to the exclusion of doors, windows or fireplaces because she believed that decoration is only valid when it is a branch of architecture—that is, when it is organic. Wharton's linking of Newland Archer's preferences in tasteful decoration to 'sincere' Eastlake is, then, a devastating criticism: he is a man of 'taste' rather than a man of principle—or at least he is a man whose principles are determined externally, according to taste" (Fryer 1986, 121).

"be a better woman" if she had a drawing room to "do over" assumes new meaning when read in the context of *The Decoration of Houses*.[32] Reflecting on Miss Bart's poignant example allows us to appreciate Wharton's profound investment in the theme of finding and making one's home, and thus improving one's quality of life.[33] Lily, reduced to tenement occupancy by the novel's close, had been physically repulsed by her aunt's "dreary" Victorian home, the "cramped flat" of her friend Gerty Farish, and the "appalling" and "mausoleum"-like house of her onetime suitor Percy Gryce (Wharton 2018, 78, 22). As Elif Armbruster has noted, Lily's "lack of attachment to a home is the strongest clue to her imminent demise."[34] Lily is, ultimately, homeless, "expatriate everywhere."

As an artist expatriated but happily rehomed in France, Edith Wharton's life actualized the possibilities of *The Decoration of Houses*. She would write, in *A Backward Glance*, that Pavillon Colombe, the stately home outside Paris where she would spend her final hours, afforded her the serenity she sought after the cultural cataclysm of the Great War: "The little house has never failed me since. As soon as I was settled in it peace and order came back into my life. I had leisure for the two pursuits which never palled, writing and gardening, and all through the years I have gone on gardening and writing" (1934, 363).

32. It would be difficult to locate a Wharton text, published or unpublished, inattentive to the connection between the psychological interior and the domestic context.

33. Wharton's philosophy on domestic spaces is not far removed from that of the American landscape designer Andrew Jackson Downing (1815–1852), who had proposed that "a good house will lead to a good civilization" and that a good home will promote the moral strength of its inhabitants. The enormously influential Downing designed villas for the wealthy, cottages for the working classes, and farmhouses for farmers. In fact, the 1859 edition of his book *A Treatise on the Theory and Practice of Landscape Gardening, Adapted to North America* (first published in 1841), was "one of the prize possessions of Wharton's library" (Lee 2007, 121).

34. "Because Lily has never been able to enjoy a true home and has never become attached to one or been able to create her own, she is lost in the truest sense of the word" (Armbruster 2019, 420).

6. Edith Wharton on the terrace at Castel Sainte Claire, circa 1920–1930. Courtesy of Lilly Library, Indiana University and the Edith Wharton Estate.

In the winter months, Wharton found equanimity at Sainte Claire du Vieux Château, her home in Hyères, overlooking the Mediterranean's "glitter of blue & gold" (Lee 2007, 547). The unassailable joy of spending her first Christmas at the south of France home is palpable in a 1920 letter to her sister-in-law Mary Cadwalader Jones:

> The little house is delicious, so friendly & comfortable & full of sun & air; but what overwhelms us all—though we thought we knew it—is the endless beauty of the view, or rather the views, for we look south, east & west, "miles & miles," & our quiet-coloured end of evening presents us with a full moon standing over the tower of the great Romanesque church just below the house, & a sunset silhouetting the "Isles d'Or" in black on a sea of silver. It is good to grow old—as well as to die—'in beauty'; & the beauty of this little place is inexhaustible. (Lewis and Lewis 1988, 436)

While neither of her postwar French properties properly would be called "little" by our standards, the history of the Hyères site seems fitting for its new owner: it originally served as a castle, later the site of a convent for the sisters of Sainte Claire. More recently, in the nineteenth century, the property had been owned by the French naval officer and archaeologist Olivier Voutier, best known for escorting the Venus de Milo from Greece to France. A worthy choice, then, for a lifelong lover of nature and beauty. When Wharton was readying to undertake the necessary renovations, introducing, for instance, such elements celebrated in *The Decoration of Houses* as marble floors, sensibly proportioned furnishings, and understated architectural accents, she declared, in a letter to Royall Tyler: "I am thrilled to the spine . . . and I feel as if I were going to get married—to the right man at last!" (Lewis and Lewis 1988, 417). Recognizing, like the heroine of "Afterward," the "opportunities to bring out the latent graces of the old place" (Wharton 1973, 61), she would ultimately locate in Sainte Claire what she called "the Great Good Place" (Lee 2007, 547). When we take in what we might call "Mrs. Wharton's view," which looks out to the Côte d'Azur and the island of Porquerolles, we see the writer's

7. Castel Sainte Claire, Hyères, France, 2023. Courtesy of Nels Pearson.

life come full circle. It is hard to imagine a more consummate declaration of self-possession than Wharton's claim, "It's only at Hyères that I own myself" (Lee 2007, 548).

The link Edith Wharton forged between owning one's self and setting up a loved home is echoed in such house and garden lifestyle forums as "The Inspired Room," "Nesting Place," and "Apartment Therapy" and in such bestselling books as Emily Henderson's *The New Design Rules: How to Decorate and Renovate, from Start to Finish* and Shea McGee's *The Art of Home*. TheNester.com posits that "home is an ever-shifting combination of grace, cozy, abundance, simplicity, form and function." Edith Wharton, who has been called a "Victorian Martha Stewart" (Perkins 2014), would agree, and her name and first book of prose are increasingly and emphatically hashtagged and pinned across social media. More than simply a historical study, *The Decoration of Houses* articulates its own design philosophy while also broadcasting a list of dos and don'ts that still make sense to modern readers (Wilson 1988, 154). *The Decoration of Houses* is arguably more

8. View from Edith Wharton's terrace at Castel Sainte Claire, Hyères, France, 2023. Courtesy of Nels Pearson.

useful than ever before in our lifetimes, particularly as a pandemic compelled many of us to reimagine, and in many cases conduct business from, our homes. More people have adjusted their habits such that the acronym WFH (work from home) is now part of the modern lexicon. The book's recommendations for honoring the architectural integrity of our living spaces and introducing more harmony, balance, symmetry, order, well-made furniture, lightly colored walls, and the right kind of light are being drawn upon to enhance the quality of our lives. Wharton and Codman's no-nonsense advice—for example, "good things do not always cost more than bad" (Wharton and Codman 1897, 176); "better to buy each year one superior piece rather than a dozen of middling quality" (194); avoid the tendency to "buy too many things, or things out of proportion with the rooms for which they are intended" (185)—is as useful to the twenty-first-century shopper as it was to the conspicuous consumer of the American 1890s. After all, Marie Kondo's call, in the best-selling *The Life-Changing*

Magic of Tidying Up: The Japanese Art of Decluttering and Organizing, to eliminate what fails to "spark joy," is a modern-day version of Wharton's insistence on banishing the "ugly," the "showy," and the "vulgar."

Given the considerable attention paid, in our twenty-first-century lives, to the relationship between domestic environments and the wellness and mindfulness of the soul, it is no exaggeration to say that Edith Wharton's philosophy of domestic aesthetics extends further than she could have imagined. It is the hope that the present volume, each chapter annotated to gloss, for the first time, Wharton's allusions to art, architecture, design, history, literature, mythology, foreign figures of speech (originally left untranslated from French, Italian, Latin, German, and Greek), and concepts unfamiliar to what the French economist Thomas Piketty has called our "new Gilded Age," will enable the reader new to, or well versed in, Edith Wharton to fully grasp the extent to which an investment in the poetics of space permeates her entire corpus. At the same time this edition seeks to support all readers in their quests to "bring out the latent graces" of their living spaces and achieve "that rare harmony of feeling which levie[s] a tax on every sense" (Wharton 2001, 323–24).

Books Consulted
by Wharton and Codman

FRENCH

Androuet du Cerceau, Jacques.
Les Plus Excellents Bâtiments de France. Paris, 1607.

Le Muet, Pierre.
Manière de Bien Bâtir pour toutes sortes de Personnes.

Oppenord, Gilles Marie.
Œuvres. 1750.

Mariette, Pierre Jean.
L'Architecture Françoise. 1727.

Briseux, Charles Étienne.
L'Art de Bâtir les Maisons de Campagne. Paris, 1743.

Lalonde, François Richard de.
Recueil de ses Œuvres.

Aviler, C. A. d'.
Cours d'Architecture. 1760.

Blondel, Jacques François.
Architecture Françoise. Paris, 1752.
Cours d'Architecture. Paris, 1771–77.

De la Distribution des Maisons de Plaisance et de la Décoration des Édifices. Paris, 1737.

Roubo, A. J., fils.
L'Art du Menuisier.

Héré de Corny, Emmanuel.
Recueil des Plans, Élévations et Coupes des Châteaux, Jardins et Dépendances que le Roi de Pologne occupe en Lorraine. Paris, n.d.

Percier et Fontaine.
Choix des plus Célèbres Maisons de Plaisance de Rome et de ses Environs. Paris, 1809.
Palais, Maisons, et autres Édifices Modernes dessinés à Rome. Paris, 1798.
Résidences des Souverains. Paris, 1833.

Krafft et Ransonnette.
Plans, Coupes, et Élévations des plus belles Maisons et Hôtels construits à Paris et dans les Environs. Paris, 1801.

Durand, Jean Nicolas Louis.
Recueil et Parallèle des Édifices de tout Genre. Paris, 1800.
Précis des Leçons d'Architecture données à l'École Royale Polytechnique. Paris, 1823.

Quatremère de Quincy, A. C.
Histoire de la Vie et des Ouvrages des plus Célèbres Architectes du XIe siècle jusqu'à la fin du XVIII siècle. Paris, 1830.

Pellassy de l'Ousle.
Histoire du Palais de Compiègne. Paris, n.d.

Letarouilly, Paul Marie.
Édifices de Rome Moderne. Paris, 1825–57.

Ramée, Daniel.
Histoire Générate de l'Architecture. Paris, 1862.
Meubles Religieux et Civils Conservés dans les princlpaux Monuments et Musées de l'Europe.

Viollet le Duc, Eugène Emmanuel.
Dictionnaire Raisonné de l'Architecture Française du XIe au XVIe siècle. Paris, 1868.

Sauvageot, Claude.
Palais, Châteaux, Hôtels et Maisons de France du XVe au XVIIIe siècle.

Daly, César.
Motifs Historiques d'Architecture et de Sculpture d'Ornement.

Rouyer et Darcel.
L'Art Architectural en France depuis François Ier jusqu'à Louis XIV.

Havard, Henry.
Dictionnaire de l'Ameublement et de la Décoration depuis le XIIIe siècle jusqu'à nos Jours. Paris, n.d.
Les Arts de l'Ameublement.

Guilmard, D.
Les Maîtres Ornemanistes. Paris, 1880.

Bauchal, Charles.
Dictionnaire des Architectes Français. Paris, 1887.

Rouaix, Paul.
Les Styles. Paris, n.d.

Bibliothèque de l'Enseignement des Beaux Arts.
Maison Quantin, Paris.

ENGLISH

Ware, Isaac.
A Complete Body of Architecture. London, 1756.

Brettincham, Matthew.
Plans, Elevations and Sections of Holkham in Norfolk, the Seat of the late Earl of Leicester. London, 1761.

Campbell, Colen.
Vitruvius Britannicus; Or, the British Architect. London, 1771.

Adam, Robert and James.
The Works in Architecture. London, 1773–1822.

Hepplewhite, A.
The Cabinet-Maker and Upholsterer's Guide.

Sheraton, Thomas.
The Cabinet-Maker's Dictionary. London, 1803.

Pain, William.
The British Palladio; Or the Builder's General Assistant. London, 1797.

Soane, Sir John.
Sketches in Architecture. London, 1793.

Hakewill, Arthur William.
General Plan and External Details, with Picturesque Illustrations, of Thorpe Hall, Peterborough.

Lewis, James.
Original Designs in Architecture.

Pyne, William Henry.
History of the Royal Residences of Windsor Castle, St. James's Palace, Carlton House, Kensington Palace, Hampton Court, Buckingham Palace, and Frogmore. London, 1819.

Gwilt, Joseph.
Encyclopedia of Architecture. New edition. Longman's, 1895.

Fergusson, James.
History of Architecture. London, 1874.
History of the Modern Styles of Architecture. Third edition, revised by Robert Kerr. London, 1891.

Gotch, John Alfred.
Architecture of the Renaissance in England.

Heaton, John Aldam.
Furniture and Decoration in England in the Eighteenth Century.

Rosengarten.
Handbook of Architectural Styles. New York, 1876.

Horne, H. P.
The Binding of Books. London, 1894.

Loftie, W. J.
Inigo Jones and Christopher Wren. London, 1893.

Kerr, Robert.
The English Gentleman's House. London, 1865.

Stevenson, J. J.
House Architecture. London, 1880.

German and Italian

Burckhardt, Jacob.
Architektur der Renaissance in Italien. Stuttgart, 1891.

Reinhardt.
Palast Architektur von Ober Italien und Toskana.

Gurlitt, Cornelius.
Geschichte des Barockstiles in Italien. Stuttgart, 1887.

Ebe, Gustav.
Die Spät-Renaissance. Berlin, 1886.
La Villa Borghese, fuori di Porta Pinciana, con l'ornamenti che si osservano nel di lei Palazzo. Roma, 1700.

Intra, G. B.
Mantova nei suoi Monumenti.

Luzio e Renier.
Mantova e Urbino. Torino-Roma, 1893.

Molmenti, Pompeo.
La Storia di Venezia nella Vita Privata. Torino, 1885.

Malamani, Vittorio.
Il Settecento a Venezia. Milano, 1895.
La Vita Italiana nel Seicento. Conferenze tenute a Firenze nel 1890.

The Decoration of Houses

Introduction

Rooms may be decorated in two ways: by a superficial application of ornament totally independent of structure, or by means of those architectural features which are part of the organism of every house, inside as well as out.

In the middle ages, when warfare and brigandage[1] shaped the conditions of life, and men camped in their castles much as they did in their tents, it was natural that decorations should be portable, and that the naked walls of the mediæval chamber should be hung with arras,[2] while a *ciel*, or ceiling, of cloth stretched across the open timbers of its roof.

When life became more secure, and when the Italian conquests of the Valois[3] had acquainted men north of the Alps with the spirit of classic tradition, proportion and the relation of voids to masses gradually came to be regarded as the chief decorative values of the interior. Portable hangings were in consequence replaced by architectural ornament: in other words, the architecture of the room became its decoration.

This architectural treatment held its own through every change of taste until the second quarter of the present century; but since then various influences have combined to sever the natural connection between the outside of the modern house and its interior. In the

---

1. Highway robbery, freebooting, pillage (*OED*).

2. A tapestry, wall hanging, or curtain, especially one of Flemish origin (*American Heritage Dictionary* 2022).

3. Dynastic family that ruled France from 1328 to 1589 (*EB* 2019mm).

average house the architect's task seems virtually confined to the elevations and floor-plan. The designing of what are today regarded as insignificant details, such as mouldings, architraves, and cornices,[4] has become a perfunctory work, hurried over and unregarded; and when this work is done, the upholsterer[5] is called in to "decorate" and furnish the rooms.

As the result of this division of labor, house-decoration has ceased to be a branch of architecture. The upholsterer cannot be expected to have the preliminary training necessary for architectural work, and it is inevitable that in his hands form should be sacrificed to color and composition to detail. In his ignorance of the legitimate means of producing certain effects, he is driven to all manner of expedients, the

4. Ornamental outlines given to linear features of a building or room (*OED*); mouldings that surround a doorway or window (*OED*); projecting mouldings that crown a building or room; type of crown moulding (*OED*).

5. From the Middle English term *upholder*, "artist who held up goods," carrying the connotation of repairing furniture rather than creating new pieces, and from the seventeenth-century term *upholster*, meaning "small furniture dealer." In eighteenth-century London, upholders frequently served as interior decorators responsible for all aspects of domestic decoration. In *Town Life in Australia* (1883), R. E. N. (Richard) Twopeny observes that "one or two millionaires have had upholsterers out from Gillow's and Jackson and Graham's to furnish their houses in the latest and most correct fashion, and many colonists who go on a trip to England bring back with them drawing and dining room suites." (Gillow & Company, in business from 1862 to 1897, a British firm that engaged in the making of cabinets, chairs, and gilding, and offered such services as upholstery and interior decoration [Furniture History Society 2022]. "In the pantheon of Victorian furnishing enterprises few names are more important than those of Jackson and Graham. In business for nearly fifty years, they served the needs of numerous illustrious clients, including the Sultan of the Ottoman Empire, Queen Victoria, Napoleon III, the Grand Khedive at Cairo, and the Royal Palace" [Edwards 1998, 238–65]). Edith Wharton and Ogden Codman disclose their frustration at the Victorian era's overreliance on the upholsterer with such jabs as "what the modern upholsterer fails to understand" and "the modern upholsterer pads and puffs his seats as though they were to form the furniture of a lunatic's cell," and by suggesting one might refer to him "more fitly" as "the house-dressmaker." They recommend that the decorator instead conceive of the home architecturally.

result of which is a piling up of heterogeneous ornament, a multiplication of incongruous effects; and lacking, as he does, a definite first
conception, his work becomes so involved that it seems impossible for
him to make an end.

The confusion resulting from these unscientific methods has
reflected itself in the lay mind, and house-decoration has come to be
regarded as a black art[6] by those who have seen their rooms subjected
to the manipulations of the modern upholsterer. Now, in the hands
of decorators who understand the fundamental principles of their art,
the surest effects are produced, not at the expense of simplicity and
common sense, but by observing the requirements of both. These
requirements are identical with those regulating domestic architecture, the chief end in both cases being the suitable accommodation of
the inmates of the house.

The fact that this end has in a measure been lost sight of is perhaps sufficient warrant for the publication of this elementary sketch.
No study of *house-decoration as a branch of architecture* has for at least
fifty years been published in England or America; and though France
is always producing admirable monographs on isolated branches of
this subject, there is no modern French work corresponding with
such comprehensive manuals as d'Aviler's *Cours d'Architecture* or Isaac
Ware's *Complete Body of Architecture.*[7]

The attempt to remedy this deficiency in some slight degree has
made it necessary to dwell at length upon the strictly architectural
principles which controlled the work of the old decorators. The effects
that they aimed at having been based mainly on the due adjustment

6. Suspicious or sinister practice, akin to witchcraft; used similarly by Wharton
to describe Old New York's distrust of the art of writing: "In the eyes of our provincial society authorship was still regarded as something between a black art and a form
of manual labour" (*OED*).

7. By architect Charles Augustin d'Aviler (1653–1701), defines French architectural terms and advises on specific architectural styles (Cabestan 2012); by English
architect Isaac Ware (1704–66), containing encyclopedic definitions and engravings
of architectural terms (Metropolitan Museum of Art n.d.).

of parts, it has been impossible to explain their methods without assuming their standpoint—that of *architectural proportion*—in contradistinction to the modern view of house-decoration as *superficial application of ornament*. When house-decoration was a part of architecture all its values were founded on structural modifications; consequently it may seem that ideas to be derived from a study of such methods suggest changes too radical for those who are not building, but are merely decorating. Such changes, in fact, lie rather in the direction of alteration than of adornment; but it must be remembered that the results attained will be of greater decorative value than were an equal expenditure devoted to surface-ornament. Moreover, the great decorators, if scrupulous in the observance of architectural principles, were ever governed, in the use of ornamental detail, by the σωφροσύνη,[8] the "wise moderation," of the Greeks; and the rooms of the past were both simpler in treatment and freer from mere embellishments than those of to-day.

Besides, if it be granted for the sake of argument that a reform in house-decoration, if not necessary, is at least desirable, it must be admitted that such reform can originate only with those whose means permit of any experiments which their taste may suggest. When the rich man demands good architecture his neighbors will get it too. The vulgarity of current decoration has its source in the indifference of the wealthy to architectural fitness. Every good moulding, every carefully studied detail, exacted by those who can afford to indulge their taste, will in time find its way to the carpenter-built cottage. Once the right precedent is established, it costs less to follow than to oppose it.

In conclusion, it may be well to explain the seeming lack of accord between the arguments used in this book and the illustrations chosen

8. Greek: "prudence." In the context of architectural principles, it can be rendered as "wise moderation" insofar as making a sound judgment entails an observance of balanced boundaries. The use of "wise" emphasizes the moral tinge that Wharton and Codman ascribe to architectural character; note, too, the authors' use of the morally coded *good* and *bad* to describe art, architecture, and design throughout. Thank you to Myrto Drizou for her kind assistance with this translation.

1. Italian Gothic Chest. Museum of the Bargello, Florence.

to interpret them.[9] While much is said of simplicity, the illustrations used are chiefly taken from houses of some importance. This has been done in order that only such apartments as are accessible to the traveller might be given as examples. Unprofessional readers will probably be more interested in studying rooms that they have seen, or at least heard of, than those in the ordinary private dwelling; and the arguments advanced are indirectly sustained by the most ornate rooms here shown, since their effect is based on such harmony of line

9. With this disclaimer, Wharton and Codman anticipate the following criticism articulated by a reviewer: "The illustrations, however, are largely drawn from just such magnificent places of temporary abode or festal use, so that to a person turning over the leaves of this book a false idea of its contents is conveyed" ("Hints for Home Decoration" 1898, 20).

that their superficial ornament might be removed without loss to the composition.

Moreover, as some of the illustrations prove, the most magnificent palaces of Europe contain rooms as simple as those in any private house; and to point out that simplicity is at home even in palaces is perhaps not the least service that may be rendered to the modern decorator.

1

The Historical Tradition

The last ten years have been marked by a notable development in architecture and decoration, and while France will long retain her present superiority in these arts, our own advance is perhaps more significant than that of any other country.[1] When we measure the work recently done in the United States by the accepted architectural standards of ten years ago, the change is certainly striking, especially in view of the fact that our local architects and decorators are without the countless advantages in the way of schools, museums and libraries which are at the command of their European colleagues. In Paris, for instance, it is impossible to take even a short walk without finding inspiration in those admirable buildings, public and private, religious and secular, that bear the stamp of the most refined taste the world has known since the decline of the arts in Italy; and probably all American architects will acknowledge that no amount of travel abroad and study at home can compensate for the lack of daily familiarity with such monuments.

It is therefore all the more encouraging to note the steady advance in taste and knowledge to which the most recent architecture in America bears witness. This advance is chiefly due to the fact that American

1. The authors nod to the work of such firms as McKim, Mead & White, which paved the way for the American Renaissance in architecture. Charles F. McKim (1847–1909), William R. Mead (1846–1928), and Stanford White (1853–1906) were trained in the Beaux-Arts tradition in Paris, a style that was prominent from the 1830s to the end of the nineteenth century and was informed by French neoclassicism and Gothic and Renaissance elements. They were collectively responsible for such august American structures as the Brooklyn Museum and the Boston Public Library.

architects are beginning to perceive two things that their French colleagues, among all the modern vagaries of taste, have never quite lost sight of: first that architecture and decoration, having wandered since 1800 in a labyrinth of dubious eclecticism,[2] can be set right only by a close study of the best models; and secondly that, given the requirements of modern life, these models are chiefly to be found in buildings erected in Italy after the beginning of the sixteenth century,[3] and in other European countries after the full assimilation of the Italian influence.

As the latter of these propositions may perhaps be questioned by those who, in admiring the earlier styles, sometimes lose sight of their relative unfitness for modern use, it must be understood at the outset that it implies no disregard for the inherent beauties of these styles. It would be difficult, assuredly, to find buildings better suited to their original purpose than some of the great feudal castles, such as Warwick in England, or Langeais in France; and as much might be said of the grim machicolated palaces of republican Florence or Siena; but our whole mode of life has so entirely changed since the days in which these buildings were erected that they no longer answer to our needs.[4]

2. Throughout their treatise, Edith Wharton and Ogden Codman Jr. lament the state of nineteenth-century architecture and design, arguing that the nadir of 1840 to 1890, which they liken to a "confusion resulting from...unscientific methods," emerged from the "piling up of heterogeneous ornament, [and] a multiplication of incongruous effects." Their solution was to return to the simpler and architecturally correct styles of architecture and design associated with Louis XIV, XV, and XVI. In their chapter on fireplaces, they cite "the general decline of taste which marked the middle of the present century." One of the more memorable edits from typed manuscript to first edition is the insertion of the (much gentler) "labyrinth of dubious eclecticism" in place of the original "hopeless quagmire of vulgarity and wrongness."

3. The authors suggest that Renaissance Italian architecture of the 1500s proves the most admirable models for Americans to emulate. In *Italian Villas and Their Gardens*, Wharton praises Italy's command of form and symmetry, citing "Roman art" as "the true source of modern architecture" (1904, 86).

4. Warwick: medieval castle situated in Warwickshire, England and developed from an original built by William the Conqueror (1028–87) in 1068. Langeais (short

It is only necessary to picture the lives led in those days to see how far removed from them our present social conditions are. Inside and outside the house, all told of the unsettled condition of country or town, the danger of armed attack, the clumsy means of defence, the insecurity of property, the few opportunities of social intercourse as we understand it. A man's house was in very truth his castle in the middle ages, and in France and England especially it remained so until the end of the sixteenth century.

Thus it was that many needs arose: the tall keep of masonry where the inmates, pent up against attack, awaited the signal of the watchman who, from his platform or *échauguette*,[5] gave warning of assault; the ponderous doors, oak-ribbed and metal-studded, with doorways often narrowed to prevent entrance of two abreast, and so low that the incomer had to bend his head; the windows that were mere openings or slits, narrow and high, far out of the assailants' reach, and piercing the walls without regard to symmetry—not, as Ruskin would have us believe, because irregularity was thought artistic,[6] but because the

---

for Château de Langeais): medieval castle, later rebuilt as a château, in Indre-et-Loire, France, on a promontory created by the small valley of the Roumer River at the opening to the Loire Valley. Machicolated (French: *mâchicoulis*): floor opening between the supporting corbels of a battlement, through which stones, or other objects, could be dropped on attackers at the base of a defensive wall.

5. French: a special kind of watchtower; a wall-mounted turret suspended from the stone wall or the corner of one, usually during the late medieval period (thank you to Joel Goldfield for research assistance).

6. John Ruskin (1819–1900): foremost Victorian art critic who insisted on "truth," and therefore irregularity, in depictions of nature. In the chapter "The Nature of Gothic" from *The Stones of Venice*, vol. 2 (1853), Ruskin observes: "And in all things that live there are certain irregularities and deficiencies which are not only signs of life, but sources of beauty. No human face is exactly the same in its lines on each side, no leaf perfect in its lobes, no branch in its symmetry. All admit irregularity as they imply change; and to banish imperfection is to destroy expression, to check exertion, to paralyze vitality." Describing her discovery of the formidable Victorian in her father's library, Wharton notes, "His wonderful cloudy pages gave me back the image of the beautiful Europe I had lost, & woke in me the habit of

mediæval architect, trained to the uses of necessity, knew that he must design openings that should afford no passage to the besiegers' arrows, no clue to what was going on inside the keep. But to the reader familiar with Viollet-le-Duc,[7] or with any of the many excellent works on English domestic architecture, further details will seem superfluous. It is necessary, however, to point out that long after the conditions of life in Europe had changed, houses retained many features of the feudal period. The survival of obsolete customs which makes the study of sociology so interesting, has its parallel in the history of architecture. In the feudal countries especially, where the conflict between the great nobles and the king was of such long duration that civilization spread very slowly, architecture was proportionately slow to give up many of its feudal characteristics. In Italy, on the contrary, where one city after another succumbed to some accomplished condottiere who between his campaigns read Virgil and collected antique marbles,[8] the rugged little republics were soon converted into brilliant courts where, life being relatively secure, social intercourse rapidly developed. This

---

precise visual observation" (2016, 195). She notes that "Ruskin fed me with visions of Italy for which I had never ceased to pine" (1934, 71), acknowledges the "incomparable service" his work did for her developing aesthetic (2016, 195), and admits she could not "disown [her] debt to Ruskin" (2016, 203). Nevertheless, Wharton's love of symmetry, which she drew from her immersion in the Italian scene, compelled her to part ways with Ruskin, who is rather severely taken to task in the third chapter of this book.

7. Eugène-Emmanuel Viollet-le-Duc (1814–79): French Gothic Revival architect, who worked extensively on restoring French medieval buildings, including Notre-Dame de Paris. Wharton would later disclose, in *A Motor-Flight through France*, her misgivings regarding the alterations he made to these structures: "It was Viollet-le-Duc who added the west front and towers to this high ancient pile; and for once his audacious hand was so happily inspired that, at the first glimpse of his twin spires soaring above the roofs of Clermont, one forgives him—for the moment—the wrong he did to Blois, to Pierrefonds and Carcassonne" (Wharton 1907).

8. Leaders (or warlords) of the professional, military-free companies (or mercenaries) contracted by the Italian city-states and the papacy from the late Middle Ages through the Renaissance.

change of conditions brought with it the paved street and square, the large-windowed palaces with their great court-yards and stately open staircases, and the market-place with its loggia[9] adorned with statues and marble seats.

Italy, in short, returned instinctively to the Roman ideal of civic life: the life of the street, the forum and the baths. These very conditions, though approaching so much nearer than feudalism to our modern civilization, in some respects make the Italian architecture of the Renaissance less serviceable as a model than the French and English styles later developed from it. The very dangers and barbarities of feudalism had fostered and preserved the idea of home as of something private, shut off from intrusion; and while the Roman ideal flowered in the great palace with its galleries, loggias and saloons, itself a kind of roofed-in forum, the French or English feudal keep became, by the same process of growth, the modern private house. The domestic architecture of the Renaissance in Italy offers but two distinctively characteristic styles of building: the palace and the villa or hunting-lodge.[†] There is nothing corresponding in interior arrangements with the French or English town house, or the *manoir* where the provincial nobles lived all the year round. The villa was a mere perch used for a few weeks of gaiety in spring or autumn; it was never a home as the French or English country-house was. There were, of course, private houses in Renaissance Italy, but these were occupied rather by shopkeepers,

9. Covered exterior gallery or corridor, usually on an upper level, or sometimes ground level. The outer wall is open to the elements, typically supported by a series of columns or arches.

† Charming as the Italian villa is, it can hardly be used in our Northern States without certain modifications, unless it is merely occupied for a few weeks in midsummer; whereas the average French or English country house built after 1600 is perfectly suited to our climate and habits. The chief features of the Italian villa are the open central *cortile* and the large saloon two stories high. An adaptation of these better suited to a cold climate is to be found in the English country houses built in the Palladian manner after its introduction by Inigo Jones. See Campbell's *Vitruvius Britannicus* for numerous examples. († indicates original footnote written by Wharton and Codman.)

craftsmen, and the *bourgeoisie* than by the class which in France and
England lived in country houses or small private hôtels. The elevations
of these small Italian houses are often admirable examples of domestic
architecture, but their planning is rudimentary, and it may be said that
the characteristic tendencies of modern house-planning were developed rather in the mezzanin[10] or low-studded intermediate story of the
Italian Renaissance palace than in the small house of the same period.

It is a fact recognized by political economists that changes in manners and customs, no matter under what form of government, usually originate with the wealthy or aristocratic minority, and are thence
transmitted to the other classes. Thus the *bourgeois* of one generation
lives more like the aristocrat of a previous generation than like his own
predecessors. This rule naturally holds good of house-planning, and it
is for this reason that the origin of modern house-planning should be
sought rather in the prince's mezzanin than in the small middle-class
dwelling. The Italian mezzanin probably originated in the habit of
building certain very high-studded saloons and of lowering the ceiling
of the adjoining rooms. This created an intermediate story, or rather
scattered intermediate rooms, which Bramante was among the first
to use in the planning of his palaces; but Bramante did not reveal the
existence of the mezzanin in his façades, and it was not until the time
of Peruzzi and his contemporaries that it became, both in plan and
elevation, an accepted part of the Italian palace.[11] It is for this reason that the year 1500 is a convenient point from which to date the

10. Also mezzanine, an intermediate floor between main floors of a building,
and therefore typically not counted among the total number of floors. Often, a mezzanine has a low ceiling and is projected in the form of a balcony.

11. Donato Bramante (1444–1514): first Italian architect to introduce the High
Renaissance into architecture. The style, which appeared at the beginning of the
sixteenth century, was characterized by reinterpreting classical forms and was concentrated in Rome. Bramante's Tempietto (c. 1502), a small, circular chapel in the
courtyard of San Pietro in Montorio in Rome, is considered the archetypal example
of High Renaissance architecture. Peruzzi: Baldassare Peruzzi (1481–1536): Italian
architect and contemporary of Bramante, known for his Renaissance palace, Mas-
simo alle Colonne (c. 1536), in which he curved the façade of the building to match

beginning of modern house-planning; but it must be borne in mind that this date is purely arbitrary, and represents merely an imaginary line drawn between mediæval and modern ways of living and house-planning, as exemplified respectively, for instance, in the ducal palace of Urbino, built by Luciano da Laurano about 1468,[12] and the palace of the Massimi alle Colonne in Rome, built by Baldassare Peruzzi during the first half of the sixteenth century.

The lives of the great Italian nobles were essentially open-air lives: all was organized with a view to public pageants, ceremonies and entertainments. Domestic life was subordinated to this spectacular existence, and instead of building private houses in our sense, they built palaces, of which they set aside a portion for the use of the family. Every Italian palace has its mezzanin or private apartment; but this part of the building is now seldom seen by travellers in Italy. Not only is it usually inhabited by the owners of the palace but, its decorations being simpler than those of the *piano nobile*, or principal story,[13] it is not thought worthy of inspection. As a matter of fact, the treatment of the mezzanin was generally most beautiful, because most suitable; and while the Italian Renaissance palace can seldom serve as a model for a modern private house, the decoration of the mezzanin rooms is full of appropriate suggestion.

In France and England, on the other hand, private life was gradually, though slowly, developing along the lines it still follows in the present day. It is necessary to bear in mind that what we call modern

---

the slight curvature of the road, thus breaking with traditional architectural principles by organizing the design of the structure around its site.

12. Luciano da Laurano (ca. 1420–79): also Laurana, Italian architect and principal designer of the Palazzo Ducale in Urbino (1475), thought to have been responsible for the construction of the courtyard and entrance.

13. Italian for "noble floor"; in architecture, the main floor of a Renaissance building. In the typical palazzo, erected by an Italian prince, the main reception rooms were in an upper story, usually one immediately above the basement or ground floor. The term also refers to the main floors of similarly constructed buildings of the English Palladian style of the eighteenth century and of those built in England and the United States during the Renaissance revival of the mid- and late nineteenth century.

civilization was a later growth in these two countries than in Italy. If this fact is insisted upon, it is only because it explains the relative unsuitability of French Renaissance or Tudor and Elizabethan architecture to modern life.[14] In France, for instance, it was not until the Fronde was subdued and Louis XIV firmly established on the throne, that the elements which compose what we call modern life really began to combine.[15] In fact, it might be said that the feudalism of which the Fronde was the lingering expression had its counterpart in the architecture of the period. While long familiarity with Italy was beginning to tell upon the practical side of house-planning, many obsolete details were still preserved. Even the most enthusiastic admirer of the French Renaissance would hardly maintain that the houses of that period are what we should call in the modern sense "convenient." It would be impossible for a modern family to occupy with any degree of comfort the Hôtel Voguë at Dijon,[16] one of the best examples (as originally planned) of sixteenth-century domestic architecture in France.[†] The same objection applies to the furniture

14. Coinciding with the ascension of Tudor monarchs in Britain from 1485 to 1603, the mainly domestic style of Tudor architecture features decorative half-timbering and large, rectangular windows. The low Tudor arch was a characteristic feature. Elizabethan style, a type of Renaissance architecture during the 1558–1603 reign of Queen Elizabeth I (1533–1603), overlapping the final years of Tudor architecture.

15. A series of civil wars in France from 1648 to 1653 in reaction to the policies enacted under Cardinal de Richelieu (1585–1642), chief minister (1624–42) to Louis XIII (1610–43), that weakened the influence of the nobility and reduced the power of Parlements. The outcomes of the Fronde paved the way for Louis XIV (1638–1715), also known as the Sun King, who ruled France from 1643 to 1715 and is considered a symbol of absolute monarchy. His reign was characterized by the expansion of French influence in Europe, the establishment of overseas colonies, the waging of three major wars, and the revocation of the Edict of Nantes (1598), which had granted rights to Huguenots.

16. The French spelling would be Hôtel de Vogüé, so *vɔgɥe*. The authors' spelling would produce *vɔge*. Renaissance-inspired mansion in eastern France built in 1614 after the French Wars of Religion (1562–98). Credit: Joel Goldfield (see also Rey 1981, 1929).

† The plan of the Hôtel Voguë has been greatly modified.

of the period. This arose from the fact that, owing to the unsettled state of the country, the landed proprietor always carried his furniture with him when he travelled from one estate to another. Furniture, in the vocabulary of the middle ages, meant something which may be transported: "Meubles sont apelez qu'on peut transporter"—hence the lack of variety in furniture before the seventeenth century, and also its unsuitableness to modern life. Chairs and cabinets that had to be carried about on mule-back were necessarily somewhat stiff and angular in design. It is perhaps not too much to say that a comfortable chair, in our self-indulgent modern sense, did not exist before the Louis XIV armchair (see plate 4); and the cushioned *bergère*, the ancestor of our upholstered easy-chair, cannot be traced back further than the Regency.[17] Prior to the time of Louis XIV, the most luxurious people had to content themselves with hard straight-backed seats. The necessities of transportation permitted little variety of design, and every piece of furniture was constructed with the double purpose of being easily carried about and of being used as a trunk (see plate 1). As Havard says, "Tout meuble se traduisait par un coffre."[18] The unvarying design of the cabinets is explained by the fact that they were made to form two trunks,[†] and even the chairs and settles had hollow seats which could be packed with the owners' wardrobe (see plate 2). The king himself, when he went from one château to another, carried all his furniture with him, and it is thus not surprising that lesser people contented themselves with a few substantial chairs and cabinets, and

17. Bergère: enclosed French armchair (with upholstered arms and back) on an upholstered frame fashionable in the eighteenth century. Regency: period when France was ruled, from 1715 to 1723, by Philippe II, Duke of Orléans (1674–1723), nephew of the recently deceased Louis XIV.

18. "Any piece of furniture resulted in a chest" or "All furniture required a chest" from volume 3 of *Dictionnaire de l'Ameublement et de la Décoration depuis le XIIIᵉ siècle jusqu'à nos jours* (Dictionary of Furnishings and Decoration from the Thirteenth Century to the Present), by art historian Henry Havard (1838–1921) (see Books Consulted). Credit: Joel Goldfield.

† Cabinets retained this shape after the transporting of furniture had ceased to be a necessity (see plate 3).

2. French Chairs, XV and XVI Centuries. From the Gavet Collection.

enough arras or cloth of Douai[19] to cover the draughty walls of their country-houses. One of Madame de Sévigné's letters gives an amusing instance of the scarceness of furniture even in the time of Louis XIV.[20]

19. Town in the Nord department of northern France, known for its wool.

20. Marie de Rabutin-Chantal, marquise de Sévigné (1626–96): aristocrat whose letters made her a major figure of seventeenth-century French literature. Wharton and Codman appear to be referring to the famous "Lettre de l'Incendie," describing an overnight fire that engulfed the home of Madame de Sévigné's neighbors and old friends, the Comte de Guitaut and his pregnant wife: "*Cependant, vers les cinq heures du matin, il fallut songer à Mme de Guitaut: je lui offris mon lit; mais Mme Guéton la mit dans le sien, parce qu'elle a plusieurs chambres meublées* [However, around five o'clock in the morning, it was time to think of Mme de Guitaut; I offered her my bed; but Mme Guéton

In describing a fire in a house near her own hôtel in Paris, she says that one or two of the persons from the burning house were brought to her for shelter, because it was known in the neighborhood (at that time a rich and fashionable one) that she had *an extra bed* in the house!

It was not until the social influences of the reign of Louis XIV were fully established that modern domestic life really began. Tradition ascribes to Madame de Rambouillet a leading share in the advance in practical house-planning;[21] but probably what she did is merely typical of the modifications which the new social conditions were everywhere producing. It is certain that at this time houses and rooms first began to be comfortable. The immense cavernous fireplaces originally meant for the roasting of beeves and the warming of a flock of frozen retainers— "les grandes antiquailles de cheminées," as Madame de Sévigné called them—were replaced by the compact chimney-piece of modern times.[22] Cushioned *bergères* took the place of the throne-like seats of Louis XIII, screens kept off unwelcome draughts, Savonnerie or moquette carpets[23] covered the stone or marble floors, and grandeur gave way to luxury.[†]

---

gave her hers since she has several furnished rooms]" (Madame de Sévigné to Madame de Grignan, February 20, 1671, reprinted in *Lettres de Madame de Sévigné, de sa Famille et de ses Amis* 1862, 75). Madame Guéton was her tenant next door at the time, which perhaps explains the remark that the "extra bed" was in Madame de Sévigné's home.

21. Catherine de Vivonne, marquise de Rambouillet (1588–1665), French aristocrat known for hosting salons (*EB* 2019i).

22. Plural for *beef* or *beef creatures*. *Les grandes antiquailles de cheminées*: French for "grand old antique chimneys." Credit: Joel Goldfield. *Antiquailles* has become synonymous with "kitsch," "knickknack," or "old junk."

23. French pile carpeting, usually large, made at the Savonnerie workshop or in that manner and style. The Savonnerie factory (named for its former soap factory site) was established in Paris in 1627 at the Hospice de la Savonnerie at Chaillot by royal order to provide pile carpets for use in the king's palace and as royal gifts. Moquette: carpet or upholstery fabric having a velvety pile; in modern times can mean wall-to-wall carpeting. Credit: Joel Goldfield.

[†] It must be remembered that in describing the decoration of any given period, we refer to the private houses, not the royal palaces, of that period. Versailles was more splendid than any previous palace; but private houses at that date were less splendid, though far more luxurious, than during the Renaissance.

English architecture having followed a line of development so similar that it need not here be traced, it remains only to examine in detail the opening proposition, namely, that modern architecture and decoration, having in many ways deviated from the paths which the experience of the past had marked out for them, can be reclaimed only by a study of the best models.

It might of course be said that to attain this end originality is more necessary than imitativeness. To this it may be replied that no lost art can be re-acquired without at least for a time going back to the methods and manner of those who formerly practised it; or the objection may be met by the question, What is originality in art? Perhaps it is easier to define what it is *not*; and this may be done by saying that it is never a wilful rejection of what have been accepted as the necessary laws of the various forms of art. Thus, in reasoning, originality lies not in discarding the necessary laws of thought, but in using them to express new intellectual conceptions; in poetry, originality consists not in discarding the necessary laws of rhythm, but in finding new rhythms within the limits of those laws. Most of the features of architecture that have persisted through various fluctuations of taste owe their preservation to the fact that they have been proved by experience to be necessary; and it will be found that none of them precludes the exercise of individual taste, any more than the acceptance of the syllogism or of the laws of rhythm prevents new thinkers and new poets from saying what has never been said before. Once this is clearly understood, it will be seen that the supposed conflict between originality and tradition is no conflict at all.[†]

[†] "Si l'on dispose un édifice d'une manière convenable à l'usage auquel on le destine, ne différera-t-il pas sensiblement d'un autre édifice destiné à un autre usage? N'aura-t-il pas naturellement un caractère, et, qui plus est, son caractère propre?" J. N. L. Durand. *Précis des Leçons d'Architecture données à l'École Royale Polytechnique.* Paris, 1823. (Editor's translation: "If you arrange a building in a manner suitable for its intended use, will it not differ noticeably from another building intended for another use? Will it not naturally have a character, and what is more, its own character?" Jean-Nicolas-Louis Durand, *Details of the Architecture Lessons given at the École Royale Polytechnique*, Paris, 1823.) Credit: Joel Goldfield.

In citing logic and poetry, those arts have been purposely chosen of which the laws will perhaps best help to explain and illustrate the character of architectural limitations. A building, for whatever purpose erected, must be built in strict accordance with the requirements of that purpose; in other words, it must have a reason for being as it is and must be as it is for that reason. Its decoration must harmonize with the structural limitations (which is by no means the same thing as saying that all decoration must be structural), and from this harmony of the general scheme of decoration with the building, and of the details of the decoration with each other, springs the rhythm that distinguishes architecture from mere construction. Thus all good architecture and good decoration (which, it must never be forgotten, *is only interior architecture*) must be based on rhythm and logic. A house, or room, must be planned as it is because it could not, in reason, be otherwise; must be decorated as it is because no other decoration would harmonize as well with the plan.

Many of the most popular features in modern house-planning and decoration will not be found to stand this double test. Often (as will be shown further on) they are merely survivals of earlier social conditions, and have been preserved in obedience to that instinct that makes people cling to so many customs the meaning of which is lost. In other cases they have been revived by the archæologizing spirit which is so characteristic of the present time, and which so often leads its possessors to think that a thing must be beautiful because it is old and appropriate because it is beautiful.

But since the beauty of all such features depends on their appropriateness, they may in every case be replaced by a more suitable form of treatment without loss to the general effect of house or room. It is this which makes it important that each room (or, better still, all the rooms) in a house should receive the same style of decoration. To some people this may seem as meaningless a piece of archaism as the habit of using obsolete fragments of planning or decoration; but such is not the case. It must not be forgotten, in discussing the question of reproducing certain styles, that the essence of a style lies not in its use of ornament, but in its handling of proportion. Structure conditions

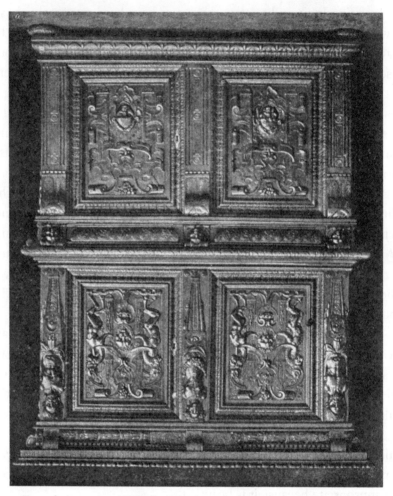

3. French Armoire, XVI Century.

ornament, not ornament structure. That is, a room with unsuitably proportioned openings, wall-spaces and cornice might receive a surface application of Louis XV or Louis XVI ornament and not represent either of those styles of decoration; whereas a room constructed according to the laws of proportion accepted in one or the other of those periods, in spite of a surface application of decorative detail widely different in character—say Romanesque or Gothic—would yet maintain its distinctive style, because the detail, in conforming with the laws of proportion governing the structure of the room, must necessarily conform with its style.[24] In other words, decoration is always subservient to proportion; and a room, whatever its decoration may be, must represent the style to which its proportions belong. The less cannot include the greater. Unfortunately it is usually by ornamental details, rather than by proportion, that people distinguish one style from another. To many persons, garlands, bow-knots, quivers, and a great deal of gilding represent the Louis XVI style; if they object to these, they condemn the style. To an architect familiar with the subject the same style means something absolutely different. He knows that a Louis XVI room may exist without any of these or similar characteristics; and he often deprecates their use as representing the cheaper and more trivial effects of the period, and those that have most helped to vulgarize it.[25] In fact, in nine cases out of ten his use of them is a concession to the client who, having asked for a Louis XVI room, would not know he had got it were these details left out.[†]

Another thing which has perhaps contributed to make people distrustful of "styles" is the garbled form in which they are presented

24. Louis XV (1710–74): penultimate king of France, whose poor rule led to the decline of royal authority (*EB* 2019x). In furniture, the Louis XV style is characterized by rich ornamentation and floral decoration (*EB* 2018e). Louis XVI (1754–93): the last French king before the French Revolution of 1789, who was guillotined on charges of counterrevolution. In furniture, the Louis XVI style marked the transition between rococo and neoclassicism; Romanesque architecture, popular in the eleventh and twelfth centuries, which combined Roman, Byzantine, and local Germanic traditions and was characterized by semicircular arches, barrel vaults, and towers (*EB* 2017e). Gothic architecture, popular between the twelfth and sixteenth centuries, was characterized by masonry buildings with cavernous spaces and tracery and was particularly known for rib vaults, flying buttresses, and rose windows (*EB* 2019q).

25. Wharton and Codman reference the Gilded Age predilection for celebrating the eighteenth-century French monarchy as seen, for example, in the Breakers (Vanderbilt mansion in Newport) and the Henry Flagler mansion (West Palm, Florida), which prominently display portraits of French kings and queens.

† It must not be forgotten that the so-called "styles" of Louis XIV, Louis XV and Louis XVI were, in fact, only the gradual development of one organic style, and hence differed only in the superficial use of ornament.

by some architects. After a period of eclecticism that has lasted long enough to make architects and decorators lose their traditional habits of design, there has arisen a sudden demand for "style." It necessarily follows that only the most competent are ready to respond to this unexpected summons. Much has to be relearned, still more to be unlearned. The essence of the great styles lay in proportion and the science of proportion is not to be acquired in a day. In fact, in such matters the cultivated layman, whether or not he has any special familiarity with the different schools of architecture, is often a better judge than the half-educated architect. It is no wonder that people of taste are disconcerted by the so-called "colonial" houses where stair-rails are used as roof-balustrades and mantel-friezes[26] as exterior entablatures, or by Louis XV rooms where the wavy movement which, in the best rococo,[27] was always an ornamental incident and never broke up the main lines of the design, is suffered to run riot through the whole treatment of the walls, so that the bewildered eye seeks in vain for a straight line amid the whirl of incoherent curves.

To conform to a style, then, is to accept those rules of proportion which the artistic experience of centuries has established as the best, while within those limits allowing free scope to the individual requirements which must inevitably modify every house or room adapted to the use and convenience of its occupants.

There is one thing more to be said in defence of conformity to style; and that is, the difficulty of getting rid of style. Strive as we may for originality, we are hampered at every turn by an artistic tradition of over two thousand years. Does any but the most inexperienced architect really think that he can ever rid himself of such an inheritance?

26. Screens formed by railings designed to prevent roofs from falling; mantel-friezes, long, horizontal panels or bands with elaborate decorations, usually placed on the mantel of a fireplace, that were instead used as assemblages of horizontal moldings and bands located immediately above the columns of classical buildings or similar structural supports in non-classical buildings (*EB* 2017b).

27. Style of eighteenth-century Parisian interior design characterized by lightness, elegance, and use of curving, natural forms (*EB* 2019ii).

4. French Sofa and Armchair, Louis XIV Period. From the Château de Bercy.

He may mutilate or misapply the component parts of his design, but he cannot originate a whole new architectural alphabet. The chances are that he will not find it easy to invent one wholly new moulding.

The styles especially suited to modern life have already been roughly indicated as those prevailing in Italy since 1500, in France from the time of Louis XIV, and in England since the introduction of the Italian manner by Inigo Jones;[28] and as the French and English styles

28. Inigo Jones (1573–1652): architect who founded the English classic tradition of architecture. Jones, cited in the first footnote of the first edition of *The Decoration of Houses*, was the first to employ Vitruvian rules of proportion and symmetry in his buildings. The Vitruvian style originates from Marcus Vitruvius Pollio (81–15 BCE), Roman author, architect, and engineer. His discussion of perfect proportion in architecture and human beings inspired Leonardo da Vinci's Vitruvian Man.

are perhaps more familiar to the general reader, the examples given will usually be drawn from these. Supposing the argument in favor of these styles to have been accepted, at least as a working hypothesis, it must be explained why, in each room, the decoration and furniture should harmonize. Most people will admit the necessity of harmonizing the colors in a room, because a feeling for color is more general than a feeling for form; but in reality the latter is the more important in decoration, and it is the feeling for form, and not any archæological affectation, which makes the best decorators insist upon the necessity of keeping to the same style of furniture and decoration. Thus the massive dimensions and heavy panelling of a seventeenth-century room would dwarf a set of eighteenth-century furniture; and the wavy, capricious movement of Louis XV decoration would make the austere yet delicate lines of Adam furniture look stiff and mean.[29]

Many persons object not only to any attempt at uniformity of style, but to the use of any recognized style in the decoration of a room. They characterize it, according to their individual views, as "servile," "formal," or "pretentious."

It has already been suggested that to conform within rational limits to a given style is no more servile than to pay one's taxes or to write according to the rules of grammar. As to the accusations of formality and pretentiousness (which are more often made in America than elsewhere), they may probably be explained by the fact that most Americans necessarily form their idea of the great European styles from public buildings and palaces. Certainly, if an architect were to propose to his client to decorate a room in a moderate-sized house in the Louis XIV style, and if the client had formed his idea of that

---

Jones's first major work was the Queen's House built in Greenwich in 1616 for King James I's wife, Anne (Summerson 2019).

29. Style made popular by Scottish architect and interior designer Robert Adam (1728–92), characterized by an experimental freedom and combination of multiple architectural styles to produce Gothic decoration within Neoclassical design. Here, Wharton and Codman are remarking on the asymmetry, whimsy, and constant curving and curling of the Louis XV style (Millikin 2019).

style from the state apartments in the palace at Versailles,[30] he would be justified in rejecting the proposed treatment as absolutely unsuitable to modern private life; whereas the architect who had gone somewhat more deeply into the subject might have singled out the style as eminently suitable, having in mind one of the simple panelled rooms, with tall windows, a dignified fireplace, large tables and comfortable arm-chairs, which were to be found in the private houses of the same period (see plate 5). It is the old story of the two knights fighting about the color of the shield.[31] Both architect and client would be right, but they would be looking at the different sides of the question. As a matter of fact, the bed-rooms, sitting-rooms, libraries and other private apartments in the smaller dwelling-houses built in Europe between 1650 and 1800 were far simpler, less pretentious and more practical in treatment than those in the average modern house.

It is therefore hoped that the antagonists of "style," when they are shown that to follow a certain style is not to sacrifice either convenience

30. Seventeenth-century French structure originally constructed as Louis XIII's hunting pavilion; eventually transformed by his son, Louis XIV, when the French court was installed at the site in 1682. A succession of kings continued to embellish the palace up until the French Revolution. Wharton would be buried at the Cimetière des Gonards in the village of Versailles, an approximately thirty-minute walk from the château.

31. This allusion was evidently so perplexing that it prompted the Scribner's editor to ask for clarification. At the close of a letter to Mr. Brownell dated October 5, 1897, and archived at Princeton University's Firestone Library, Wharton attaches the following postscript: "The reference to the knights fighting about the colour of the shield, marked by you with a query, is taken from chap. I of Herbert Spencer's 'First Principals.'" Spencer refers to "that perennially significant fable concerning those knights who fought about the color of a shield of which neither looked at more than one face. Each combatant, seeing clearly his own aspect of the question, has charged his opponent with stupidity or dishonesty in not seeing the same aspect of it; while each has wanted the candor to go over to his opponent's side and find out how it was that he saw everything so differently." In the medieval allegory of "the gold and silver shield," two knights approach a shield from opposite directions and come to blows arguing about its color, only to be told that they were both right as the shield was painted a different color on each side.

5. Room in the Grand Trianon, Versailles. (Example of Simple Louis XIV Decoration.)

or imagination, but to give more latitude to both, will withdraw an opposition which seems to be based on a misapprehension of facts.

Hitherto architecture and decoration have been spoken of as one, as in any well-designed house they ought to be. Indeed, it is one of the numerous disadvantages of the present use of styles, that unless the architect who has built the house also decorates it, the most hopeless discord is apt to result. This was otherwise before our present desire for variety had thrown architects, decorators, and workmen out of the regular routine of their business. Before 1800 the decorator called upon to treat the interior of a house invariably found a suitable background prepared for his work, while much in the way of detail was intrusted to the workmen, who were trained in certain traditions

6. French Armchair, Louis XV Period.

instead of being called upon to carry out in each new house the vagaries of a different designer.

But it is with the decorator's work alone that these pages are concerned, and the above digression is intended to explain why his task is now so difficult, and why his results are so often unsatisfactory to himself as well as to his clients. The decorator of the present day may be compared to a person who is called upon to write a letter in the

English language, but is ordered, in so doing, to conform to the Chinese or Egyptian rules of grammar, or possibly to both together.

By the use of a little common sense and a reasonable conformity to those traditions of design which have been tested by generations of architects, it is possible to produce great variety in the decoration of rooms without losing sight of the purpose for which they are intended. Indeed, the more closely this purpose is kept in view, and the more clearly it is expressed in all the details of each room, the more pleasing that room will be, so that it is easy to make a room with tinted walls, deal furniture and dimity curtains more beautiful,[32] because more logical and more harmonious, than a ball-room lined with gold and marbles, in which the laws of rhythm and logic have been ignored.

32. Inexpensive style at the time, made of pine; dimity curtains, lightweight, usually white, sheer cotton fabric commonly used for bed upholstery and curtains. In acknowledging the use of these relatively affordable materials, Wharton and Codman make it clear they are targeting not only the excessively wealthy but also the upper middle class.

2

Rooms in General

Before beginning to decorate a room it is essential to consider for what purpose the room is to be used. It is not enough to ticket it with some such general designation as "library," "drawing-room," or "den." The individual tastes and habits of the people who are to occupy it must be taken into account; it must be not "a library," or "a drawing-room," but the library or the drawing-room best suited to the master or mistress of the house which is being decorated. Individuality in house-furnishing has seldom been more harped upon than at the present time. That cheap originality which finds expression in putting things to uses for which they were not intended is often confounded with individuality; whereas the latter consists not in an attempt to be different from other people at the cost of comfort, but in the desire to be comfortable in one's own way, even though it be the way of a monotonously large majority. It seems easier to most people to arrange a room like some one else's than to analyze and express their own needs. Men, in these matters, are less exacting than women, because their demands, besides being simpler, are uncomplicated by the feminine tendency to want things because other people have them, rather than to have things because they are wanted.

But it must never be forgotten that every one is unconsciously tyrannized over by the wants of others—the wants of dead and gone predecessors, who have an inconvenient way of thrusting their different habits and tastes across the current of later existences. The unsatisfactory relations of some people with their rooms are often to be explained in this way. They have still in their blood the traditional uses to which these rooms were put in times quite different from the present. It is only an unconscious extension of the conscious habit which old-fashioned people have of clinging to their parents' way of living. The difficulty of reconciling these instincts with our own comfort and convenience, and the various compromises to which they lead in the arrangement of our rooms, will be more fully dealt with in the following chapters. To go to the opposite extreme and discard things because they are old-fashioned is equally unreasonable. The golden mean lies in trying to arrange our houses with a view to our own comfort and convenience; and it will be found that the more closely we follow this rule the easier our rooms will be to furnish and the pleasanter to live in.

People whose attention has never been specially called to the *raison d'être* of house-furnishing sometimes conclude that because a thing is unusual it is artistic, or rather that through some occult process the most ordinary things become artistic by being used in an unusual manner; while others, warned by the visible results of this theory of furnishing, infer that everything artistic is unpractical. In the Anglo-Saxon mind beauty is not spontaneously born of material wants, as it is with the Latin races. We have to *make* things beautiful; they do not grow so of themselves. The necessity of making this effort has caused many people to put aside the whole problem of beauty and fitness in household decoration as something mysterious and incomprehensible to the uninitiated. The architect and decorator are often aware that they are regarded by their clients as the possessors of some strange craft like black magic or astrology.

This fatalistic attitude has complicated the simple and intelligible process of house-furnishing, and has produced much of the discomfort which causes so many rooms to be shunned by everybody in the house, in spite (or rather because) of all the money and ingenuity expended on their arrangement. Yet to penetrate the mystery of house-furnishing it is only necessary to analyze one satisfactory room and to notice wherein its charm lies. To the fastidious eye it will, of course, be found in fitness of proportion, in the proper use of each moulding and in the harmony of all the decorative processes; and even to those who think themselves indifferent to such detail, much of the sense of restfulness and comfort produced by certain rooms depends on the due adjustment of their fundamental parts. Different rooms minister to different wants and while a room may be made very livable without satisfying any but the material requirements of its inmates it is evident that the perfect room should combine these qualities with what corresponds to them in a higher order of needs. At present, however, the subject deals only with the material livableness of a room, and this will generally be found to consist in the position of the doors and fireplace, the accessibility of the windows, the arrangement of the furniture, the privacy of the room and the absence of the superfluous.

The position of doors and fireplace, though the subject comes properly under the head of house-planning, may be included in this summary, because in rearranging a room it is often possible to change its openings, or at any rate, in the case of doors, to modify their dimensions.

The fireplace must be the focus of every rational scheme of arrangement. Nothing is so dreary, so hopeless to deal with, as a room in which the fireplace occupies a narrow space between two doors, so that it is impossible to sit about the hearth.[†] Next in importance come the windows. In town-houses especially, where there is so little light that every ray is precious to the reader or worker, window-space is invaluable. Yet in few rooms are the windows easy of approach, free from useless draperies and provided with easy-chairs so placed that the light falls properly on the occupant's work.

It is no exaggeration to say that many houses are deserted by the men of the family for lack of those simple comforts which they find at their clubs: windows unobscured by layers of muslin, a fireplace surrounded by easy-chairs and protected from draughts, well-appointed writing-tables and files of papers and magazines. Who cannot call to mind the dreary drawing-room, in small town-houses the only possible point of reunion for the family, but too often, in consequence of its exquisite discomfort, of no more use as a meeting-place than the vestibule or the cellar? The windows in this kind of room are invariably supplied with two sets of muslin curtains, one hanging against the

[†] There is no objection to putting a fireplace between two doors, provided both doors be at least six feet from the chimney.

panes, the other fulfilling the supererogatory duty of hanging against the former; then come the heavy stuff curtains,[1] so draped as to cut off the upper light of the windows by day, while it is impossible to drop them at night: curtains that have thus ceased to serve the purpose for which they exist. Close to the curtains stands the inevitable lamp or jardinière,[2] and the wall-space between the two windows, where a writing-table might be put, is generally taken up by a cabinet or console, surmounted by a picture made invisible by the dark shadow of the hangings. The writing-table might find place against the side-wall near either window; but these spaces are usually sacred to the piano and to that modern futility, the silver-table. Thus of necessity the writing-table is either banished or put in some dark corner, where it is little wonder that the ink dries unused and a vase of flowers grows in the middle of the blotting-pad.

The hearth should be the place about which people gather; but the mantelpiece in the average American house, being ugly, is usually covered with inflammable draperies; the fire is, in consequence, rarely lit, and no one cares to sit about a fireless hearth. Besides, on the opposite side of the room is a gap in the wall eight or ten feet wide, opening directly upon the hall, and exposing what should be the most private part of the room to the scrutiny of messengers, servants and visitors. This opening is sometimes provided with doors; but these, as a rule, are either slid into the wall or are unhung and replaced by a curtain through which every word spoken in the room must necessarily pass. In such a room it matters very little how the rest of the furniture is arranged, since it is certain that no one will ever sit in it except the luckless visitor who has no other refuge.

Even the visitor might be thought entitled to the solace of a few books; but as all the tables in the room are littered with knick-knacks,

---

1. Equivalent of heavy-duty, blackout curtains, the purpose of which was to prevent sunlight from damaging furniture. (For an excellent discussion of Victorian curtains, see Gere 1989).

2. Ornamental flowerpot or flower basket within doors, on a windowsill, or on a dining table (*M-W*).

7. French Bergère, Louis XVI Period.

it is difficult for the most philanthropic hostess to provide even this slight alleviation.

When the town-house is built on the basement plan, and the drawing-room or parlor is up-stairs, the family, to escape from its discomforts, habitually take refuge in the small room opening off the hall on the ground floor; so that instead of sitting in a room twenty or twenty-five feet wide, they are packed into one less than half that size and exposed to the frequent intrusions from which, in basement houses, the drawing-room is free. But too often even the "little room down-stairs" is arranged less like a sitting-room in a private house than a waiting-room at a fashionable doctor's or dentist's. It has the inevitable yawning gap in the wall, giving on the hall close to the front door, and is either the refuge of the ugliest and most uncomfortable furniture in the house, or, even if furnished with taste, is arranged with so little regard to comfort that one might as well make it part of the hall, as is often done in rearranging old houses. This habit of sacrificing a useful room to the useless widening of the hall is indeed the natural outcome of furnishing rooms of this kind in so unpractical a way that their real usefulness has ceased to be apparent. The science of restoring wasted rooms to their proper uses is one of the most important and least understood branches of house-furnishing.

Privacy would seem to be one of the first requisites of civilized life, yet it is only necessary to observe the planning and arrangement of the average house to see how little this need is recognized. Each room in a house has its individual uses: some are made to sleep in, others are for dressing, eating, study, or conversation; but whatever the uses of a room, they are seriously interfered with if it be not preserved as a small world by itself. If the drawing-room be a part of the hall and the library a part of the drawing-room, all three will be equally unfitted to serve their special purpose. The indifference to privacy which has sprung up in modern times, and which in France, for instance, has given rise to the grotesque conceit of putting sheets of plate-glass between two rooms, and of replacing doorways by openings fifteen feet wide, is of complex origin. It is probably due in part to the fact that many houses are built and decorated by people unfamiliar with the habits of those for whom they are building. It may be that architect and decorator live in a simpler manner than their clients, and are therefore ready to sacrifice a kind of comfort of which they do not feel the need to the "effects" obtainable by vast openings and extended "vistas." To the untrained observer size often appeals more than proportion and costliness than suitability. In a handsome house such an observer is attracted rather by the ornamental detail than by the underlying purpose of planning and decoration. He sees the beauty of the detail, but not its relation to the whole. He therefore regards it as elegant but useless; and his next step is to infer that there is an inherent elegance in what is useless.

Before beginning to decorate a house it is necessary to make a prolonged and careful study of its plan and elevations, both as a whole and in detail. The component parts of an undecorated room are its floor, ceiling, wall-spaces and openings. The openings consist of the doors, windows and fireplace; and of these, as has already been pointed out, the fireplace is the most important in the general scheme of decoration.

No room can be satisfactory unless its openings are properly placed and proportioned, and the decorator's task is much easier if he has also been the architect of the house he is employed to decorate; but as this seldom happens his ingenuity is frequently taxed to produce a good design upon the background of a faulty and illogical structure. Much may be done to overcome this difficulty by making slight changes in the proportions of the openings; and the skilful decorator, before applying his scheme of decoration, will do all that he can to correct the fundamental lines of the room. But the result is seldom so successful as if he had built the room, and those who employ different people to build and decorate their houses should at least try to select an architect and a decorator trained in the same school of composition, so that they may come to some understanding with regard to the general harmony of their work.

In deciding upon a scheme of decoration, it is necessary to keep in mind the relation of furniture to ornament, and of the room as a whole to other rooms in the house. As in a small house a very large room dwarfs all the others, so a room decorated in a very rich manner will make the simplicity of those about it look mean. Every house should be decorated according to a carefully graduated scale of ornamentation culminating in the most important room of the house; but this plan must be carried out with such due sense of the relation of the rooms to each other that there shall be no violent break in the continuity of treatment. If a white-and-gold drawing-room opens on a hall with a Brussels carpet[3] and papered walls, the drawing-room will look too fine and the hall mean.

In the furnishing of each room the same rule should be as carefully observed. The simplest and most cheaply furnished room (provided the furniture be good of its kind, and the walls and carpet unobjectionable in color) will be more pleasing to the fastidious eye than one in which gilded consoles and cabinets of buhl stand side by side with cheap machine-made furniture, and delicate old marquetry tables are covered with trashy china ornaments.[4]

It is, of course, not always possible to refurnish a room when it is redecorated. Many people must content themselves with using their old furniture, no matter how ugly and ill-assorted it may be; and it is the decorator's business to see that his background helps the furniture to look its best. It is a mistake to think that because the furniture of a room is inappropriate or ugly a good background will bring out these defects. It will, on the contrary, be a relief to the eye to escape from the bad lines of the furniture to the good lines of the walls; and should the opportunity to purchase new furniture ever come, there will be a suitable background ready to show it to the best advantage.

Most rooms contain a mixture of good, bad, and indifferent furniture. It is best to adapt the decorative treatment to the best pieces and to discard those which are in bad taste, replacing them, if necessary, by willow chairs[5] and stained deal tables until it is possible to buy something better. When the room is to be refurnished as well as redecorated the client often makes his purchases without regard to the decoration. Besides being an injustice to the decorator, inasmuch as it makes it impossible for him to harmonize his decoration with the furniture, this generally produces a result unsatisfactory to the

3. Type of carpet with the loops of the pile uncut, which became fashionable in the nineteenth century (*EB* 2005).

4. Buhl: material like brass or tortoiseshell that is often worked into ornamental patterns. Marquetry table: small table to which wood, metal, or organic materials with intricately carved patterns are affixed (*M-W*).

5. Wicker chair made of willow shoots.

8. French Bergère, Louis XVI Period.

owner of the house. Neither decoration nor furniture, however good
of its kind, can look its best unless each is chosen with reference to the
other. It is therefore necessary that the decorator, before planning his
treatment of a room, should be told what it is to contain. If a gilt set is
put in a room the walls of which are treated in low relief and painted
white, the high lights of the gilding will destroy the delicate values

of the mouldings, and the walls, at a little distance, will look like flat expanses of whitewashed plaster.[6]

When a room is to be furnished and decorated at the smallest possible cost, it must be remembered that the comfort of its occupants depends more on the nature of the furniture than of the wall-decorations or carpet. In a living-room of this kind it is best to tint the walls and put a cheerful drugget on the floor,[7] keeping as much money as possible for the purchase of comfortable chairs and sofas and substantial tables. If little can be spent in buying furniture, willow arm-chairs[†] with denim cushions and solid tables with stained legs and covers of denim or corduroy will be more satisfactory than the "parlor suit" turned out in thousands by the manufacturer of cheap furniture, or the pseudo-Georgian or pseudo-Empire of the dealer in "high-grade goods."[8] Plain bookcases may be made of deal, painted or stained; and a room treated in this way, with a uniform color on the wall, and plenty of lamps and books, is sure to be comfortable and can never be vulgar.

It is to be regretted that, in this country and in England, it should be almost impossible to buy plain but well-designed and substantial furniture. Nothing can exceed the ugliness of the current designs: the bedsteads with towering head-boards fretted by the versatile jig-saw; the "bedroom suits" of "mahoganized" cherry, bird's-eye maple, or some other crude-colored wood; the tables with meaninglessly turned

6. Gilded flatware or teacups (M-W); low relief, a carving or stamping in which the design projects only slightly from the base (EB 2016b).

7. Coarse, durable cloth, usually made of cotton or wool, used as a rug or floor covering (M-W).

† Not rattan, as the models are too bad.

8. Meaning "parlor set," as in a set of matching chairs, chaise, couch, and so on, placed in a parlor; pseudo-Georgian, English architecture that imitates the design popular between 1714 and 1830, during the reigns of the first four members of the house of Hanover, which is itself imitative of classical Greek architecture (EB 2019o). Pseudo-Empire: architecture that imitates the neoclassical art popular in France during the time of the first Empire, between 1804 and 1814, when Napoleon desired a style reminiscent of ancient Egypt and Rome (EB 2018e).

legs; the "Empire" chairs and consoles stuck over with ornaments of cast bronze washed in liquid gilding; and, worst of all, the supposed "Colonial" furniture,[9] that unworthy travesty of a plain and dignified style. All this showy stuff has been produced in answer to the increasing demand for cheap "effects" in place of unobtrusive merit in material and design; but now that an appreciation of better things in architecture is becoming more general, it is to be hoped that the "artistic" furniture disfiguring so many of our shop-windows will no longer find a market.

There is no lack of models for manufacturers to copy, if their customers will but demand what is good. France and England, in the eighteenth century, excelled in the making of plain, inexpensive furniture of walnut, mahogany, or painted beechwood (see plates 6–10). Simple in shape and substantial in construction, this kind of furniture was never tricked out with moulded bronzes and machine-made carving, or covered with liquid gilding, but depended for its effect upon the solid qualities of good material, good design and good workmanship. The eighteenth-century cabinet-maker did not attempt cheap copies of costly furniture; the common sense of his patrons would have resented such a perversion of taste. Were the modern public as fastidious, it would soon be easy to buy good furniture for a moderate price; but until people recognize the essential vulgarity of the pinchbeck[10] article flooding our shops and overflowing upon our sidewalks,

9. Style of architecture found in North America, beginning in the years preceding the American Revolution. While there are many versions of colonial architecture, Edith Wharton and Ogden Codman Jr. are likely referring to the New England colonial, where houses and furniture were predominantly made of wood and hand-hewn oak, or the Dutch colonial, popular in the Hudson River Valley and surrounding areas, known for its use of brick in its facades. With their consistent use of scare quotes to distinguish "colonial," the authors suggest that what goes by this name is a "modest" (their term) or illegitimate copy of Georgian models (Millon et al. 2018).

10. Yellowish alloy of copper and zinc, used to imitate gold in jewelry, furniture, and the like (M-W).

manufacturers will continue to offer such wares in preference to better but less showy designs.

The worst defects of the furniture now made in America are due to an Athenian thirst for novelty, not always regulated by an Athenian sense of fitness. No sooner is it known that beautiful furniture was made in the time of Marie-Antoinette than an epidemic of supposed "Marie-Antoinette" rooms breaks out over the whole country.[11] Neither purchaser nor manufacturer has stopped to inquire wherein the essentials of the style consist. They know that the rooms of the period were usually painted in light colors, and that the furniture (in palaces) was often gilt and covered with brocade; and it is taken for granted that plenty of white paint, a pale wall-paper with bow-knots, and fragile chairs dipped in liquid gilding and covered with a flowered silk-and-cotton material, must inevitably produce a "Marie-Antoinette" room. According to the creed of the modern manufacturer, you have only to combine certain "goods" to obtain a certain style.

This quest of artistic novelties would be encouraging were it based on the desire for something better, rather than for something merely different. The tendency to dash from one style to another, without stopping to analyze the intrinsic qualities of any, has defeated the efforts of those who have tried to teach the true principles of furniture-designing by a return to the best models. If people will buy the stuff now offered them as Empire, Sheraton[12] or Louis XVI, the manufacturer is not to blame for making it. It is not the maker but the purchaser who sets the standard; and there will never be any general supply of better furniture until people take time to study the subject, and find out wherein lies the radical unfitness of what now contents them.

11. Marie-Antoinette (1755–93): Austrian queen and wife of French king Louis XVI, whose reign lasted from 1774 to 1792. Associated with courtly extravagance, she was ultimately sent to the guillotine by revolutionaries (*EB* 2019dd). Wharton strategically references her legacy in chapter 1 of *The Custom of the Country*.

12. Type of neoclassical furniture, primarily cabinets, made popular by Thomas Sheraton (1751–1806), characterized by a feminine refinement of late Georgian styles. See also chapter 13, note 5, on sideboard (*EB* 2019ll).

Until this golden age arrives the householder who cannot afford to buy old pieces, or to have old models copied by a skilled cabinet-maker, had better restrict himself to the plainest of furniture, relying for the embellishment of his room upon good bookbindings and one or two old porcelain vases for his lamps.

Concerning the difficult question of color, it is safe to say that the fewer the colors used in a room, the more pleasing and restful the result will be. A multiplicity of colors produces the same effect as a number of voices talking at the same time. The voices may not be discordant, but continuous chatter is fatiguing in the long run. Each room should speak with but one voice: it should contain one color, which at once and unmistakably asserts its predominance, in obedience to the rule that where there is a division of parts one part shall visibly prevail over all the others.

To attain this result, it is best to use the same color and, if possible, the same material, for curtains and chair-coverings. This produces an impression of unity and gives an air of spaciousness to the room. When the walls are simply panelled in oak or walnut, or are painted in some neutral tones, such as gray and white, the carpet may contrast in color with the curtains and chair-coverings. For instance, in an oak-panelled room crimson curtains and chair-coverings may be used with a dull green carpet, or with one of dark blue patterned in subdued tints; or the color-scheme may be reversed, and green hangings and chair-coverings combined with a plain crimson carpet.

Where the walls are covered with tapestry, or hung with a large number of pictures, or, in short, are so treated that they present a variety of colors, it is best that curtains, chair-coverings and carpet should all be of one color and without pattern. Graduated shades on the same color should almost always be avoided; theoretically they seem harmonious, but in reality the light shades look faded in proximity with the darker ones. Though it is well, as a rule, that carpet and hangings should match, exception must always be made in favor of a really fine old Eastern rug. The tints of such rugs are too subdued, too subtly harmonized by time, to clash with any colors the room may contain; but those who cannot cover their floors in this

9. French Sofa, Louis XV Period. Tapestry Designed by Boucher.

way will do well to use carpets of uniform tint, rather than the gaudy rugs now made in the East. The modern red and green Smyrna or Turkey carpet is an exception.[13] Where the furniture is dark and substantial, and the predominating color is a strong green or crimson, such a carpet is always suitable. These Smyrna carpets are usually well designed; and if their colors be restricted to red and green, with small admixture of dark blue, they harmonize with almost any style of decoration. It is well, as a rule, to shun the decorative

13. Turkey carpet: small carpet traditionally used as a prayer rug; reminiscent of sixteenth-century Ottoman court rugs and known for their unique color scheme, characterized by a vibrant red, as well as yellow and violet—"Smyrna carpet" (*EB* 1998d).

10. French Marquetry Table, Louis XVI Period.

schemes concocted by the writers who supply our newspapers with hints for "artistic interiors." The use of such poetic adjectives as jonquil-yellow, willow-green, shell-pink, or ashes-of-roses, gives to these descriptions of the "unique boudoir" or "ideal summer room" a charm which the reality would probably not possess. The arrangements suggested are usually cheap devices based upon the mistaken idea that defects in structure or design may be remedied by an overlaying of color or ornament. This theory often leads to the spending of much more money than would have been required to make one or two changes in the plan of the room, and the result is never satisfactory to the fastidious.

There are but two ways of dealing with a room which is fundamentally ugly: one is to accept it, and the other is courageously to correct its ugliness. Half-way remedies are a waste of money and serve rather to call attention to the defects of the room than to conceal them.

3

Walls

Proportion is the good breeding of architecture. It is that something, indefinable to the unprofessional eye, which gives repose and distinction to a room: in its origin a matter of nice mathematical calculation, of scientific adjustment of voids and masses, but in its effects as intangible as that all-pervading essence which the ancients called the soul.

It is not proposed to enter here into a technical discussion of the delicate problem of proportion. The decorator, with whom this book is chiefly concerned, is generally not consulted until the house that he is to decorate has been built—and built, in all probability, quite without reference to the interior treatment it is destined to receive. All he can hope to do is, by slight modifications here and there in the dimensions or position of the openings, to re-establish that harmony of parts so frequently disregarded in modern house-planning. It often happens, however, that the decorator's desire to make these slight changes, upon which the success of his whole scheme depends, is a source of perplexity and distress to his bewildered client, who sees in it merely the inclination to find fault with another's work. Nothing can be more natural than this attitude on the part of the client. How is he to decide between the architect, who has possibly disregarded in some measure the claims of symmetry and proportion in planning the interior of the house, and the decorator who insists upon those claims without being able to justify his demands by any explanation comprehensible to the unprofessional? It is inevitable that the decorator, who comes last, should fare worse, especially as he makes his appearance at a time when contractors' bills are pouring in, and the proposition to move a mantelpiece or change the dimensions of a door opens fresh vistas of expense to the client's terrified imagination.

Undoubtedly these difficulties have diminished in the last few years. Architects are turning anew to the lost tradition of symmetry and to a scientific study of the relation between voids and masses, and the decorator's task has become correspondingly easier. Still, there are many cases where his work is complicated by some trifling obstacle, the removal of which the client opposes only because he cannot in imagination foresee the improvement which would follow. If the client permits the change to be made, he has no difficulty in appreciating the result: he cannot see it in advance.

A few words from Isaac Ware's admirable chapter on "The Origin of Proportions in the Orders"[†] may serve to show the importance of proportion in all schemes of decoration, and the necessity of conforming to certain rules that may at first appear both arbitrary and incomprehensible.

"An architect of genius," Ware writes (alluding to the latitude which the ancients allowed themselves in using the orders), "will think himself happy, in designing a building that is to be enriched with the Doric order,[1] that he has all the latitude between two and a half and seventeen for the projecture of its capital; that he can proportion this projecture to the general idea of his building anywhere between these extremes and show his authority. This is an happiness to the person of real genius; . . . but as all architects are not, nor can be expected to be, of this stamp, it is needful some standard should be established, founded upon what a good taste shall most admire in the antique, and fixed as a model from which to work, or as a test to which we may have recourse in disputes and controversies."

If to these words be added his happy definition of the sense of proportion as "fancy under the restraint and conduct of judgment," and his closing caution that "it is mean in the undertaker of a great work

---

[†] *A Complete Body of Architecture*, book 2, chap. 3.

1. Type of classical architecture, invented in the seventh century, characterized by simple, baseless columns and broad capitals (Bush-Brown et al. 2018).

to copy strictly, and it is dangerous to give a loose to fancy *without a perfect knowledge how far a variation may be justified*," the unprofessional reader may form some idea of the importance of proportion and of the necessity for observing its rules.

If proportion is the good breeding of architecture, symmetry, or the answering of one part to another, may be defined as the sanity of decoration. The desire for symmetry, for balance, for rhythm in form as well as in sound, is one of the most inveterate of human instincts. Yet for years Anglo-Saxons have been taught that to pay any regard to symmetry in architecture or decoration is to truckle to one of the meanest forms of artistic hypocrisy. The master who has taught this strange creed, in words magical enough to win acceptance for any doctrine, has also revealed to his generation so many of the forgotten beauties of early art that it is hard to dispute his principles of æsthetics. As a guide through the byways of art, Mr. Ruskin is entitled to the reverence and gratitude of all; but as a logical exponent of the causes and effects of the beauty he discovers, his authority is certainly open to question. For years he has spent the full force of his unmatched prose in denouncing the enormity of putting a door or a window in a certain place in order that it may correspond to another; nor has he scrupled to declare to the victims of this practice that it leads to abysses of moral as well as of artistic degradation.

Time has taken the terror from these threats and architects are beginning to see that a regard for external symmetry, far from interfering with the requirements of house-planning, tends to produce a better, because a more carefully studied, plan, as well as a more convenient distribution of wall-space; but in the lay mind there still lingers not only a vague association between outward symmetry and interior discomfort, between a well-balanced façade and badly distributed rooms, but a still vaguer notion that regard for symmetry indicates poverty of invention, lack of ingenuity and weak subservience to a meaningless form.

What the instinct for symmetry means, philosophers may be left to explain; but that it does exist, that it means something, and that it is most strongly developed in those races which have reached the highest artistic civilization, must be acknowledged by all students of sociology. It is, therefore, not superfluous to point out that, in interior decoration as well as in architecture, a regard for symmetry, besides satisfying a legitimate artistic requirement, tends to make the average room not only easier to furnish, but more comfortable to live in.

As the effect produced by a room depends chiefly upon the distribution of its openings, it will be well to begin by considering the treatment of the walls. It has already been said that the decorator can often improve a room, not only from the artistic point of view, but as regards the comfort of its inmates, by making some slight change in the position of its openings. Take, for instance, a library in which it is necessary to put the two principal bookcases one on each side of a door or fireplace. If this opening is in the *centre* of one side of the room, the wall-decorations may be made to balance, and the bookcases may be of the same width—an arrangement which will give to the room an air of spaciousness and repose. Should the wall-spaces on either side of the opening be of unequal extent, both decorations and bookcases must be modified in size and design; and not only does the problem become more difficult, but the result, because necessarily less simple, is certain to be less satisfactory. Sometimes, on the other hand, convenience is sacrificed to symmetry; and in such cases it is the decorator's business to remedy this defect, while preserving to the eye the aspect of symmetry. A long narrow room may be taken as an example. If the fireplace is in the centre of one of the long sides of the room, with a door directly opposite, the hearth will be without privacy and the room virtually divided into two parts, since, in a narrow room, no one cares to sit in a line with the doorway. This division of the room makes it more difficult to furnish and less comfortable to live in, besides wasting all the floor-space between the chimney and the door. One way of overcoming the difficulty is to move the door some distance down the long side of the room, so that the space about the fireplace is no longer a thoroughfare, and the privacy of the greater part of the room is preserved, even if the door be left open. The removal of the door from the centre of one side of the room having disturbed the equilibrium of the openings, this equilibrium may be restored by placing in a line with

11. Drawing-Room in Berkeley Square, London. XVIII Century.

the door, at the other end of the same side-wall, a piece of furniture corresponding as nearly as possible in height and width to the door. This will satisfy the eye, which in matters of symmetry demands, not absolute similarity of detail, but merely correspondence of outline and dimensions.

It is idle to multiply examples of the various ways in which such readjustments of the openings may increase the comfort and beauty of a room. Every problem in house decoration demands a slightly different application of the same general principles, and the foregoing instances are intended only to show how much depends upon the placing of openings and how reasonable is the decorator's claim to have a share in planning the background upon which his effects are to be produced.

It may surprise those whose attention has not been turned to such matters to be told that in all but the most cheaply constructed houses the interior walls are invariably treated as an order. In all houses, even of the poorest kind, the walls of the rooms are finished by a plain projecting board adjoining the floor, surmounted by one or more mouldings. This base, as it is called, is nothing more nor less than the part of an order between shaft and floor, or shaft and pedestal, as the case may be. If it be next remarked that the upper part of the wall, adjoining the ceiling, is invariably finished by a moulded projection corresponding with the crowning member of an order, it will be clear that the shaft, with its capital, has simply been omitted, or that the uniform wall-space between the base and cornice has been regarded as replacing it. In rooms of a certain height and importance the column or pilaster is frequently restored to its proper place between base and cornice; but where such treatment is too monumental for the dimensions of the room, the main lines of the wall-space should none the less be regarded as distinctly architectural, and the decoration applied should be subordinate to the implied existence of an order. (For the application of an order to walls, see plates 42 and 50.)

Where the shafts are omitted, the eye undoubtedly feels a lack of continuity in the treatment: the cornice seems to hang in air and the effect produced is unsatisfactory. This is obviated by the use of panelling, the vertical lines carried up at intervals from base to cornice satisfying the need for some visible connection between the upper and lower members of the order. Moreover, if the lines of the openings are carried up to the cornice (as they are in all well-designed schemes of decoration), the openings may be considered as intercolumniations[2] and the intermediate wall-spaces as the shafts or piers supporting the cornice.

In well-finished rooms the order is usually imagined as resting, not on the floor, but on pedestals, or rather on a continuous pedestal. This

2. Spaces between columns that support an arch or entablature (*EB* 1998b).

continuous pedestal, or "dado"[3] as it is usually called, is represented by a plinth surmounted by mouldings, by an intermediate member often decorated with tablets or sunk panels with moulded margins, and by a cornice. The use of the dado raises the chief wall-decoration of the room to a level with the eye and prevents its being interrupted or concealed by the furniture which may be placed against the walls. This fact makes it clear that in all well-designed rooms there should be a dado about two and a half feet high. If lower than this, it does not serve its purpose of raising the wall-decoration to a line above the furniture; while the high dado often seen in modern American rooms throws all the rest of the panelling out of scale and loses its own significance as the pedestal supporting an order.

In rooms of the sixteenth and seventeenth centuries, when little furniture was used, the dado was often richly ornamented, being sometimes painted with delicate arabesques[4] corresponding with those on the doors and inside shutters. As rooms grew smaller and the quantity of furniture increased so much that the dado was almost concealed, the treatment of the latter was wisely simplified, being reduced, as a rule, to sunk panels and a few strongly marked mouldings. The decorator cannot do better than plan the ornamentation of his dado according to the amount of furniture to be placed against the walls. In corridor or ante-chamber, or in a ball-room, the dado may receive a more elaborate treatment than is necessary in a library or drawing-room, where probably much less of it will be seen. It was not unusual,

3. In classical architecture, the plain portion between the base and cornice of the pedestal of a column and, in later architecture, the paneled, painted, or otherwise decorated lower part of a wall, up to two or three feet above the floor.

4. Decorative style characterized by intertwining reeds and curving lines. The style originated in Asia Minor by Hellenistic craftsmen, but is best known for its importance to Islam. By the Renaissance, it was adapted by European artisans for the decoration of manuscripts, walls, and furniture. Arabesque wall covering factors meaningfully into Charlotte Perkins Gilman's gothic story "The Yellow Wallpaper," published in 1892 (*EB* 2016a).

in the decoration of lobbies and corridors in old French and Italian houses, to omit the dado entirely if an order was used, thus bringing the wall-decoration down to the base-board; but this was done only in rooms or passage-ways not meant to contain any furniture.

The three noblest forms of wall-decoration are fresco-painting, paneling, and tapestry hangings.[5] In the best period of decoration all three were regarded as subordinate to the architectural lines of the room. The Italian fresco-painters, from Giotto to Tiepolo,[6] never lost

---

5. Fresco painting: oldest known and most durable painting medium, created by applying water-based paints onto a plaster wall, therefore ideal for making murals (*EB* 2014a). Paneling: decorative treatment of walls, ceilings, and doors wherein wide sheets of thin wood are framed by narrower strips of thick wood (*EB* 2011d). Tapestry hangings: in the fourteenth century, this Western European tradition for wall treatment became firmly established with centers of production in Paris and Flanders; tapestries made by Francois Boucher, "given by Louis the Fifteenth" (Wharton 2006, 325), are a sacred asset to Undine Spragg's French nobleman husband in Edith Wharton's *The Custom of the Country*. Plate 9 of this book features a Boucher tapestry.

6. Giotto di Bondone (1276?–1337): Italian painter and a pioneer of the Renaissance artistic style, best known for his frescoes in the Arena Chapel in Padua, Italy (Murray 2019a). Giovanni Battista Tiepolo (1676–1770): Italian painter known for combining baroque and rococo elements, considered the first master of the Grand Manner, or the classic art of the High Renaissance (Pallucchini 2019). Elsewhere in *The Decoration of Houses* he is "the great Tiepolo," and references appear frequently in Wharton's corpus. While her mentor and friend Charles Eliot Norton, who has been credited with establishing the liberal arts in the United States, would not have shared her esteem of Tiepolo, Wharton describes with great regard his ceiling frescoes in Venice, notwithstanding that the guidebooks discourage "undue admiration of Tiepolo" (Wharton 1998, 195). Wharton recognizes Tiepolo—whose name, she asserts, "is familiar to the cultivated minority of travelers" (199)—as a descendant of Titian and Veronese, a claim that would at the time have sounded blasphemous. In *Italian Backgrounds*, Wharton mentions Tiepolo over a dozen times. Lily Bart in *The House of Mirth* (1905) considers, but decides against, modeling her tableau vivant on Tiepolo's frescoes of the ultimately suicidal Cleopatra from the Palazzo Labia in Venice, "The Banquet of Cleopatra" (1743–50) and "The Meeting of Antony and Cleopatra" (1743–50). Tiepolo's art would figure prominently in Wharton's 1922 novel *The Glimpses of the Moon*.

12. Room in the Villa Vertemati, Near Chiavenna. XVI or Early XVII Century. (Example of Frescoed Ceiling.)

sight of the interrelation between painting and architecture. It matters not if the connection between base and cornice be maintained by actual pilasters or mouldings, or by their painted or woven imitations. The line, and not the substance, is what the eye demands. It is a curious perversion of artistic laws that has led certain critics to denounce painted architecture or woven mouldings. As in imaginative literature the author may present to his reader as possible anything that he has the talent to make the reader accept, so in decorative art the artist is justified in presenting to the eye whatever his skill can devise to satisfy its requirements; nor is there any insincerity in this proceeding. Decorative art is not an exact science. The decorator is not a chemist or a physiologist; it is part of his mission, not to explain illusions, but to produce them. Subject only to laws established by the limitations of the eye, he is master of the domain of fancy, of that *pays bleu*[7] of the impossible that it is his privilege to throw open to the charmed imagination.

Of the means of wall-decoration already named, fresco-painting and stucco-panelling were generally preferred by Italian decorators, and wood-panelling and tapestries by those of northern Europe. The use of arras naturally commended itself to the northern noble, shivering in his draughty castles and obliged to carry from one to another the furniture and hangings that the unsettled state of the country made it impossible to leave behind him. Italy, however, long supplied the finest designs to the tapestry-looms of northern Europe, as the Italian painters provided ready-made backgrounds of peaked hills, winding torrents and pinnacled cities to the German engravers and the Flemish painters of their day.

Tapestry, in the best periods of house-decoration, was always subordinated to the architectural lines of the room (see plate 11). Where it was not specially woven for the panels it was intended to fill, the subdivisions of the wall-spaces were adapted to its dimensions. It was carefully fitted into the panelling of the room, and never made to turn an angle, as wall-paper does in modern rooms, nor combined with other odds and ends of decoration. If a room was tapestried, it was tapestried, not decorated in some other way, with bits of tapestry hung here and there at random over the fundamental lines of the decoration. Nothing can be more beautiful than tapestry properly used; but hung up without regard to the composition of the room, here turning an angle, there covering a part of the dado or overlapping a pilaster, it not only loses its own value, but destroys the whole scheme of decoration with which it is thus unmeaningly combined.

7. French: literally, "blue country." Well acquainted with the works of Charles Baudelaire (1821–67), Edith Wharton and Ogden Codman Jr. likely allude to the sense of a dreamland or land of ideals in his poem "La Lune offensée" (1868, posthumous). Here Wharton and Codman celebrate the innovative possibilities of the home decorator. Thank you to Joel Goldfield for the Baudelaire allusion.

Italian panelling was of stone, marble or stucco, while in northern Europe it was so generally of wood that (in England especially) the term *panelling* has become almost synonymous with *wood-panelling*, and in some minds there is a curious impression that any panelling not of wood is a sham. As a matter of fact, wood-panelling was used in northern Europe simply because it kept the cold out more successfully than a *revétement* of stone or plaster;[8] while south of the Alps its use was avoided for the equally good reason that in hot climates it attracts vermin.

If priority of use be held as establishing a standard in decoration, wood-panelling should be regarded as a sham and plaster-panelling as its lawful prototype; for the use of stucco in the panelling of walls and ceilings is highly characteristic of Roman interior decoration, and wood-panelling as at present used is certainly of later origin. But nothing can be more idle than such comparisons, nor more misleading than the idea that stucco is a sham because it seeks to imitate wood. It does not seek to imitate wood. It is a recognized substance, of incalculable value for decorative effect, and no more owes its place in decoration to a fancied resemblance to some other material than the nave of a cathedral owes its place in architecture to the fancied resemblance to a ship.

In the hands of a great race of artistic *virtuosi* like the Italians, stucco has produced effects of beauty which in any other substance would have lost something of their freshness, their plastic spontaneity. From the delicate traceries of the Roman baths and the loveliness of Agostino da [di] Duccio's chapel-front at Perugia, to the improvised bravura treatment of the Farnese theatre at Parma,[9] it has served,

8. French: "coating."

9. Agostino Di Duccio (1418–81?): early Renaissance sculptor whose style is characterized by flat forms and an emphasis on linear decoration. One of his two major works was the series of reliefs created for the Oratory of San Bernardino in Perugia, to which Wharton and Codman refer (*EB* 2019b). Farnese theatre at Parma: Teatro Farnese, in Parma, Italy, the first example of the modern playhouse. With its baroque style and proscenium arch, it was an important work of Renaissance

through every phase of Italian art, to embody the most refined and studied, as well as the most audacious and ephemeral, of decorative conceptions.

It must not be supposed that because painting, panelling and tapestry are the noblest forms of wall-decoration, they are necessarily the most unattainable. Good tapestry is, of course, very expensive, and even that which is only mediocre is beyond the reach of the average purchaser; while stuff hangings and wallpapers, its modern successors, have less to recommend them than other forms of wall-decoration. With painting and panelling the case is different. When painted walls were in fashion, there existed, below the great creative artists, schools of decorative designers skilled in the art of fresco-decoration, from the simplest kind to the most ornate. The demand for such decoration would now call forth the same order of talent, and many artists who are wasting their energies on the production of indifferent landscapes and unsuccessful portraits might, in the quite different field of decorative painting, find the true expression of their talent.

To many minds the mention of a frescoed room suggests the image of a grandiose saloon, with gods and goddesses of heroic size crowding the domed ceiling and lofty walls; but the heroic style of fresco-painting is only one of its many phases. To see how well this form of decoration may be adapted to small modern rooms and to our present way of living, it is only necessary to study the walls of the little Pompeian houses, with their delicate arabesques and slender, fanciful figures, or to note the manner in which the Italian painters treated the small rooms of the casino or garden-pavilion which formed part of every Italian country-seat. Examples of this light style of decoration may be found in the Casino del grotto in the grounds of the Palazzo del T at Mantua, in some of the smaller rooms of the hunting-lodge of Stupinigi near Turin, and in the casino of the Villa Valmarana near Vicenza, where the frescoes are by Tiepolo; while in France a pleasing

---

architecture. It has since been rebuilt following its destruction during World War II (*EB* 2010b).

instance of the same style of treatment is seen in the small octagonal pavilion called the Belvédère, frescoed by Le Riche, in the gardens of the Petit Trianon at Versailles.[10]

As regards panelling, it has already been said that if the effect produced be satisfactory to the eye, the substance used is a matter of indifference. Stone-panelling has the merit of solidity, and the outlines of massive stone mouldings are strong and dignified; but the same effect may be produced in stucco, a material as well suited to the purpose as stone, save for its greater fragility. Wood-panelling is adapted to the most delicate carving, greater sharpness of edge and clearness of undercutting being obtainable than in stucco: though this qualification applies only to the moulded stucco ornaments used from economy, not to those modelled by hand. Used in the latter way, stucco may be made to produce the same effects as carved wood, and for delicacy of modelling in low relief it is superior to any other material. There is, in short, little to choose between the different substances, except in so far as one or the other may commend itself to the artist as more peculiarly suited to the special requirements of his design, or to the practical conditions regulating his work.

It is to this regard for practical conditions, and not to any fancied superiority over other materials, that the use of wood-panelling

10. (Also Palazzo del Tèl; the authors follow Vasari's spelling): summer palace near Mantua, Italy, designed by Giulio Romano (1499?–1546), who is also responsible for its many frescoes, including life-size portraits of the original owner's horses and the Sala dei Giganti, which depicts the giants of Greek myth storming Mount Olympus (*EB* 2019ee). Stupinigi: Palazzina di caccia of Stupinigi, royal hunting lodge in Turin, Italy, built by architect Filippo Juvarra (1678–1736) in 1732, characterized by its baroque style and its highly decorated dome. Villa Valmarana: Palazzina in the Villa Valmarana ai Nani, a Renaissance villa, built in the sixteenth century, with its frescoes painted by Tiepolo and his son Giandomenico that depicted idyllic scenes of peasants and merchants (Villa Valmarana ai Nani n.d.). The Belvédère: small gazebo-like lounge in the English Gardens of Versailles (Château de Versailles, "The English Garden"); designed by Richard Mique (1720–94) in 1781 for Marie-Antoinette, but the walls surrounding the four patio doors are frescoed by Francois Le Riche, while the ceiling was painted by Jean-Jacques Lagrenée (1739-1821) (Web Gallery of Art, "Frescoes").

13. Drawing-Room at Easton Neston Hall, England. Built by Nicholas Hawkesmoor, 1702. (Example of Stucco Decoration.)

in northern Europe may most reasonably be attributed. Not only was wood easy to obtain, but it had the additional merit of keeping out the cold: two qualities sufficient to recommend it to the common sense of French and English architects. From the decorative point of view it has, when unpainted, one undeniable advantage over stucco—that is, beauty of color and veining. As a background for the dull gilding of old picture-frames, or as a setting for tapestry, nothing can surpass the soft rich tones of oak or walnut panelling, undefaced by the application of a shiny varnish.

With the introduction of the orders into domestic architecture and the treatment of interior walls with dado and cornice, the panelling of the wall-space between those two members began to assume definite proportions. In England and France, before that time, wall-panels were often divided into small equal-sized rectangles which, from lack of any central motive, produced a most inadequate impression. Frequently, too, in the houses of the Renaissance the panelling, instead of being carried up to the ceiling, was terminated two or three feet below it—a form of treatment that reduced the height of the room and broke the connection between walls and ceiling. This awkward device of stunted panelling, or, as it might be called, of an unduly heightened dado, has been revived by modern decorators; and it is not unusual to see the walls of a room treated, as regards their base-board and cornice, as part of an order, and then panelled up to within a foot or two of the cornice, without apparent regard to the true *raison d'être* of the dado (see plate 12).

If, then, the design of the wall-panelling is good, it matters little whether stone, stucco, or wood be used. In all three it is possible to obtain effects ranging from the grandeur of the great loggia of the Villa Madama[11] to the simplicity of any wood-panelled parlor in a New England country-house, and from the greatest costliness to an outlay little larger than that required for the purchase of a good wall-paper.

It was well for the future of house-decoration when medical science declared itself against the use of wall-papers.[12] These hangings have, in fact, little to recommend them. Besides being objectionable on sanitary grounds, they are inferior as a wall-decoration to any form of treatment, however simple, that maintains, instead of effacing, the architectural lines of a room. It was the use of wall-paper that led to the obliteration of the over-door and over-mantel, and to the gradual submerging under a flood of pattern of all the main lines of the wall-spaces. Its merits are that it is cheap, easy to put on and easy to remove. On the other hand, it is readily damaged, soon fades, and cannot be

11. Royal rural house at the foot of Monte Mario near Rome. Its first architect was Raphael (1483–1520), who began building in 1518. As Wharton and Codman note, its most extravagant room is the loggia, an open-sided gallery, which has richly colored decorations, including small frescoes of mythological figures.

12. Wharton and Codman's wholesale dismissal of wallpaper, on grounds sanitary and aesthetic, provides an important context for Charlotte Perkins Gilman's "The Yellow Wall-paper."

cleaned; while from the decorative point of view there can be no comparison between the flat meanderings of wall-paper pattern and the strong architectural lines of any scheme of panelling, however simple. Sometimes, of course, the use of wall-paper is a matter of convenience, since it saves both time and trouble; but a papered room can never, decoratively or otherwise, be as satisfactory as one in which the walls are treated in some other manner.

The hanging of walls with chintz[13] or any other material is even more objectionable than the use of wall-paper, since it has not the saving merit of cheapness. The custom is probably a survival of the time when wall-decorations had to be made in movable shape; and this facility of removal points to the one good reason for using stuff hangings. In a hired house, if the wall-decorations are ugly, and it is necessary to hide them, the rooms may be hung with stuff which the departing tenant can take away. In other words, stuff hangings are serviceable if used as a tent; as a permanent mode of decoration they are both unhealthy and inappropriate. There is something unpleasant in the idea of a dust-collecting fabric fixed to the wall, so that it cannot be shaken out at will like a curtain. Textile fabrics are meant to be moved, folded, shaken: they have none of the qualities of permanence and solidity which we associate with the walls of a room. The much-derided marble curtains of the Jesuit church in Venice are no more illogical than stuff wall-hangings.[14]

In decorating the walls of a room, the first point to be considered is whether they are to form a background for its contents, or to be in themselves its chief decoration. In many cases the disappointing

13. From the Hindi word *chint*, meaning "spotted," "variegated," "speckled," or "sprayed": "The term was appropriated in [the] English-speaking world in the eighteenth century to reference industrially printed cottons" notes Sarah Fee in *Cloth That Changed the World: The Art and Fashion of Indian Chintz* (2020): "In popular imagination, over the nineteenth century, the term became associated with floral designs and heavy glazing."

14. Church of Santa Maria Assunta, also known as I Gesuiti.

effects of wall-decoration are due to the fact that this important distinction has been overlooked. In rooms that are to be hung with prints or pictures, the panelling or other treatment of the walls should be carefully designed with a view to the size and number of the pictures. Pictures should never be hung against a background of pattern. Nothing is more distressing than the sight of a large oil-painting in a ponderous frame seemingly suspended from a spray of wild roses or any of the other naturalistic vegetation of the modern wall-paper. The overlaying of pattern is always a mistake. It produces a confusion of line in which the finest forms lose their individuality and significance.

It is also important to avoid hanging pictures or prints too close to each other. Not only do the colors clash, but the different designs of the frames, some of which may be heavy, with deeply recessed mouldings, while others are flat and carved in low relief, produce an equally discordant impression. Every one recognizes the necessity of selecting the mouldings and other ornamental details of a room with a view to their position in the scheme of decoration; but few stop to consider that in a room hung with pictures, the frames take the place of wall-mouldings, and consequently must be chosen and placed as though they were part of a definite decorative composition.

Pictures and prints should be fastened to the wall, not hung by a cord or wire, nor allowed to tilt forward at an angle. The latter arrangement is specially disturbing since it throws the picture-frames out of the line of the wall. It must never be forgotten that pictures on a wall, whether set in panels or merely framed and hung, inevitably become a part of the wall-decoration. In the seventeenth and eighteenth centuries, in rooms of any importance, pictures were always treated as a part of the decoration, and frequently as panels sunk in the wall in a setting of carved wood or stucco mouldings (see paintings in plates 5 and 19). Even when not set in panels, they were always fixed to the wall, and their frames, whether of wood or stucco, were made to correspond with the ornamental detail of the rest of the room. Beautiful examples of this mode of treatment are seen in many English interiors of the seventeenth and eighteenth centuries,[†] and some of the finest carvings of Grinling Gibbons were designed for this purpose.[15]

Even where the walls are not to be hung with pictures, it is necessary to consider what kind of background the furniture and objects of art require. If the room is to be crowded with cabinets, bookcases and other tall pieces, and these, as well as the tables and mantel-shelf, are to be covered with porcelain vases, bronze statuettes, ivories, Chinese monsters and Chelsea groups,[16] a plain background should be provided for this many-colored medley. Should the room contain only a few important pieces of furniture, and one or two vases or busts, the walls against which these strongly marked objects are to be placed may receive a more decorative treatment. It is only in rooms used for entertaining, dining, or some special purpose for which little furniture is required, that the walls should receive a more elaborate scheme of decoration.

Where the walls are treated in an architectural manner, with a well-designed dado and cornice, and an over-mantel and over-doors connecting the openings with the cornice, it will be found that in a room of average size the intervening wall-spaces may be tinted in a uniform color and left unornamented. If the fundamental lines are right, very little decorative detail is needed to complete the effect; whereas, when the lines are wrong, no overlaying of ornamental odds and ends, in the way of pictures, bric-à-brac and other improvised expedients, will conceal the structural deficiencies.

[†] See the saloon at Easton Neston, built by Nicholas Hawkesmoor [sic] (plate 13), and various examples given in Pyne's *Royal Residences*.

15. Grinling Gibbons (1648–1721): Dutch-English woodcarver and sculptor known for his decorative woodwork and ornamentation, as seen in St. James's Church and St. Paul's Cathedral (*EB* 2019r).

16. Miniature porcelain figurines from eighteenth-century England popular in the nineteenth century.

4

Doors

The fate of the door in America has been a curious one, and had the other chief features of the house—such as windows, fireplaces, and stairs—been pursued with the same relentless animosity by architects and decorators, we should no longer be living in houses at all. First, the door was slid into the wall; then even its concealed presence was resented, and it was unhung and replaced by a portière;[1] while of late it has actually ceased to form a part of house-building, and many recently built houses contain doorways *without doors*. Even the front door, which might seem to have too valid a reason for existence to be disturbed by the variations of fashion, has lately had to yield its place, in the more pretentious kind of house, to a wrought-iron gateway lined with plate-glass,[2] against which, as a climax of inconsequence, a thick curtain is usually hung.

It is not difficult to explain such architectural vagaries. In general, their origin is to be found in the misapplication of some serviceable feature and its consequent rejection by those who did not understand that it had ceased to be useful only because it was not properly used.

In the matter of doors, such an explanation at once presents itself. During the latter half of the eighteenth century it occurred to some

1. Curtain that hangs in a doorway in the United States in lieu of a door and that replaced the pocket door, a popular style in Victorian homes (*M-W*).
2. Victorian homes traditionally had front doors with large, impressive panels of stained glass framed with brass, wood, or intricate ironwork. This was done to enhance the overall effect and status of the home (Old English Doors n.d.).

14. Doorway with Marble Architrave, Ducal Palace, Mantua. XVI Century.

ingenious person that when two adjoining rooms were used for entertaining, and it was necessary to open the doors between them, these doors might be in the way; and to avoid this possibility, a recess was formed in the thickness of the wall, and the door was made to slide into it.

This idea apparently originated in England, for sliding doors, even in the present day, are virtually unknown on the continent; and Isaac Ware, in the book already quoted, speaks of the sliding door as having been used "at the house, late Mr. de Pestre's, near Hanover Square," and adds that "the manner of it there may serve as an example to other builders," showing it to have been a novelty which he thought worthy of imitation.[3]

English taste has never been so sure as that of the Latin races; and it has, moreover, been perpetually modified by a passion for contriving all kinds of supposed "conveniences," which instead of simplifying life not unfrequently tend to complicate it. Americans have inherited this trait, and in both countries the architect or upholsterer who can present a new and more intricate way of planning a house or of making a piece of furniture, is more sure of a hearing than he who follows the accepted lines.

It is doubtful if the devices to which so much is sacrificed in English and American house-planning always offer the practical advantages attributed to them. In the case of the sliding door these advantages are certainly open to question, since there is no reason why a door should not open into a room. Under ordinary circumstances, doors should always be kept shut; it is only, as Ware points out, when two adjoining rooms are used for entertaining that it is necessary to leave the door between them open. Now, between two rooms destined for entertaining, a double door (*à deux battants*) is always preferable to a single one; and as an opening four feet six inches wide is sufficient in such cases, each of the doors will be only two feet three inches wide, and therefore cannot encroach to any serious extent on the floor-space of the room. On the other hand, much has been sacrificed to the supposed "convenience" of the sliding door: first, the decorative effect of a well-panelled door, with hinges, box-locks[4] and handle of finely

---

3. Edith Wharton and Ogden Codman Jr. quote from chapter 15 of Ware's book in which, to their chagrin, he approves what they deride as the "ingenious" idea of a sliding door, describing "a cavity somewhat more than equal to the depth and substance of the door in the thickness of the wall. Into this the door may slide by a gentle touch, and remain undiscovered; and a handsome brass ring being fixed to the edge, it may come out again when it is to be shut with as slight a motion. This is done, at the house late Mr. De Pestres', near Hanover Square, and the manner of it there may serve as an example to other builders" (Ware, 459).

4. Ornate lock, typically bronze, featured on Victorian doors.

chiselled bronze; secondly, the privacy of both rooms, since the difficulty of closing a heavy sliding door always leads to its being left open, with the result that two rooms are necessarily used as one. In fact, the absence of privacy in modern houses is doubtless in part due to the difficulty of closing the doors between the rooms.

The sliding door has led to another abuse in house-planning: the exaggerated widening of the doorway. While doors were hung on hinges, doorways were of necessity restricted to their proper dimensions; but with the introduction of the sliding door, openings eight or ten feet wide became possible. The planning of a house is often modified by a vague idea on the part of its owners that they may wish to give entertainments on a large scale. As a matter of fact, general entertainments are seldom given in a house of average size; and those who plan their houses with a view to such possibilities sacrifice their daily comfort to an event occurring perhaps once a year. But even where many entertainments are to be given large doorways are of little use. Any architect of experience knows that ease of circulation depends far more on the planning of the house and on the position of the openings than on the actual dimensions of the latter. Indeed, two moderate-sized doorways leading from one room to another are of much more use in facilitating the movements of a crowd than one opening ten feet wide.

Sliding doors have been recommended on the ground that their use preserves a greater amount of wall-space; but two doorways of moderate dimensions, properly placed, will preserve as much wall-space as one very large opening and will probably permit a better distribution of panelling and furniture. There was far more wall-space in seventeenth- and eighteenth-century rooms than there is in rooms of the same dimensions in the average modern American house; and even where this space was not greater in actual measurement, more furniture could be used, since the openings were always placed with a view to the proper arrangement of what the room was to contain.

According to the best authorities, the height of a well-proportioned doorway should be twice its width; and as the height is necessarily regulated by the stud of the room, it follows that the width varies; but it is obvious that no doorway should be less than six feet high nor less than three feet wide.

When a doorway is over three feet six inches wide, a pair of doors should always be used; while a single door is preferable in a narrow opening.

In rooms twelve feet or less in height, doorways should not be more than nine feet high. The width of openings in such rooms is therefore restricted to four feet six inches; indeed, it is permissible to make the opening lower and thus reduce its width to four feet; six inches of additional wall-space are not to be despised in a room of average dimensions.

The treatment of the door forms one of the most interesting chapters in the history of house-decoration. In feudal castles the interior doorway, for purposes of defense, was made so small and narrow that only one person could pass through at a time, and was set in a plain lintel or architrave of stone, the door itself being fortified by bands of steel or iron, and by heavy bolts and bars. Even at this early period it seems probable that in the chief apartments the lines of the doorway were carried up to the ceiling by means of an over-door of carved wood, or of some painted decorative composition.[†] This connection between the doorway and the ceiling, maintained through all the subsequent phases of house-decoration, was in fact never disregarded until the beginning of the present century.

It was in Italy that the door, in common with the other features of private dwellings, first received a distinctly architectural treatment. In Italian palaces of the fifteenth century the doorways were usually framed by architraves of marble, enriched with arabesques, medallions and processional friezes in low relief, combined with disks of colored marble. Interesting examples of this treatment are seen in the apartments of Isabella of Este in the ducal palace at Mantua (see plate 14), in the ducal palace at Urbino, and in the Certosa of Pavia—some of the smaller doorways in this monastery being decorated with medallion

---

[†] See Viollet-le-Duc, *Dictionnaire raisonné de l'Architecture française*, under *Porte*.

portraits of the Sforzas, and with other low reliefs of extraordinary beauty.[5]

The doors in Italian palaces were usually of inlaid wood, elaborate in composition and affording in many cases beautiful instances of that sense of material limitation that preserves one art from infringing upon another. The intarsia doors[6] of the palace at Urbino are among the most famous examples of this form of decoration. It should be noted that many of the woods used in Italian marquetry were of a light shade, so that the blending of colors in Renaissance doors produces a sunny golden-brown tint in perfect harmony with the marble architrave of the doorway. The Italian decorator would never have permitted so harsh a contrast as that between the white trim and the mahogany doors of English eighteenth-century houses. This juxtaposition of colors was disapproved by French decorators also, and was seldom seen except in England and in the American houses built under English influence. It should be observed, too, that the polish given to hard-grained wood in England, and imitated in the wood-varnish of the present day, was never in favor in Italy and France. Shiny surfaces were always disliked by the best decorators.

The classic revival in Italy necessarily modified the treatment of the doorway. Flat arabesques and delicately chiselled medallions gave way to a plain architrave, frequently masked by an order; while the over-door[7] took the form of a pediment, or, in the absence of shafts,

5. Isabella of Este (1474–1539): Marchioness of Mantua and major patron of the arts during the Renaissance. The doorway in question is decorated with a marble architrave, which contains a small frieze. Palazzo Ducale di Urbino: Renaissance palace in central Italy, which now operates as the National Gallery of the Marches, with a major collection of artwork and a *studiolo* (study) with intarsia paneling, specifically on the doors of the throne room (*EB* 2010c). Certosa di Pavia: monastery in Lombardy, Italy, with a decorative entryway (Certosa di Pavia n.d.). Sforza: important family of the Italian Renaissance that ruled Milan for almost a century. Some of its members are buried in the Certosa di Pavia (*EB* 2017f).

6. A form of wood inlay, resembling mosaic, often used in panels in chapels and private studies (*EB* 2018g).

7. A painting, panel, or decorative piece over a doorframe (*M-W*).

of a cornice or entablature resting on brackets. The use of a pediment over interior doorways was characteristic of Italian decoration.

In studying Italian interiors of this period from photographs or modern prints, or even in visiting the partly dilapidated palaces themselves, it may at first appear that the lines of the doorway were not always carried up to the cornice. Several causes have combined to produce this impression. In the first place, the architectural treatment of the over-door was frequently painted on the wall, and has consequently disappeared with the rest of the wall-decoration (see plate 15). Then, again, Italian rooms were often painted with landscapes and out-of-door architectural effects, and when this was done the doorways were combined with these architectural compositions, and were not treated as part of the room, but as part of what the room *pretended to be*. In the suppressed Scuola della Carità (now the Academy of Fine Arts) at Venice, one may see a famous example of this treatment in the doorway under the stairs leading up to the temple, in Titian's[8] great painting of the "Presentation of the Virgin."† Again, in the high-studded Italian saloons containing a musician's gallery, or a clerestory, a cornice was frequently carried around the walls at suitable height above the lower range of openings, and the decorative treatment above the doors, windows and fireplace extended only to this cornice, not to the actual ceiling of the room.

Thus it will be seen that the relation between the openings and cornice in Italian decoration was in reality always maintained except

---

8. Titian (1488/90–1576): Italian Renaissance master, considered the most important of the sixteenth-century Venetian school. In *A Backward Glance*, Wharton's friend Robert S. Minturn is described as a "grave young man whose pensive dusky head was so like that of a Titian portrait" (1934, 156); in Wharton's story "The Confessional" (1901), Roberto has features resembling those of Minturn, "a melancholy musing face such as you may see in some of Titian's portraits of young men" (322).

† This painting has now been restored to its proper position in the Scuola della Carità, and the door which had been *painted in* under the stairs has been removed to make way for the actual doorway around which the picture was originally painted.

where the decorator chose to regard them as forming a part, not of the room, but of some other architectural composition.

In the sixteenth century the excessive use of marquetry was abandoned, doors being panelled, and either left undecorated or painted with those light animated combinations of figure and arabesque which Raphael borrowed from the Roman fresco-painters, and which since his day have been peculiarly characteristic of Italian decorative painting.[†]

Wood-carving in Italy was little used in house-decoration, and, as a rule, the panelling of doors was severely architectural in character, with little of the delicate ornamentation marking the French work of the seventeenth and eighteenth centuries.[†]

In France the application of the orders to interior doorways was never very popular, though it figures in French architectural works of the eighteenth century. The architrave, except in houses of great magnificence, was usually of wood, sometimes very richly carved. It was often surmounted by an entablature with a cornice resting on carved brackets; while the panel between this and the ceiling-cornice was occupied by an over-door consisting either of a painting, of a carved panel or of a stucco or marble bas-relief. These over-doors usually corresponded with the design of the over-mantel.

Great taste and skill were displayed in the decoration of door-panels and embrasure.[9] In the earlier part of the seventeenth century, doors and embrasures were usually painted, and nothing in the way of decorative painting can exceed in beauty and fitness the French compositions of this period.[†]

During the reign of Louis XIV, doors were either carved or painted, and their treatment ranged from the most elaborate decoration to the

[†] See the doors of the Sala dello Zodiaco in the ducal palace at Mantua (plate 16).

[†] Some rooms of the rocaille period, however, contain doors as elaborately carved as those seen in France (see the doors in the royal palace at Genoa, plate 34).

9. Opening in a wall with thicker sides that flare outward, usually used in fortification for the firing of a cannon (M-W).

[†] See the doors at Vaux-le-Vicomte and in the Palais de Justice at Rennes.

15. Sala dei Cavalli, Palazzo del T, Mantua. XVI Century. (Example of Painted Architectural Decoration.)

simplest panelling set in a plain wooden architrave. In some French doors of this period painting and carving were admirably combined; and they were further ornamented by the chiselled locks and hinges for which French locksmiths were famous. So important a part did these locks and hinges play in French decoration that Lebrun himself is said to have designed those in the Galerie d'Apollon, in the Louvre, when he composed the decoration of the room.[10] Even in the simplest private houses, where chiselled bronze was too expensive a luxury, and wrought-iron locks and hinges, with plain knobs of brass or iron, were used instead, such attention was paid to both design and execution that it is almost impossible to find in France an old lock or hinge, however

10. Charles Le Brun (1619–90): French painter who created and supervised the production of works of art commissioned by the French government under Louis XIV, including the Galerie d'Apollon, a hall in the Louvre, known for its detailed paintings on the walls and ceilings (*EB* 2019j).

plain, that is not well designed and well made (see plate 17). The miserable commercial article that disgraces our modern doors would not have been tolerated in the most unpretentious dwelling.

The mortise-lock[11] now in use in England and America first made its appearance toward the end of the eighteenth century in England, where it displaced the brass or iron box-lock; but on the Continent it has never been adopted. It is a poor substitute for the box-lock, since it not only weakens but disfigures the door, while a well-designed box-lock is both substantial and ornamental (see plate 17).

In many minds the Louis XV period is associated with a general waviness of line and excess of carving. It has already been pointed out that even when the rocaille manner was at its height the main lines of a room were seldom allowed to follow the capricious movement of the ornamental accessories.[12] Openings being the leading features of a room, their main lines were almost invariably respected; and while considerable play of movement was allowed in some of the accessory mouldings of the over-doors and over-mantels, the plan of the panel, in general symmetrical, was in many cases a plain rectangle.[†]

During the Louis XV period the panelling of doors was frequently enriched with elaborate carving; but such doors are to be found only in palaces, or in princely houses like the Hôtels de Soubise, de Rohan, or de Toulouse (see plate 18).[13] In the most magnificent apartments, moreover, plain panelled doors were as common as those adorned with carving; while in the average private hôtel, even where much ornament was lavished on the panelling of the walls, the doors were left plain.

11. Lock that fits into a groove or slot purposely cut into a door or piece of furniture (M-W).

12. An aspect of the rococo style, characterized by stylized rocklike and scroll ornamentation reflecting the architectural response to the sterility of the baroque style (EB 2018n).

† Only in the most exaggerated German baroque were the vertical lines of the door-panels sometimes irregular.

13. Mansions in Paris built for royal families or nobles tightly connected to them (Archives Nationales n.d.).

Towards the close of this reign, when the influence of Gabriel[14] began to simplify and restrain the ornamental details of house-decoration, the panelled door was often made without carving and was sometimes painted with attenuated arabesques and grisaille medallions, relieved against a gold ground. Gabriel gave the key-note of what is known as Louis XVI decoration, and the treatment of the door in France followed the same general lines until the end of the eighteenth century. As the classic influence became more marked, paintings in the over-door and over-mantel were replaced by low or high reliefs in stucco: and towards the end of the Louis XVI period a processional frieze in the classic manner often filled the entablature above the architrave of the door (see plate 16).

Doors opening upon a terrace, or leading from an antechamber into a summer-parlor, or *salon frais*, were frequently made of glass; while in gala rooms, doors so situated as to correspond with the windows of the room were sometimes made of looking-glass. In both these instances the glass was divided into small panes, with such strongly marked mouldings that there could not be a moment's doubt of the apparent, as well as the actual, solidity of the door. In good decorative art first impressions are always taken into account, and the immediate satisfaction of the eye is provided for.

In England the treatment of doorway and door followed in a general way the Italian precedent. The architrave, as a rule, was severely architectural, and in the eighteenth century the application of an order was regarded as almost essential in rooms of a certain importance. The door itself was sometimes inlaid,[†] but oftener simply panelled (see plate 11).

In the panelling of doors, English taste, except when it closely followed Italian precedents, was not always good. The use of a pair of doors in one opening was confined to grand houses, and in the average

---

14. Ange-Jacques Gabriel (1698–1782): French architect who worked on many royal palaces under Louis XV (*EB* 2019c).

† The inlaid doors of Houghton Hall, the seat of Sir Robert Walpole, were noted for their beauty and costliness. The price of each was £200.

dwelling single doors were almost invariably used, even in openings over three feet wide. The great width of some of these single doors led to a curious treatment of the panels, the door being divided by a central stile, which was sometimes beaded, as though, instead of a single door, it were really a pair held together by some invisible agency. This central stile is almost invariably seen in the doors of modern American houses.

Towards the middle of the eighteenth century the use of highly polished mahogany doors became general in England. It has already been pointed out that the juxtaposition of a dark-colored door and a white architrave was not approved by French and Italian architects. Blondel, in fact, expressly states that such contrasts are to be avoided, and that where walls are pale in tint the door should never be dark: thus in vestibules and ante-chambers panelled with Caen stone he recommends painting the doors a pale shade of gray.[15]

In Italy, when doors were left unpainted they were usually made of walnut, a wood of which the soft, dull tone harmonizes well with almost any color, whether light or dark; while in France it would not be easy to find an unpainted door, except in rooms where the wall-panelling is also of natural wood.

In the better type of house lately built in America there is seen a tendency to return to the use of doors hung on hinges. These, however, have been so long out of favor that the rules regulating their dimensions have been lost sight of, and the modern door and architrave are seldom satisfactory in these respects. The principles of proportion have been further disturbed by a return to the confused and hesitating system of panelling prevalent in England during the Tudor and Elizabethan periods.[16]

15. Jacques-François Blondel (1705–74): French architect during the reign of Louis XV; came from an architectural family and was versed in the rococo style, but he eventually rejected such style (*EB* 2019s). Caen stone: a specific type of yellowish limestone from the city of Caen in western France, favored by masons for being easy to carve and mold (Canterbury Historical and Archaeological Society n.d.).

16. See chapter 1, note 14, on Tudor and Elizabethan; derivative of the Perpendicular Gothic style (*EB* 2010a); both styles are characterized by an emphasis on

16. Door in the Sala dello Zodiaco, Ducal Palace, Mantua. XVIII Century.

The old French and Italian architects never failed to respect that rule of decorative composition which prescribes that where there is any division of parts, one part shall unmistakably predominate. In

_____

vertical lines, which presented itself in intricate wood paneling, to which Wharton and Codman are referring (*EB* 2011e).

conformity with this rule, the principal panel in doors of French or Italian design is so much higher than the others that these are at once seen to be merely accessory; whereas many of our modern doors are cut up into so many small panels, and the central one so little exceeds the others in height, that they do not "compose."

The architrave of the modern door has been neglected for the same reasons as the window-architrave. The use of the heavy sliding door, which could not be opened or shut without an effort, led to the adoption of the portière; and the architrave, being thus concealed, was no longer regarded as a feature of any importance in the decoration of the room.

The portière has always been used, as old prints and pictures show; but, like the curtain, in earlier days it was simply intended to keep out currents of air, and was consequently seldom seen in well-built houses, where double sets of doors served far better to protect the room from draughts. In less luxurious rooms, where there were no double doors, and portières had to be used, these were made as scant and unobtrusive as possible. The device of draping stuffs about the doorway, thus substituting a textile architrave for one of wood or stone, originated with the modern upholsterer; and it is now not unusual to see a wide opening with no door in it, enclosed in yards and yards of draperies which cannot even be lowered at will.

The portière, besides causing a break in architectural lines, has become one of the chief expenses in the decoration of the modern room; indeed, the amount spent in buying yards of plush or damask,[17] with the addition of silk cord, tassels, gimp and fringe, often makes it necessary to slight the essential features of the room; so that an ugly mantelpiece or ceiling is preserved because the money required to replace it has been used in the purchase of portières. These superfluous

17. Elaborately patterned fabric originating in Damascus and woven on a Jacquard loom. Traditionally only made from silk, but cotton, linen, and rayon are now widely used. In Wharton's *The House of Mirth* (1905) and *The Custom of the Country* (1913) pink damask is associated with hotel-leasing nouveau riche women.

draperies are, in fact, more expensive than a well-made door with hinges and box-lock of chiselled bronze.

The general use of the portière has also caused the disappearance of the over-door. The lines of the opening being hidden under a mass of drapery, the need of connecting them with the cornice was no longer felt, and one more feature of the room passed out of the architect's hands into those of the upholsterer, or, as he might more fitly be called, the house-dressmaker.

The return to better principles of design will do more than anything else to restore the architectural lines of the room. Those who use portières generally do so from an instinctive feeling that a door is an ugly thing that ought to be hidden, and modern doors are in fact ugly; but when architects give to the treatment of openings the same attention they formerly received, it will soon be seen that this ugliness is not a necessity, and portières will disappear with the return of well-designed doors.

Some general hints concerning the distribution of openings have been given in the chapter on walls. It may be noted in addition that while all doorways in a room should, as a rule, be of one height, there are cases where certain clearly subordinate openings may be lower than those which contain doors *à deux battants*.[18] In such cases the panelling of the door must be carefully modified in accordance with the dimensions of the opening, and the treatment of the over-doors in their relation to each other must be studied with equal attention. Examples of such adaptations are to be found in many old French and Italian rooms.[†]

Doors should always swing *into* a room. This facilitates entrance and gives the hospitable impression that everything is made easy to those who are coming in. Doors should furthermore be so hung that they screen that part of the room in which the occupants usually sit. In

18. French: sets of double doors.

† See a room in the Ministère de la Marine at Paris, where a subordinate door is cleverly treated in connection with one of more importance.

17. Examples of Modern French Locksmiths' Work.

small rooms, especially those in town houses, this detail cannot be too carefully considered. The fact that so many doors open in the wrong way is another excuse for the existence of portières.

A word must also be said concerning the actual making of the door. There is a general impression that veneered doors or furniture are cheap substitutes for articles made of solid blocks of wood. As a matter of fact, owing to the high temperature of American houses, all well-made wood-work used in this country is of necessity composed of at least three, and often of five, layers of wood. This method of veneering, in which the layers are so placed that the grain runs in different directions, is the only way of counteracting the shrinking and swelling of the wood under artificial heat.

To some minds the concealed door represents one of those architectural deceptions which no necessity can excuse. It is certain that the concealed door is an expedient, and that in a well-planned house there should be no need for expedients, unless the architect is hampered by limitations of space, as is the case in designing the average American town house. Architects all know how many principles of beauty and fitness must be sacrificed to the restrictions of a plot of ground twenty-five feet wide by seventy-five or a hundred in length. Under such conditions, every device is permissible that helps to produce an effect of spaciousness and symmetry without interfering with convenience: chief among these contrivances being the concealed door.

Such doors are often useful in altering or adding to a badly planned house. It is sometimes desirable to give increased facilities of communication without adding to the visible number of openings in any one room; while in other cases the limited amount of wall-space may make it difficult to find place for a doorway corresponding in dimensions with the others; or, again, where it is necessary to make a closet under the stairs, the architrave of a visible door may clash awkwardly with the string-board.[19]

Under such conditions the concealed door naturally suggests itself. To those who regard its use as an offense against artistic integrity, it must once more be pointed out that architecture addresses itself not to the moral sense, but to the eye. The existing confusion on this point is partly due to the strange analogy drawn by modern critics between artistic sincerity and moral law. Analogies are the most dangerous form of reasoning: they connect resemblances, but disguise facts; and

19. Boards used on a set of stairs to cover the vertical ends of the steps; also known as risers (*M-W*).

18. Carved Door, Palace of Versailles. Louis XV Period. (Showing Painted Over-Door.)

in this instance nothing can be more fallacious than to measure the architect's action by an ethical standard.

"Sincerity," in many minds, is chiefly associated with speaking the truth; but architectural sincerity is simply obedience to certain visual requirements, one of which demands that what are at once seen to be the main lines of a room or house shall be acknowledged as such in the application of ornament. The same architectural principles demand that the main lines of a room shall not be unnecessarily interrupted; and in certain cases it would be bad taste to disturb the equilibrium of wall-spaces and decoration by introducing a visible door leading to some unimportant closet or passageway, of which the existence need not be known to any but the inmates of the house. It is in such cases that the concealed door is a useful expedient. It can hardly be necessary to point out that it would be a great mistake to place a concealed door in a main opening. These openings should always be recognized as one of the chief features of the room, and so treated by the decorator; but this point has already been so strongly insisted upon that it is reverted to here only in order to show how different are the requirements which justify concealment.

The concealed door has until recently been used so little by American architects that its construction is not well understood, and it is often hung on ordinary visible hinges, instead of being swung on a pivot. There is no reason why, with proper care, a door of this kind should not be so nicely adjusted to the wall-panelling as to be practically invisible; and to fulfil this condition is the first necessity of its construction (see concealed door in plate 45).

5

Windows

In the decorative treatment of a room the importance of openings can hardly be overestimated. Not only do they represent the three chief essentials of its comfort—light, heat and means of access—but they are the leading features in that combination of voids and masses that forms the basis of architectural harmony. In fact, it is chiefly because the decorative value of openings has ceased to be recognized that modern rooms so seldom produce a satisfactory and harmonious impression. It used to be thought that the effect of a room depended on the treatment of its wall-spaces and openings; now it is supposed to depend on its curtains and furniture. Accessory details have crowded out the main decorative features; and, as invariably happens when the relation of parts is disturbed, everything in the modern room has been thrown out of balance by this confusion between the essential and the incidental in decoration.[†]

The return to a more architectural treatment of rooms and to a recognition of the decorative value of openings, besides producing much better results, would undoubtedly reduce the expense of house-decoration. A small quantity of ornament, properly applied, will produce far more effect than ten times its amount used in the wrong way; and it will be found that when decorators rely for their effects on the

---

[†] As an example of the extent to which openings have come to be ignored as factors in the decorative composition of a room, it is curious to note that in Eastlake's well-known *Hints on Household Taste* no mention is made of doors, windows or fireplaces. Compare this point of view with that of the earlier decorators, from Vignola to Roubo and Ware.

treatment of openings, the rest of the room will require little ornamentation. The crowding of rooms with furniture and bric-à-brac
is doubtless partly due to an unconscious desire to fill up the blanks
caused by the lack of architectural composition in the treatment of
the walls.

The importance of connecting the main lines of the openings
with the cornice having been explained in the previous chapter, it is
now necessary to study the different openings in turn, and to see in
how many ways they serve to increase the dignity and beauty of their
surroundings.

As light-giving is the main purpose for which windows are made,
the top of the window should be as near the ceiling as the cornice will
allow. Ventilation, the secondary purpose of the window, is also better served by its being so placed, since an opening a foot wide near
the ceiling will do more towards airing a room than a space twice as
large near the floor. In our northern States, where the dark winter days
and the need of artificial heat make light and ventilation so necessary,
these considerations are especially important. In Italian palaces the
windows are generally lower than in more northern countries, since
the greater intensity of the sunshine makes a much smaller opening
sufficient; moreover, in Italy, during the summer, houses are not kept
cool by letting in the air, but by shutting it out.

Windows should not exceed five feet in width, while in small
rooms openings three feet wide will be found sufficient. There are
practical as well as artistic reasons for observing this rule, since a sash-
window containing a sheet of glass more than five feet wide cannot
be so hung that it may be raised without effort; while a casement, or
French window, though it may be made somewhat wider, is not easy to
open if its width exceeds six feet.[1]

The next point to consider is the distance between the bottom of
the window and the floor. This must be decided by circumstances,

1. Casement: window made of panels of glass that opens by one panel sliding
vertically or horizontally. French window: window opening outward through the use
of hinges (Sash Window Workshop n.d.).

such as the nature of the view, the existence of a balcony or veranda, or the wish to have a window-seat. The outlook must also be considered, and the window treated in one way if it looks upon the street, and in another if it gives on the garden or informal side of the house. In the country nothing is more charming than the French window opening to the floor. On the more public side of the house, unless the latter gives on an enclosed court, it is best that the windows should be placed about three feet from the floor, so that persons approaching the house may not be able to look in. Windows placed at this height should be provided with a fixed seat, or with one of the little settees with arms, but without a back, formerly used for this purpose.

Although for practical reasons it may be necessary that the same room should contain some windows opening to the floor and others raised several feet above it, the tops of all the windows should be on a level. To place them at different heights serves no useful end, and interferes with any general scheme of decoration and more specially with the arrangement of curtains.

Mullions dividing a window in the centre should be avoided whenever possible, since they are an unnecessary obstruction to the view.[2] The chief drawback to a casement window is that its sashes join in the middle; but as this is a structural necessity, it is less objectionable. If mullions are required, they should be so placed as to divide the window into three parts, thus preserving an unobstructed central pane. The window called Palladian illustrates this point.[3]

Now that large plate-glass windows have ceased to be a novelty, it will perhaps be recognized that the old window with subdivided panes had certain artistic and practical merits that have of late been disregarded.

2. Thin piece of wood or metal that divides two windows or panels of glass in a window (*M-W*).

3. Most popular during the seventeenth and eighteenth centuries; composed of three parts, which include a large central section with an arched top and two shorter, square sections on each side (*EB* 2016c).

Where there is a fine prospect, windows made of a single plate of glass are often preferred; but it must be remembered that the subdivisions of a sash, while obstructing the view, serve to establish a relation between the inside of the house and the landscape, making the latter what, *as seen from a room*, it logically ought to be: a part of the wall-decoration, in the sense of being subordinated to the same general lines. A large unbroken sheet of plate-glass interrupts the decorative scheme of the room, just as in verse, if the distances between the rhymes are so great that the ear cannot connect them, the continuity of sound is interrupted. Decoration must rhyme to the eye, and to do so must be subject to the limitations of the eye, as verse is subject to the limitations of the ear. Success in any art depends on a due regard for the limitations of the sense to which it appeals.

The effect of a perpetually open window, produced by a large sheet of plate-glass, while it gives a sense of coolness and the impression of being out of doors, becomes for these very reasons a disadvantage in cold weather.

It is sometimes said that the architects of the eighteenth century would have used large plates of glass in their windows had they been able to obtain them; but as such plates were frequently used for mirrors, it is evident that they were not difficult to get, and that there must have been other reasons for not employing them in windows; while the additional expense could hardly have been an obstacle in an age when princes and nobles built with such royal disregard of cost. The French, always logical in such matters, having tried the effect of plate-glass, are now returning to the old fashion of smaller panes; and in many of the new houses in Paris, where the windows at first contained large plates of glass, the latter have since been subdivided by a network of narrow mouldings applied to the glass.

As to the comparative merits of French, or casement, and sash windows, both arrangements have certain advantages. In houses built in the French or Italian style, casement windows are best adapted to the general treatment; while the sash-window is more in keeping in English houses. Perhaps the best way of deciding the question is to remember that "les fenêtres sont intimement liées aux grandes lignes de l'architecture," and to conform to the rule suggested by this axiom.[4]

The two common objections to French windows—that they are less convenient for ventilation, and that they cannot be opened without letting in cold air near the floor—are both unfounded. All properly made French windows have at the top an impost or stationary part containing small panes, one of which is made to open, thus affording perfect ventilation without draught. Another expedient, seen in one of the rooms of Mesdames de France at Versailles,[5] is a small pane in the main part of the window, opening on hinges of its own. (For examples of well-designed French windows, see plates 30 and 31.)

Sash-windows have the disadvantage of not opening more than half-way, a serious drawback in our hot summer climate. It is often said that French windows cannot be opened wide without interfering with the curtains; but this difficulty is easily met by the use of curtains made with cords and pulleys, in the sensible old-fashioned manner. The real purpose of the window-curtain is to regulate the amount of light admitted to the room, and a curtain so arranged that it cannot be drawn backward and forward at will is but a meaningless accessory. It was not until the beginning of the present century that curtains were used without regard to their practical purpose. The window-hangings of the middle ages and of the Renaissance were simply straight pieces of cloth or tapestry hung across the window without any attempt at drapery, and regarded not as part of the decoration of the room, but as a necessary protection against draughts. It is probably for this reason that in old prints and pictures representing the rooms of wealthy people, curtains are so seldom seen. The better the house, the less need there was for curtains. In the engravings of Abraham Bosse,[6] which so faithfully represent the interior decoration of every class of French

4. French: "windows are intrinsically tied to the main architectural design."

5. Honorary title of the royal daughters of Louis XV, who all lived at Versailles before fleeing during the French Revolution.

6. Abraham Bosse (1604–76): French artist best known for his engravings that depicted the fashions and customs of the era (*EB* 2019a).

house during the reign of Louis XIII, it will be noticed that in the richest apartments there are no window-curtains. In all the finest rooms of the seventeenth and eighteenth centuries the inside shutters and embrasures of the windows were decorated with a care which proves that they were not meant to be concealed by curtains (see the painted embrasures of the saloon in the Villa Vertemati, plate 44). The shutters in the state apartments of Fouquet's château of Vaux-le-Vicomte, near Melun, are painted on both sides with exquisite arabesques;[7] while those in the apartments of Mesdames de France, on the ground floor of the palace of Versailles, are examples of the most beautiful carving. In fact, it would be more difficult to cite a room of any importance in which the windows were not so treated, than to go on enumerating examples of what was really a universal custom until the beginning of the present century. It is known, of course, that curtains were used in former times: prints, pictures and inventories alike prove this fact; but the care expended on the decorative treatment of windows makes it plain that the curtain, like the portière, was regarded as a necessary evil rather than as part of the general scheme of decoration. The meagreness and simplicity of the curtains in old pictures prove that they were used merely as window shades or sun-blinds. The scant straight folds pushed back from the tall windows of the Prince de Conti's salon, in Olivier's charming picture of "Le Thé à l'Anglaise chez le Prince de Conti," are as obviously utilitarian as the strip of green woollen stuff hanging against the leaded casement of the mediæval bed-chamber in Carpaccio's "Dream of St. Ursula."[8]

7. Nicolas Fouquet (1615–80): finance minister for Louis XIV. His manor, Vaux-le-Vicomte, was constructed in 1661. Its interior design was supervised by Charles Le Brun, and its gardens designed by André Le Nôtre (1613–1700). The château is considered a quintessential piece of baroque residential architecture.

8. *Le Thé à l'Anglaise chez le Prince de Conti*: a 1766 painting by Michel Barthélémy Olivier depicting a salon scene in a room with tall ceilings and floor-length windows, flanked by thin curtains (Bourdin 2013). *Dream of St. Ursula*: a 1495 painting by the Italian artist Vittore Carpaccio, in which the bottom panels of the bedchamber's walls are covered by green fabric. The painting is referenced in Edith Wharton's

19. Salon des Malachites, Grand Trianon, Versailles. Louis XIV Period. (Showing Well-Designed Window with Solid Inside Shutter, and Pictures Forming Part of Wall-Decoration.)

Another way of hanging window-curtains in the seventeenth and eighteenth centuries was to place them inside the architrave, so that they did not conceal it. The architectural treatment of the trim, and the practice prevalent at that period of carrying the windows up to the cornice, made this a satisfactory way of arranging the curtain; but in the modern American house, where the trim is usually bad, and where there is often a dreary waste of wall-paper between the window and the ceiling, it is better to hang the curtains close under the cornice.

False Dawn, the first of the four-part novella *Old New York* (1924) (Web Gallery of Art n.d.).

It was not until the eighteenth century that the window-curtain was divided in the middle; and this change was intended only to facilitate the drawing of the hangings, which, owing to the increased size of the windows, were necessarily wider and heavier. The curtain continued to hang down in straight folds, pulled back at will to permit the opening of the window, and drawn at night. Fixed window-draperies, with festoons[9] and folds so arranged that they cannot be lowered or raised, are an invention of the modern upholsterer. Not only have these fixed draperies done away with the true purpose of the curtain, but they have made architects and decorators careless in their treatment of openings. The architrave and embrasure of a window are now regarded as of no more importance in the decorative treatment of a room than the inside of the chimney.

The modern use of the lambrequin[10] as an ornamental finish to window-curtains is another instance of misapplied decoration. Its history is easy to trace. The mediæval bed was always enclosed in curtains hanging from a wooden framework, and the lambrequin was used as a kind of cornice to conceal it. When the use of gathered window-shades became general in Italy, the lambrequin was transferred from the bed to the window, in order to hide the clumsy bunches of folds formed by these shades when drawn up. In old prints, lambrequins over windows are almost always seen in connection with Italian shades, and this is the only logical way of using them; though they are often of service in concealing the defects of badly-shaped windows and unarchitectural trim.

Those who criticize the architects and decorators of the past are sometimes disposed to think that they worked in a certain way because they were too ignorant to devise a better method; whereas they were usually controlled by practical and artistic considerations which their critics are prone to disregard, not only in judging the work

9. Garland, or a decoration carved or painted to look like garland (*M-W*).

10. Valance. In *A Backward Glance*, Wharton despairs of "the upholsterers...who crammed every room with curtains, lambrequins," and other "sumptuous excesses" of the Gilded Age (*M-W*).

of the past, but in the attempt to make good its deficiencies. Thus the cabinet-makers of the Renaissance did not make straight-backed wooden chairs because they were incapable of imagining anything more comfortable, but because the former were better adapted than cushioned arm-chairs to the *déplacements*[11] so frequent at that period. In like manner, the decorator who regarded curtains as a necessity rather than as part of the decoration of the room knew (what the modern upholsterer fails to understand) that, the beauty of a room depending chiefly on its openings, to conceal these under draperies is to hide the key of the whole decorative scheme.

The muslin window-curtain is a recent innovation. Its only purpose is to protect the interior of the room from public view: a need not felt before the use of large sheets of glass, since it is difficult to look through a subdivided sash from the outside. Under such circumstances muslin curtains are, of course, useful; but where they may be dispensed with, owing to the situation of the room or the subdivision of panes, they are no loss. Lingerie effects do not combine well with architecture, and the more architecturally a window is treated, the less it need be dressed up in ruffles. To put such curtains in a window, and then loop them back so that they form a mere frame to the pane, is to do away with their real purpose, and to substitute a textile for an architectural effect. Where muslin curtains are necessary, they should be a mere transparent screen hung against the glass. In town houses especially all outward show of richness should be avoided; the use of elaborate lace-figured curtains, besides obstructing the view, seems an attempt to protrude the luxury of the interior upon the street. It is needless to point out the futility of the second layer of muslin which, in some houses, hangs inside the sash-curtains.

The solid inside shutter, now so generally discarded, save in France, formerly served the purposes for which curtains and shades are used, and, combined with outside blinds, afforded all the protection that a

11. French: "movements of people or objects." Here the term refers to changes of residence.

window really requires (see plate 19). These shutters should be made with solid panels, not with slats, their purpose being to darken the room and keep out the cold, while the light is regulated by the outside blinds. The best of these is the old-fashioned hand-made blind, with wide fixed slats, still to be seen on old New England houses and always used in France and Italy: the frail machine-made substitute now in general use has nothing to recommend it.

6

Fireplaces

The fireplace was formerly always regarded as the chief feature of the room, and so treated in every well-thought-out scheme of decoration.

The practical reasons which make it important that the windows in a room should be carried up to the cornice have already been given, and it has been shown that the lines of the other openings should be extended to the same height. This applies to fireplaces as well as to doors, and, indeed, as an architectural principle concerning all kinds of openings, it has never been questioned until the present day. The hood of the vast Gothic fireplace always descended from the springing of the vaulted roof, and the monumental chimney-pieces of the Renaissance followed the same lines (see plate 20). The importance of giving an architectural character to the chimney-piece is insisted on by Blondel, whose remark, "Je voudrais n'appliquer à une cheminée que des ornements convenables à l'architecture," is a valuable axiom for the decorator.[1] It is a mistake to think that this treatment necessitates a large mantel-piece and a monumental style of panelling. The smallest mantel, surmounted by a picture or a mirror set in simple mouldings, may be as architectural as the great chimney-pieces at Urbino or Cheverny[2] all depends on the spirit of the treatment and on the proper relation of the different members used. Pajou's monument

1. "I would only like to add fireplace embellishments suitable for the architecture."

2. Château in the Loire Valley of France, in which the fireplaces are adorned with golden embellishments (Château de Cheverny n.d.).

20. Mantelpiece in Ducal Palace, Urbino. XV Century. (Transition between Gothic and Renaissance.)

to Madame du Barry's canary-bird is far more architectural than the Albert Memorial.[3]

3. Augustin Pajou (1730–1809): French neoclassical sculptor, best known for his portrait busts (*EB* 2019g). His patroness was Madame du Barry (1743–93), the last of the mistresses of Louis XV and subsequently executed during the French Revolution

When, in the middle ages, the hearth in the centre of the room was replaced by the wall-chimney, the fireplace was invariably constructed with a projecting hood of brick or stone, generally semicircular in shape, designed to carry off the smoke which in earlier times had escaped through a hole in the roof. The opening of the fireplace, at first of moderate dimensions, was gradually enlarged to an enormous size, from the erroneous idea that the larger the fire the greater would be the warmth of the room. By degrees it was discovered that the effect of the volume of heat projected into the room was counteracted by the strong draught and by the mass of cold air admitted through the huge chimney; and to obviate this difficulty iron doors were placed in the opening and kept closed when the fire was not burning (see plate 21). But this was only a partial remedy, and in time it was found expedient to reduce the size of both chimney and fireplace.

In Italy the strong feeling for architectural lines and the invariable exercise of common sense in construction soon caused the fireplace to be sunk into the wall, thus ridding the room of the Gothic hood, while the wall-space above the opening received a treatment of panelling, sometimes enclosed in pilasters, and usually crowned by an entablature and pediment. When the chimney was not sunk in the wall, the latter was brought forward around the opening, thus forming a flat chimney-breast[4] to which the same style of decoration could be applied. This projection was seldom permitted in Italy, where the thickness of the walls made it easy to sink the fireplace, while an unerring feeling

---

(EB 2018h). There are no existing records of a Pajou sculpture of a canary, so we might assume that Edith Wharton and Ogden Codman Jr. are making a joke to prove their point about the necessary artistic choices that must be made for beautiful architecture. Albert Memorial: also known as the Prince Consort National Memorial, is a monument located in Kensington Gardens in London, commissioned by Queen Victoria (1819–1901) in memory of her husband, Prince Albert (1819–61), and designed by George Gilbert Scott (1811–78). It was completed in 1876 and features a gilded, life-size statue of Prince Albert, alongside angels and other figures representing the four corners of the world (EB 2018c; Royal Parks n.d.).

4. Part of a wall that extends outward to cover a chimney (M-W).

for form rejected the advancing chimney-breast as a needless break in the wall-surface of the room. In France, where Gothic methods of construction persisted so long after the introduction of classic ornament, the habit of building out the chimney-breast continued until the seventeenth century, and even a hundred years later French decorators described the plan of sinking the fireplace into the thickness of the wall as the "Italian manner." The thinness of modern walls has made the projecting chimney-breast a structural necessity; but the composition of the room is improved by "furring out" the wall on each side of the fireplace in such a way as to conceal the projection and obviate a break in the wall-space.[5] Where the room is so small that every foot of space is valuable, a niche may be formed in either angle of the chimney-breast, thus preserving the floor-space which would be sacrificed by advancing the wall, and yet avoiding the necessity of a break in the cornice. The Italian plan of panelling the space between mantel and cornice continued in favor, with various modifications, until the beginning of the present century. In early Italian Renaissance over-mantels the central panel was usually filled by a bas-relief; but in the sixteenth century this was frequently replaced by a picture, not hung on the panelling, but forming a part of it.[†] In France the sculptured over-mantel followed the same general lines of development, though the treatment, until the time of Louis XIII, showed traces of the Gothic tendency to overload with ornament without regard to unity of design, so that the main lines of the composition were often lost under a mass of ill-combined detail.

In Italy the early Renaissance mantels were usually of marble. French mantels of the same period were of stone; but this material was

5. Application of wood, brick, or metal onto joists or walls in order to level the surface or to create a space for insulation (*M-W*).

† In Italy, where the walls were frescoed, the architectural composition over the mantel was also frequently painted. Examples of this are to be seen at the Villa Vertemati, near Chiavenna, and at the Villa Giacomelli, at Maser, near Treviso. This practice accounts for the fact that in many old architectural drawings of Italian interiors a blank wall-space is seen over the mantel.

so unsuited to the elaborate sculpture then in fashion that wood was sometimes used instead. For a season richly carved wooden chimney-pieces, covered with paint and gilding, were in favor; but when the first marble mantels were brought from Italy, that sense of fitness in the use of material for which the French have always been distinguished, led them to recognize the superiority of marble, and the wooden mantel-piece was discarded: nor has it since been used in France.

With the seventeenth century, French mantel-pieces became more architectural in design and less florid in ornament, and the ponderous hood laden with pinnacles, escutcheons, fortified castles and statues of saints and warriors, was replaced by a more severe decoration.[6]

Thackeray's gibe at Louis XIV[7] and his age has so long been accepted by the English-speaking races as a serious estimate of the period, that few now appreciate the artistic preponderance of France in the seventeenth century. As a matter of fact, it is to the schools of art founded by Louis XIV and to his magnificent patronage of the architects and decorators trained in these schools that we owe the preservation, in northern Europe, of that sense of form and spirit of moderation which mark the great classic tradition. To disparage the work of men like Levau, Mansart, de Cotte and Lebrun,[8] shows an

---

6. Pinnacles: conical-shaped ornament that rests atop a spire or buttress, most often used during the Romanesque and Gothic architectural movements (*EB* 2016e). Escutcheon: shield or armor-like design that can be applied to the center of pediments in furniture or to the metal plate around a keyhole (*EB* 2006).

7. William Makepeace Thackeray (1811–63): English writer best known for *Vanity Fair* (1848), which Wharton cites in *The Writing of Fiction* (1925) as a representative novel of manners (Brander 2019). Wharton and Codman refer to Thackeray's 1840 satirical print of Louis XIV called *What Makes the King?*, wherein the unrecognizable monarch appears as a short, bald, paunchy elder with walking stick and in plain clothes. He is placed between empty royal regalia at left and king in full regalia at right, suggesting that the excess of lace, wigs, and eighteenth-century frippery elevate a shriveled man to majesty (Granger Historical Picture Archive n.d.). Wharton and Codman ask the reader to reconsider seventeenth-century French architecture.

8. Louis Le Vau (1612–70): French architect who started the plans for the Palace of Versailles, but is best known for designing Vaux-le-Vicomte, whose interior

insufficient understanding, not only of what they did, but of the inheritance of confused and turgid ornament from which they freed French art.[†] Whether our individual tastes incline us to the Gothic or to the classic style, it is easy to see that a school which tried to combine the structure of the one with the ornament of the other was likely to fall into incoherent modes of expression; and this was precisely what happened to French domestic architecture at the end of the Renaissance period. It has been the fashion to describe the art of the Louis XIV period as florid and bombastic; but a comparison of the designs of Philibert de Lorme and Androuet Ducerceau[9] with those of such men as Levau and Robert de Cotte will show that what the latter did was not to introduce a florid and bombastic manner, but to discard it for what Viollet-le-Duc, who will certainly not be suspected of undue partiality for this school of architects, calls "une grandeur solide, sans faux ornements."[10] No better illustration of this can be obtained than by comparing the mantel-pieces of the respective periods.[†] The

---

décor Charles Lebrun supervised (*EB* 2018p). Mansart: Jules Hardouin-Mansart (1646–1708), city planner who completed the design of Versailles under Louis XIV, starting from Le Vau's plans (*EB* 2019v). De Cotte: Robert de Cotte (1656–1735), Mansart's student and assistant who succeeded him as first architect to the king and was responsible for the decoration of the Chapel of Versailles (*EB* 2019hh).

[†] It is to be hoped that the recently published English translation of M. Émile Bourgeois's book on Louis XIV will do much to remove this prejudice.

9. Philibert Delorme (1512?–70), French architect during the Renaissance, often praised for mastery of his materials, which was considered on par with the Italian masters, as he was able to produce original plans and buildings of similar caliber, without simply imitating them (*EB* 2019ff). Androuet Ducerceau: family of French architects who monopolized the field until the end of the seventeenth century. Jacques Androuet du Cerceau (1520–85), first member of the dynasty, worked for Charles IX and Catherine de' Medici. His son, Baptiste (1545–90), succeeded his father in his roles. Baptiste's son, Jean (1585–1649), is best known for building private homes for Louis XIII (*EB* 2011b).

10. French, originally from Viollet-le-Duc's "grandeur solide, sans faux ornements": "impressive majesty, without artificial ornamentation."

[†] It is curious that those who criticize the ornateness of the Louis XIV style are often the warmest admirers of the French Renaissance, the style of all others most

Louis XIV mantel-pieces are much simpler and more coherent in design. The caryatides[11] supporting the entablature above the opening of the earlier mantels, and the full-length statues flanking the central panel of the over-mantel, are replaced by massive and severe mouldings of the kind which the French call *mâle* (see mantels in plates 5 and 36). Above the entablature there is usually a kind of attic or high concave member of marble, often fluted, and forming a ledge or shelf just wide enough to carry the row of porcelain vases with which it had become the fashion to adorn the mantel. These vases, and the bas-relief or picture occupying the central panel above, form the chief ornament of the chimney-piece, though occasionally the crowning member of the over-mantel is treated with a decoration of garlands, masks, trophies or other strictly architectural ornament, while in Italy and England the broken pediment is frequently employed. The use of a mirror over the fireplace is said to have originated with Mansart; but according to Blondel it was Robert de Cotte who brought about this innovation, thus producing an immediate change in the general scheme of composition. The French were far too logical not to see the absurdity of placing a mirror too high to be looked into; and the concave Louis XIV member, which had raised the mantel-shelf six feet from the floor was removed[†] and the shelf placed directly over the entablature.

Somewhat later the introduction of clocks and candelabra as mantel ornaments made it necessary to widen the shelf, and this further modified the general design; while the suites of small rooms which had come into favor under the Regent[12] led to a reduction in the size

---

remarkable for its excessive use of ornament, exquisite in itself, but quite unrelated to structure and independent of general design.

    11. Marble figure, usually of a woman, used as architectural support instead of a column (*EB* 2019h).

    † It is said to have been put at this height in order that the porcelain vases should be out of reach. See Daviler, "Cours d'Architecture."

    12. Queen Regent, Marie de Médicis (1573–1642), who ruled for her son, Louis XIII, between 1610 and 1614 (*EB* 2019cc).

21. Mantelpiece in the Villa Giacomelli. At Maser, Near Treviso. XVI Century. (Showing Iron Doors in Opening.)

of mantel-pieces, and to the use of less massive and perhaps less architectural ornament.

In the eighteenth century, mantel-pieces in Italy and France were almost always composed of a marble or stone architrave surmounted by a shelf of the same material, while the over-mantel consisted of a mirror, framed in mouldings varying in design from the simplest style to the most ornate. This over-mantel, which was either of the exact width of the mantel-shelf or some few inches narrower, ended under the cornice, and its upper part was usually decorated in the same way as the over-doors in the room. If these contained paintings, a picture carrying out the same scheme of decoration was often placed in the upper part of the over-mantel; or the ornaments of carved wood or stucco filling the panels over the doors were repeated in the upper part of the mirror-frame.

In France, mirrors had by this time replaced pictures in the central panel of the over-mantel; but in Italian decoration of the same period oval pictures were often applied to the centre of the mirror, with delicate lines of ornament connecting the picture and mirror frames.[†]

The earliest fireplaces were lined with stone or brick, but in the sixteenth century the more practical custom of using iron fire-backs was introduced. At first this fire-back consisted of a small plaque of iron, shaped like a headstone, and fixed at the back of the fireplace, where the brick or stone was most likely to be calcined by the fire. When chimney-building became more scientific, the size of the fireplace was reduced, and the sides of the opening were brought much nearer the flame, thus making it necessary to extend the fire-back into a lining for the whole fireplace.

It was soon seen that besides resisting the heat better than any other substance, the iron lining served to radiate it into the room. The iron back consequently held its own through every subsequent change in the treatment of the fireplace; and the recent return, in England and America, to brick or stone is probably due to the fact that the modern iron lining is seldom well designed. Iron backs were adopted because they served their purpose better than any others; and as no new substance offering greater advantages has since been discovered, there is no reason for discarding them, especially as they are not only more practical but more decorative than any other lining. The old fire-backs (of which reproductions are readily obtained) were decorated with charming bas-reliefs, and their dark bosses, in the play of

---

[†] Examples are to be seen in several rooms of the hunting-lodge of the kings of Savoy, at Stupinigi, near Turin.

the firelight, form a more expressive background than the dead and unresponsive surface of brick or stone.

It was not uncommon in England to treat the mantel as an order crowned by its entablature. Where this was done, an intermediate space was left between mantel and over-mantel, an arrangement which somewhat weakened the architectural effect. A better plan was that of surmounting the entablature with an attic, and making the over-mantel spring directly from the latter. Fine examples of this are seen at Holkham, built by Brettingham for the Earl of Leicester about the middle of the eighteenth century.[13]

The English fireplace was modified at the end of the seventeenth century, when coal began to replace wood. Chippendale gives many designs for beautiful basket-grates, such as were set in the large fireplaces originally intended for wood; for it was not until later that chimneys with smaller openings were specially constructed to receive the fixed grate and the hob-grate.[14]

It was in England that the architectural treatment of the over-mantel was first abandoned. The use of a mirror framed in a panel over the fireplace had never become general in England, and toward the end of the eighteenth century the mantel-piece was frequently surmounted by a blank wall-space, on which a picture or a small round mirror was hung high above the shelf (see plate 47). Examples are seen in Moreland's pictures,[15] and in prints of simple eighteenth-century

13. English estate built between 1734 and 1764 under the supervision of the first Earl of Leicester, Thomas Coke (1697–1759). The plans for the Palladian-inspired estate were drawn up by Coke and William Kent, but Matthew Brettingham (1699–1769) was the supervising architect (Holkham Hall n.d.).

14. Furniture style named for English cabinetmaker Thomas Chippendale (1718–79) (*EB* 2011a). Here, Wharton and Codman refer to rococo Chippendale, popular in the 1750s and created as a response to William Kent's highly formal baroque style. Hob grate: catchall term for any sort of cast-iron grillwork that holds the coal; a hob grate is one that is supported off the ground, whereas a fixed grate, as the name suggests, is one that cannot be moved.

15. Paintings of George Moreland (1763–1804), sometimes spelled Morland: English landscape artist.

English interiors; but this treatment is seldom found in rooms of any architectural pretensions.

The early American fireplace was merely a cheap provincial copy of English models of the same period. The application of the word "Colonial" to pre-Revolutionary architecture and decoration has created a vague impression that there existed at that time an American architectural style. As a matter of fact, "Colonial" architecture is simply a modest copy of Georgian models; and "Colonial" mantel-pieces were either imported from England by those who could afford it, or were reproduced in wood from current English designs. Wooden mantels were, indeed, not unknown in England, where the use of a wooden architrave led to the practice of facing the fireplace with Dutch tiles; but wood was used, both in England and America, only from motives of cheapness, and the architrave was set back from the opening only because it was unsafe to put an inflammable material so near the fire.

After 1800 all the best American houses contained imported marble mantel-pieces. These usually consisted of an entablature resting on columns or caryatides, with a frieze in low relief representing some classic episode, or simply ornamented with bucranes[16] and garlands. In the general decline of taste which marked the middle of the present century, these dignified and well-designed mantel-pieces were replaced by marble arches containing a fixed grate. The hideousness of this arched opening soon produced a distaste for marble mantels in the minds of a generation unacquainted with the early designs. This distaste led to a reaction in favor of wood, resulting in the displacement of the architrave and the facing of the space between architrave and opening with tiles, iron or marble.

People are beginning to see that the ugliness of the marble mantel-pieces of 1840–60 does not prove that wood is the more suitable material to employ. There is indeed something of unfitness in the use of an inflammable material surrounding a fireplace. Everything about

16. Decorative motif often seen on friezes or lintels above Doric columns that represents an ox that is sacrificed in a religious ritual; better known as a bucranium (*EB* 2018d).

the hearth should not only be, but *look*, fire-proof. The chief objection to wood is that its use necessitates the displacement of the architrave, thus leaving a flat intermediate space to be faced with some fire-proof material. This is an architectural fault. A door of which the architrave should be set back eighteen inches or more to admit of a facing of tiles or marble would be pronounced unarchitectural; and it is usually admitted that all classes of openings should be subject to the same general treatment.

Where the mantel-piece is of wood, the setting back of the architrave is a necessity; but, curiously enough, the practice has become so common in England and America that even where the mantel is made of marble or stone it is set back in the same way; so that it is unusual to see a modern fireplace in which the architrave defines the opening. In France, also, the use of an inner facing (called a *retrécissement*)[17] has become common, probably because such a device makes it possible to use less fuel, while not disturbing the proportions of the mantel as related to the room.

The reaction from the bare stiff rooms of the first quarter of the present century—the era of mahogany and horsehair—resulted, some twenty years since, in a general craving for knick-knacks; and the latter soon spread from the tables to the mantel, especially in England and America, where the absence of the architectural over-mantel left a bare expanse of wall above the chimney-piece.

The use of the mantel as a bric-à-brac shelf led in time to the lengthening and widening of this shelf, and in consequence to the enlargement of the whole chimney-piece.

Mantels which in the eighteenth century would have been thought in scale with rooms of certain dimensions would not be considered too small and insignificant. The use of mantel-pieces, besides throwing everything in the room out of scale, is a structural mistake, since the excessive projection of the mantel has a tendency to make the fire

17. Set of upper and lateral pieces of a fireplace that connect with the mantel at a shallow angle (Chimney Safety Institute of America 2022).

smoke; indeed, the proportions of the old mantels, far from being arbitrary, were based as much on practical as on artistic considerations.
Moreover, the use of long, wide shelves has brought about the accumulation of superfluous knick-knacks, whereas a smaller mantel, if architecturally designed, would demand only its conventional *garniture* of
clock and candlesticks.[18]

The device of concealing an ugly mantel-piece by folds of drapery brings an inflammable substance so close to the fire that there is
a suggestion of danger even where there is no actual risk. The lines
of a mantel, however bad, represent some kind of solid architrave,—
a more suitable setting for an architectural opening than flimsy festoons of brocade or plush. Any one who can afford to replace an ugly
chimney-piece by one of good design will find that this change does
more than any other to improve the appearance of a room. Where a
badly designed mantel cannot be removed, the best plan is to leave it
unfurbelowed,[19] simply placing above it a mirror or panel to connect
the lines of the opening with the cornice.

The effect of a fireplace depends much upon the good taste and
appropriateness of its accessories. Little attention is paid at present to
the design and workmanship of these and like necessary appliances;
yet if good of their kind they add more to the adornment of a room
than a multiplicity of useless knick-knacks.

Andirons should be of wrought-iron, bronze or ormolu.[20] Substances which require constant polishing, such as steel or brass, are
unfitted to a fireplace. It is no longer easy to buy the old bronze andirons of French or Italian design, with pedestals surmounted by statuettes of nymph or faun, to which time has given the iridescence that

18. Set of decorative objects; embellishments (*M-W*).

19. Extravagant or garish flounce on women's clothing. Wharton and Codman
recommend leaving a badly designed mantel simple and without decoration (*M-W*).

20. Metal support, usually found in pairs, that holds the burning firewood. In
A Backward Glance, Wharton relishes her eagle andirons inherited from her great
grandfather, Major General Ebenezer Stevens (*M-W*). Ormolu: gilded brass or
bronze (*M-W*).

modern bronze-workers vainly try to reproduce with varnish. These bronzes, and the old ormolu andirons, are now almost introuvables;[21] but the French artisan still copies the old models with fair success (see plates 5 and 36). Andirons should not only harmonize with the design of the mantel but also be in scale with its dimensions. In the fireplace of a large drawing-room, boudoir andirons would look insignificant; while the monumental Renaissance fire-dogs[22] would dwarf a small mantel and make its ornamentation trivial.

If andirons are gilt, they should be of ormolu. The cheaper kinds of gilding are neither durable nor good in tone, and plain iron is preferable to anything but bronze or fire-gilding. The design of shovel and tongs should accord with that of the andirons: in France such details are never disregarded. The shovel and tongs should be placed upright against the mantel-piece, or rest upon hooks inserted in the architrave: the brass or gilt stands now in use are seldom well designed. Fenders, being merely meant to protect the floor from sparks,[23] should be as light and easy to handle as possible: the folding fender of wire-netting is for this reason preferable to any other, since it may be shut and put away when not in use. The low guards of solid brass in favor in England and America not only fail to protect the floor, but form a permanent barrier between the fire and those who wish to approach it; and the latter objection applies also to the massive folding fender that is too heavy to be removed.

Coal-scuttles,[24] like andirons, should be made of bronze, ormolu or iron. The unnecessary use of substances which require constant polishing is one of the mysteries of English and American housekeeping: it is difficult to see why a housemaid should spend hours in polishing brass or steel fenders, andirons, coal-scuttles and door-knobs, when all these articles might be made of some substance that does not need daily cleaning.

21. French: "impossible to find."
22. Andirons; also called dog irons (Buffalo as an Architectural Museum n.d.).
23. Low gate or metal screen before an open fireplace (*M-W*).
24. Hod; trough or bucket that holds coal.

Where wood is burned, no better wood-box can be found than an old carved chest, either one of the Italian *cassoni*,[25] with their painted panels and gilded volutes, or a plain box of oak or walnut with well-designed panels and old iron hasps. The best substitute for such a chest is a plain wicker basket, without ornamentation, enamel paint or gilding. If an article of this kind is not really beautiful, it had better be as obviously utilitarian as possible in design and construction.

A separate chapter might be devoted to the fire-screen, with its carved frame and its panel of tapestry, needlework, or painted arabesques. Of all the furniture of the hearth, it is that upon which most taste and variety of invention have been spent; and any of the numerous French works on furniture and house-decoration will supply designs which the modern decorator might successfully reproduce (see plate 22). So large is the field from which he may select his models, that it is perhaps more to the purpose to touch upon the styles of fire-screens to be avoided: such as the colossal brass or ormolu fan, the stained-glass screen, the embroidered or painted banner suspended on a gilt rod, or the stuffed bird spread out in a broiled attitude against a plush background.

In connection with the movable fire-screen, a word may be said of the fire-boards[26] which, until thirty or forty years ago, were used to close the opening of the fireplace in summer. These fire-boards are now associated with old-fashioned boarding-house parlors, where they are still sometimes seen, covered with a paper like that on the walls, and looking ugly enough to justify their disuse. The old fire-boards were very different: in rooms of any importance they were beautifully decorated, and in Italian interiors, where the dado was often painted, the same decoration was continued on the fire-boards. Sometimes the latter were papered; but the paper used was designed expressly for the

25. Italian chests, usually used as marriage chests, and the most elaborately decorated piece of furniture of the Renaissance.

26. Also called chimney board; panel designed to cover a fireplace during the warm months of the year; commonly used during the later eighteenth and early nineteenth centuries, effectively reducing the number of insects, birds, and squirrels that might enter a house through an open chimney.

22. French Fire-Screen, Louis XIV Period. From the Château of Anet.

purpose, with a decorative composition of flowers, landscapes, or the ever-amusing *chinoiseries*[27] on which the eighteenth-century designer played such endless variations.

27. French: imitation or evocation of Chinese motifs and techniques in Western art, furniture, and architecture, especially in the eighteenth century; unnecessary complications.

Whether the fireplace in summer should be closed by a board, or left open, with the logs laid on the irons, is a question for individual taste; but it is certain that if the painted fire-board were revived, it might form a very pleasing feature in the decoration of modern rooms. The only possible objection to its use is that it interferes with ventilation by closing the chimney-opening; but as fire-boards are used only at a season when all the windows are open, this drawback is hardly worth considering.

In spite of the fancied advancement in refinement and luxury of living, the development of the modern heating apparatus seems likely, especially in America, to do away with the open fire. The temperature maintained in most American houses by means of hot-air or hot-water pipes is so high that even the slight additional warmth of a wood fire would be unendurable. Still there are a few exceptions to this rule, and in some houses the healthy glow of open fires is preferred to the parching atmosphere of steam. Indeed, it might almost be said that the good taste and *savoir-vivre*[28] of the inmates of a house may be guessed from the means used for heating it. Old pictures, old furniture and fine bindings cannot live in a furnace-baked atmosphere; and those who possess such treasures and know their value have an additional motive for keeping their houses cool and well ventilated.

No house can be properly aired in winter without the draughts produced by open fires. Fortunately, doctors are beginning to call attention to this neglected detail of sanitation; and as dry artificial heat is the main source of throat and lung diseases, it is to be hoped that the growing taste for open-air life and outdoor sports will bring about a desire for better ventilation, and a dislike for air-tight stoves, gas-fires and steam-heat.

Aside from the question of health and personal comfort, nothing can be more cheerless and depressing than a room without fire on a winter day. The more torrid the room, the more abnormal is the contrast between the cold hearth and the incandescent temperature.

28. French: "good living"; the art of knowing how to live well.

Without a fire, the best-appointed drawing-room is as comfortless as the shut-up "best parlor" of a New England farm-house. The empty fireplace shows that the room is not really lived in and that its appearance of luxury and comfort is but a costly sham prepared for the edification of visitors.

7

Ceilings and Floors

To attempt even an outline of the history of ceilings in domestic architecture would exceed the scope of this book; nor would it serve any practical purpose to trace the early forms of vaulting and timbering which preceded the general adoption of the modern plastered ceiling. To understand the development of the modern ceiling, however, one must trace the two very different influences by which it has been shaped: that of the timber roof of the North and that of the brick or stone vault of the Latin builders. This twofold tradition has curiously affected the details of the modern ceiling. During the Renaissance, flat plaster ceilings were not infrequently coffered with stucco panels exactly reproducing the lines of timber framing; and in the Villa Vertemati, near Chiavenna,[1] there is a curious and interesting ceiling of carved wood made in imitation of stucco (see plate 23); while one of the rooms in the Palais de Justice at Rennes[2] contains an elaborate vaulted ceiling constructed entirely of wood, with mouldings nailed on (see plate 24).

1. Now called the Palazzo Vertemate Franchi and located in Prosto di Piuro, Italy. Commissioned in the latter half of the sixteenth century by the Vertemate Franchi brothers, though the architects remain unknown. Best known for embroidered wooden ceilings (Palazzo Vertemate Franchi n.d.).

2. Originally created to house the Parliament of Brittany at Rennes in the seventeenth century and renovated after a 1994 fire, the Palais de Justice (courthouse) acquired its current name once it started serving as a court of appeals in the nineteenth century. Thank you to Joel Goldfield.

In northern countries, where the ceiling was simply the under side of the wooden floor,[†] it was natural that its decoration should follow the rectangular subdivisions formed by open timber-framing. In the South, however, where the floors were generally of stone, resting on stone vaults, the structural conditions were so different that although the use of caissons[3] based on the divisions of timber-framing was popular both in the Roman and Renaissance periods, the architect always felt himself free to treat the ceiling as a flat, undivided surface prepared for the application of ornament.

The idea that there is anything unarchitectural in this method comes from an imperfect understanding of the construction of Roman ceilings. The vault was the typical Roman ceiling, and the vault presents a smooth surface, without any structural projections to modify the ornament applied to it. The panelling of a vaulted or flat ceiling was as likely to be agreeable to the eye as a similar treatment of the walls; but the Roman coffered ceiling[4] and its Renaissance successors were the result of a strong sense of decorative fitness rather than of any desire to adhere to structural limitations.

Examples of the timbered ceiling are, indeed, to be found in Italy as well as in France and England; and in Venice the flat wooden ceiling, panelled upon structural lines, persisted throughout the Renaissance period; but in Rome, where the classic influences were always much stronger, and where the discovery of the stucco ceilings of ancient baths and palaces produced such lasting effects upon the architecture of the early Renaissance, the decorative treatment of the stone vault was transferred to the flat or coved Renaissance ceiling without a thought

[†] In France, until the sixteenth century, the same word—*plancher*—was used to designate both floor and ceiling.

3. Watertight chamber used as a foundation for a building during construction (*M-W*). Edith Wharton and Ogden Codman Jr. are referring to the architectural use of caissons having to do with ceilings, "*Vide laissé par l'assemblage des solives d'un plafond—Compartiment creux, orné de moulures*" (Empty area formed by the assembly of the ceiling joists—hollow compartment decorated with moldings). (Paul 1978, 236). Credit: Joel Goldfield.

4. Recessed panel in a vault or ceiling (*M-W*).

of its being inapplicable or "insincere." The fear of insincerity, in the sense of concealing the anatomy of any part of a building, troubled the Renaissance architect no more than it did his Gothic predecessor, who had never hesitated to stretch a "ciel" of cloth or tapestry over the naked timbers of the mediæval ceiling. The duty of exposing structural forms—an obligation that weighs so heavily upon the conscience of the modern architect—is of very recent origin. Mediæval as well as Renaissance architects thought first of adapting their buildings to the uses for which they were intended and then of decorating them in such a way as to give pleasure to the eye; and the maintenance of that relation which the eye exacts between main structural lines and their ornamentation was the only form of sincerity which they knew or cared about.

If a flat ceiling rested on a well-designed cornice, or if a vaulted or coved ceiling sprang obviously from walls capable of supporting it, the Italian architect did not allow himself to be hampered by any pedantic conformity to structural details. The eye once satisfied that the ceiling had adequate support, the fit proportioning of its decoration was considered far more important than mere technical fidelity to the outline of floor-beams and joists. If the Italian decorator wished to adorn a ceiling with carved or painted panels he used the lines of the timbering to frame his panels, because they naturally accorded with his decorative scheme; while, were a large central painting to be employed, or the ceiling to be covered with reliefs in stucco, he felt no more hesitation in deviating from the lines of the timbering than he would have felt in planning the pattern of a mosaic or a marble floor without reference to the floor-beams beneath it.

In France and England it was natural that timber-construction should long continue to regulate the design of the ceiling. The Roman vault lined with stone caissons, or with a delicate tracery of stucco-work, was not an ever-present precedent in northern Europe. Tradition pointed to the open-timbered roof; and as Italy furnished numerous and brilliant examples of decorative treatment adapted to this form of ceiling, it was to be expected that both in France and England the national form should be preserved long after Italian influences had established themselves in both countries. In fact, it is interesting to

23. Carved Wooden Ceiling, Villa Vertemati. XVI Century. (Showing influence of Stucco Decoration.)

note that in France, where the artistic feeling was much finer, and the
sense of fitness and power of adaptation were more fully developed,
than in England, the lines of the timbered ceiling persisted throughout the Renaissance and Louis XIII periods; whereas in England the
Elizabethan architects, lost in the mazes of Italian detail, without a
guiding perception of its proper application, abandoned the timbered
ceiling, with its eminently architectural subdivisions, for a flat plaster
surface over which geometrical flowers in stucco meandered in endless
sinuosities,⁵ unbroken by a single moulding, and repeating themselves

5. Curve, bend, or turn; winding path (*M-W*).

with the maddening persistency of wall-paper pattern. This style of ornamentation was done away with by Inigo Jones and his successors, who restored the architectural character of the ceiling, whether flat or vaulted; and thereafter panelling persisted in England until the French Revolution brought about the general downfall of taste.[†]

In France, at the beginning of the eighteenth century, the liking for *petits appartements*[6] led to greater lightness in all kinds of decorative treatment; and the ceilings of the Louis XV period, while pleasing in detail, are open to the criticism of being somewhat weak in form. Still, they are always *compositions*, and their light traceries, though perhaps too dainty and fragile in themselves, are so disposed as to form a clearly marked design, instead of being allowed to wander in a monotonous network over the whole surface of the ceiling, like the ubiquitous Tudor rose.[7] Isaac Ware, trained in the principles of form which the teachings of Inigo Jones had so deeply impressed upon English architects, ridicules the "petty wildnesses" of the French style; but if the Louis XV ceiling lost for a time its architectural character, this was soon to be restored by Gabriel and his followers, while at the same period in England the forcible mouldings of Inigo Jones's school were fading into the ineffectual grace of Adam's laurel-wreaths and velaria.[8]

In the general effect of the room, the form of the ceiling is of more importance than its decoration. In rooms of a certain size and height, a flat surface overhead looks monotonous, and the ceiling should be

---

[†] For a fine example of an English stucco ceiling, see plate 13.

6. French, classified as any suite in a palace where the royal family actually lives and operates (Château de Fontainebleau n.d.).

7. Symbol of the House of Tudor. During the War of the Roses, Henry VII (1457–1509), a Lancastrian, defeated Yorkist king Richard III (1452–85) and married his niece Elizabeth (1466–1503), heiress of the House of York. The Tudor rose is both red and white, representing the union of the Lancastrians and the Yorkists, respectively (*EB* 2018f).

8. Reference to Inigo Jones and Robert Adam, discussed in chapter 1, notes 28 and 29. Velarium: awning or cover placed over a Roman amphitheater (*M-W*).

24. Ceiling in Palais de Justice, Rennes. Louis XIV Period. (Wooden Ceiling Imitating Masonry Vaulting and Stucco Ornamentation.)

vaulted or coved.[†] Endless modifications of this form of treatment are to be found in the architectural treatises of the seventeenth and eighteenth centuries, as well as in the buildings of that period.

A coved ceiling greatly increases the apparent height of a low-studded room; but rooms of this kind should not be treated with an order, since the projection of the cornice below the springing of the cove will lower the walls so much as to defeat the purpose for which the cove has been used. In such rooms the cove should rise directly from the walls; and this treatment suggests the important rule that

[†] The flat Venetian ceilings, such as those in the ducal palace, with their richly carved wood-work and glorious paintings, beautiful as they have been made by art, are not so fine architecturally as a domed or coved ceiling.

where the cove is not supported by a cornice the ceiling decoration should be of very light character. A heavy panelled ceiling should not rest on the walls without the intervention of a strongly profiled cornice. The French Louis XV decoration, with its fanciful embroidery of stucco ornament, is well suited to coved ceilings springing directly from the walls in a room of low stud; while a ceiling divided into panels with heavy architectural mouldings, whether it be flat or vaulted, looks best when the walls are treated with a complete order.

Durand,[9] in his lectures on architecture, in speaking of cornices lays down the following excellent rules: "Interior cornices must necessarily differ more or less from those belonging to the orders as used externally, though in rooms of reasonable height these differences need be but slight; but if the stud be low, as sometimes is inevitable, the cornice must be correspondingly narrowed, and given an excessive projection, in order to increase the apparent height of the room. Moreover, as in the interior of the house the light is much less bright than outside, the cornice should be so profiled that the juncture of the mouldings shall form not right angles, but acute angles, with spaces between the mouldings serving to detach the latter still more clearly from each other."

The choice of the substance out of which a ceiling is to be made depends somewhat upon the dimensions of the room, the height of the stud and the decoration of the walls. A heavily panelled wooden ceiling resting upon walls either frescoed or hung with stuff is likely to seem oppressive; but, as in all other kinds of decoration, the effect produced depends far more upon the form and the choice of ornamental detail than upon the material used. Wooden ceilings, however, both from the nature of the construction and the kind of ornament which may most suitably be applied to them, are of necessity rather heavy in appearance, and should therefore be used only in large and high-studded rooms the walls of which are panelled in wood.[†]

9. Jean-Nicolas-Louis Durand (1760–1834): French author, teacher, and architect; an important figure in neoclassicism.

† For an example of a wooden ceiling which is too heavy for the wall-decoration below it, see plate 44.

Stucco and fresco-painting are adapted to every variety of decoration, from the light traceries of a boudoir ceiling to the dome of the *salon à l'Italienne*;[10] but the design must be chosen with strict regard to the size and height of the room and to the proposed treatment of its walls. The cornice forms the connecting link between walls and ceiling and it is essential to the harmony of any scheme of decoration that this important member should be carefully designed. It is useless to lavish money on the adornment of walls and ceiling connected by an ugly cornice.

The same objections extend to the clumsy plaster mouldings which in many houses disfigure the ceiling. To paint or gild a ceiling of this kind only attracts attention to its ugliness. When the expense of removing the mouldings and filling up the holes in the plaster is considered too great, it is better to cover the bulbous rosettes and pendentives with kalsomine than to attempt their embellishment by means of any polychrome decoration.[11] The cost of removing plaster ornaments is not great, however, and a small outlay will replace an ugly cornice by one of architectural design; so that a little economy in buying window-hangings or chair-coverings often makes up for the additional expense of these changes. One need only look at the ceilings in the average modern house to see what a thing of horror plaster may become in the hands of an untrained "designer."

The same general principles of composition suggested for the treatment of walls may be applied to ceiling-decoration. Thus it is essential that where there is a division of parts, one part shall perceptibly predominate; and this, in a ceiling, should be the central division. The chief defect of the coffered Renaissance ceiling is the lack of

10. French: Italian-style lounge (Meubliz n.d.).

11. Rosette: decorative, flower-shaped ornament carved out of stone or wood found across Western architecture (Buffalo as an Architectural Museum n.d.). Pendentive: triangular segment used in architecture within a dome for support, found most commonly in Romanesque and Islamic architecture, specifically in Byzantine churches (*EB* 2016d). Kalsomine: better known as calcimine; white or pale blue wash used on plastered surfaces (*M-W*).

this predominating part. Great as may have been the decorative skill expended on the treatment of beams and panels, the coffered ceiling of equal-sized divisions seems to press down upon the spectator's head; whereas the large central panel gives an idea of height that the great ceiling-painters were quick to enhance by glimpses of cloud and sky, or some aerial effect, as in Mantegna's incomparable ceiling of the Sala degli Sposi in the ducal palace of Mantua.[12]

Ceiling-decoration should never be a literal reproduction of wall-decoration. The different angle and greater distance at which ceilings are viewed demand a quite different treatment and it is to the disregard of this fact that most badly designed ceilings owe their origin. Even in the high days of art there was a tendency on the part of some decorators to confound the two plane surfaces of wall and ceiling, and one might cite many wall-designs which have been transferred to the ceiling without being rearranged to fit their new position. Instances of this kind have never been so general as in the present day. The reaction from the badly designed mouldings and fungoid growths that characterized the ceilings of forty years ago has led to the use of attenuated laurel-wreaths combined with other puny attributes taken from Sheraton cabinets and Adam mantel-pieces. These so-called ornaments, always somewhat lacking in character, become absolutely futile when viewed from below.

This pressed-flower ornamentation is a direct precedent to the modern ceiling covered with wall-paper. One would think that the inappropriateness of this treatment was obvious; but since it has become popular enough to warrant the manufacture of specially designed ceiling-papers, some protest should be made. The necessity for hiding

12. Andrea Mantegna (1431–1506): Italian artist, best known for mastery of perspective and highly realistic interpretations of architecture; most famous work is the *Camera degli Sposi*, which Wharton and Codman refer to as the *Sala degli Sposi*, in the Palazzo Ducale in Mantua (Sheard 2019). The decoration consists of lifelike architectural elements on all four walls and ceiling; from ground level, these elements look three-dimensional. For example, the ceiling is flat but appears concave through Mantegna's use of perspective. In chapter 9, Wharton and Codman suggest Mantegna's *Triumphs of Caesar* as suitable for a small entryway.

cracks in the plaster is the reason most often given for papering ceilings; but the cost of mending cracks is small and a plaster ceiling lasts much longer than is generally thought. It need never be taken down unless it is actually falling; and as well-made repairs strengthen and improve the entire surface, a much-mended ceiling is stronger than one that is just beginning to crack. If the cost of repairing must be avoided, a smooth white lining-paper should be chosen in place of one of the showy and vulgar papers which serve only to attract attention.

Of all forms of ceiling adornment painting is the most beautiful. Italy, which contains the three perfect ceilings of the world—those of Mantegna in the ducal palace of Mantua (see plate 25), of Perugino in the Sala del Cambio at Perugia and of Araldi in the Convent of St. Paul at Parma—is the best field for the study of this branch of art.[13] From the semi-classical vaults of the fifteenth century, with their Roman arabesques and fruit-garlands framing human figures detached as mere ornament against a background of solid color, to the massive goddesses and broad Virgilian landscapes of the Carracci and to the piled-up perspectives of Giordano's school of prestidigitators,[14] culminating in the great Tiepolo, Italian art affords examples of every temperament applied to the solution of one of the most interesting problems in decoration.

13. Perugino (1450?–1523): Italian Renaissance painter of the Umbria school, who painted a fresco in the Sala dell'Udienza in the Collegio del Cambio, the currency exchange in Perugia, Italy (Murray 2019b). The ceiling is particularly important as Perugino's student, Raphael, assisted in the painting. Alessandro Araldi (1460?–1530?): Italian Renaissance painter based in Parma. Little is known about him, but it has been proven that he painted the fresco in the apartment of Abbess Giovanna da Piacenza in the Benedictine Convent of Saint Paul. The fresco depicts scenes from both the Old and New Testaments.

14. Family of Italian Renaissance artists, consisting of two brothers, Agostino (1557–1602) and Annibale (1560–1609), and cousin Lodovico (1555–1619). The best-known frescoes were done by Annibale and have two defining characteristics: idyllic, pastoral landscapes and oversized figures from Greek and Roman classics (*EB* 2019d). Luca Giordano (1634–1705): Neapolitan painter gifted with the ability to create pastiche paintings in the style of almost any artist (*EB* 2019z).

25. Ceiling of the Sala delgi Sposi, Ducal Palace, Mantua. By Andrea
Mantegna, 1474.

Such ceilings as those on which Raphael and Giovanni da Udine[15]
worked together, combining painted arabesques and medallions with

15. Giovanni da Udine (1487–1564): student of Raphael who helped him carry
out the frescoes in the Loggia di Psiche in the Villa Farnesina.

stucco reliefs, are admirably suited to small low-studded rooms and might well be imitated by painters incapable of higher things.

There is but one danger in adapting this decoration to modern use—that is, the temptation to sacrifice scale and general composition to the search after refinement of detail. It cannot be denied that some of the decorations of the school of Giovanni da Udine are open to this criticism. The ornamentation of the great loggia of the Villa Madama is unquestionably out of scale with the dimensions of the structure. Much exquisite detail is lost in looking up past the great piers and the springing of the massive arches to the lace-work that adorns the vaulting. In this case the composition is less at fault than the scale: the decorations of the semi-domes at the Villa Madama, if transferred to a small mezzanin room, would be found to "compose" perfectly. Charming examples of the use of this style in small apartments may be studied in the rooms of the Casino del Grotto, near Mantua.[16]

The tendency of many modern decorators to sacrifice composition to detail, and to neglect the observance of proportion between ornament and structure, makes the adaptation of Renaissance stucco designs a somewhat hazardous undertaking; but the very care required to preserve the scale and to accentuate the general lines of the design affords good training in the true principles of composition.

Equally well suited to modern use are the designs in arabesque with which, in France, Bérain[17] and his followers painted the ceilings of small rooms during the Louis XIV period (see plate 26). With the opening of the eighteenth century the Bérain arabesques, animated by the touch of Watteau, Huet and J.-B. Leprince,[18] blossomed into

16. A suite once used for servants and courtiers in the Palazzo del Te in Mantua. The ceiling is slightly domed and contains elaborate decoration.

17. Jean Berain, the Elder (1637–1711): royal designer to Louis XIV, known as tastemaker; inspired by Oriental art, which, in turn, influenced other rococo artists (*EB* 2019t).

18. Antoine Watteau (1684–1721): French painter influenced by commedia dell'arte and opera ballet, which allowed him to bring unprecedented whimsy and theatricality to classic art (*EB* 2019f). Paul Huet (1803–69): French painter who

trellis-like designs alive with birds and monkeys, Chinese mandarins balancing umbrellas, and nymphs and shepherdesses under slender classical ruins. Side by side with the monumental work of such artists as Lebrun and Lesueur, Coypel, Vouet and Natoire,[19] this light style of composition was always in favor for the decoration of *petits apparte-ments*: the most famous painters of the day did not think it beneath them to furnish designs for such purposes (see plate 27).

In moderate-sized rooms which are to be decorated in a simple and inexpensive manner, a plain plaster ceiling with well-designed cornice is preferable to any device for producing showy effects at small cost. It may be laid down as a general rule in house-decoration that what must be done cheaply should be done simply. It is better to pay for the best plastering than to use a cheaper quality and then to cover the cracks with lincrusta[20] or ceiling-paper. This is true of all such expedients: let the fundamental work be good in design and quality and the want of ornament will not be felt.

In America the return to a more substantial way of building and the tendency to discard wood for brick or stone whenever possible will doubtless lead in time to the use of brick, stone or marble floors. These floors, associated in the minds of most Americans with shivering expeditions through damp Italian palaces, are in reality perfectly

---

specialized in creating Romantic landscapes. Jean-Baptiste Le Prince (1734–81): French printmaker, credited with creating aquatint by making colorful prints using granulated resin.

19. Eustache Le Sueur (1617–55): baroque painter, known for religious scenes and painstaking attention to detail (*EB* 2019l). Antoine Coypel (1661–1722): first painter to Louis XIV, known for biblical paintings, which combine the lightness of the rococo style with baroque drama (*EB* 2019e). Simon Vouet (1590–1649): first painter to Louis XIII, known for introducing Italianate baroque style into France, his style characterized by soft and smooth anatomy modeled after classics and bright colors (*EB* 2019jj). Charles Joseph Natoire (1700–1777): rococo artist, a director of the French Academy in Rome.

20. Deeply embossed wallcovering, invented by Frederick Walton, launched in 1877, and used in a host of applications from royal homes to railway carriages.

suited to the dry American climate, and even the most anæmic person could hardly object to brick or marble covered by heavy rugs.

The inlaid marble floors of the Italian palaces, whether composed of square or diamond-shaped blocks, or decorated with a large design in different colors, are unsurpassed in beauty; while in high-studded rooms where there is little pattern on the walls and a small amount of furniture, elaborately designed mosaic floors with sweeping arabesques and geometrical figures are of great decorative value.

Floors of these substances have the merit of being not only more architectural in character, more solid and durable, but also easier to keep clean. This should especially commend them to the hygienically-minded American housekeeper, since floors that may be washed are better suited to our climate than those which must be covered with a nailed-down carpet.

Next in merit to brick or marble comes the parquet[21] of oak or other hard wood; but even this looks inadequate in rooms of great architectural importance. In ball-rooms a hard-wood floor is generally regarded as a necessity; but in vestibule, staircase, dining-room or saloon, marble is superior to anything else. The design of the parquet floor should be simple and unobtrusive. The French, who brought this branch of floor-laying to perfection, would never have tolerated the crudely contrasted woods that make the modern parquet so aggressive. Like the walls of a room, the floor is a background: it should not furnish pattern, but set off whatever is placed upon it. The perspective effects dear to the modern floor-designer are the climax of extravagance. A floor should not only be, but appear to be, a perfectly level surface, without simulated bosses or concavities.

In choosing rugs and carpets the subject of design should be carefully studied. The Oriental carpet-designers have always surpassed their European rivals. The patterns of Eastern rugs are invariably well composed, with skilfully conventionalized figures in flat unshaded

21. Geometric pattern of inlaid wood (*M-W*).

colors. Even the Oriental rug of the present day is well drawn; but the colors used by Eastern manufacturers since the introduction of aniline dyes[22] are so discordant that these rugs are inferior to most modern European carpets.

In houses with deal floors, nailed-down carpets are usually considered a necessity, and the designing of such carpets has improved so much in the last ten or fifteen years that a sufficient choice of unobtrusive geometrical patterns may now be found. The composition of European carpets woven in one piece, like rugs, has never been satisfactory. Even the splendid *tapis de Savonnerie*[23] made in France at the royal manufactory during the seventeenth and eighteenth centuries were not so true to the best principles of design as the old Oriental rugs. In Europe there was always a tendency to transfer wall or ceiling-decoration to floor-coverings. Such incongruities as architectural mouldings, highly modelled trophies and human masks appear in most of the European carpets from the time of Louis XIV to the present day; and except when copying Eastern models the European designers were subject to strange lapses from taste. There is no reason why a painter should not simulate loggia and sky on a flat plaster ceiling, since no one will try to use this sham opening as a means of exit; but the carpet-designer who puts picture-frames and human faces under foot, though he does not actually deceive, produces on the eye a momentary startling sense of obstruction. Any *trompe-l'œil*[24] is

22. Organic base first discovered by distillation of indigo, which was subsequently formed into a strong purple dye. During the authors' lifetime, dyeing wood floors was a popular practice; any synthetic dye came to be known as an aniline dye. Today, this dyeing is mostly done using pigmented stains (*WOOD Magazine* 2018).

23. See chapter 1, note 23 (*EB* 2008).

24. Tricking the eye; technique used in painting to create an optical illusion that deceives the viewer into thinking the object in question exists in three dimensions; began with ancient Greeks and enthusiastically adopted by early Renaissance muralists (*EB* 2014b).

26. Ceiling in the Style of Bérain. Louis XIV Period.

permissible in decorative art if it gives an impression of pleasure; but the inherent sense of fitness is shocked by the act of walking upon upturned faces.

Recent carpet-designs, though usually free from such obvious incongruities, have seldom more than a negative merit. The unconventionalized flower still shows itself, and even when banished from the centre of the carpet lingers in the border which accompanies it. The vulgarity of these borders is the chief objection to using carpets of European manufacture as rugs, instead of nailing them to the floor. It is difficult to find a border that is not too wide, and of which the design is a simple conventional figure in flat unshaded colors. If used at all, a carpet with a border should always be in the form of a rug, laid in

27. Ceiling in the Château of Chantilly. Louis XV Period. (Example of Chinoiserie Decoration.)

the middle of the room, and not cut to follow all the ins and outs of the floor, as such adaptation not only narrows the room but emphasizes any irregularity in its plan.

In houses with deal floors, where nailed-down carpets are used in all the rooms, a restful effect is produced by covering the whole of each story with the same carpet, the door-sills being removed so that the carpet may extend from one room to another. In small town houses, especially, this will be found much less fatiguing to the eye than the usual manner of covering the floor of each room with carpets differing in color and design.

Where several rooms are carpeted alike, the floor-covering chosen should be quite plain, or patterned with some small geometrical figure in a darker shade of the foundation color; and green, dark blue or red will be found most easy to combine with the different color-schemes of the rooms.

Pale tints should be avoided in the selection of carpets. It is better that the color-scale should ascend gradually from the dark tone of floor or carpet to the faint half-tints of the ceiling. The opposite combination—that of a pale carpet with a dark ceiling—lowers the stud and produces an impression of top-heaviness and gloom; indeed, in a room where the ceiling is overladen, a dark rich-toned carpet will do much to lighten it, whereas a pale floor-covering will bring it down, as it were, on the inmates' heads.

Stair-carpets should be of a strong full color and, if possible, without pattern. It is fatiguing to see a design meant for a horizontal surface constrained to follow the ins and outs of a flight of steps; and the use of pattern where not needed is always meaningless, and interferes with a decided color-effect where the latter might have been of special advantage to the general scheme of decoration.

8

Entrance and Vestibule

The decoration of the entrance necessarily depends on the nature of the house and its situation. A country house, where visitors are few and life is simple, demands a less formal treatment than a house in a city or town; while a villa in a watering-place where there is much in common with town life has necessarily many points of resemblance to a town house.

It should be borne in mind of entrances in general that, while the main purpose of a door is to admit, its secondary purpose is to exclude. The outer door, which separates the hall or vestibule from the street, should clearly proclaim itself an effectual barrier. It should look strong enough to give a sense of security, and be so plain in design as to offer no chance of injury by weather and give no suggestion of interior decoration.

The best ornamentation for an entrance-door is simple panelling, with bold architectural mouldings and as little decorative detail as possible. The necessary ornament should be contributed by the design of locks, hinges and handles. These, like the door itself, should be strong and serviceable, with nothing finikin[1] in their treatment, and made of a substance which does not require cleaning. For the latter reason, bronze and iron are more fitting than brass or steel.

In treating the vestibule, careful study is required to establish a harmony between the decorative elements inside and outside the house. The vestibule should form a natural and easy transition from

---

1. Excessively fastidious and precise; finicky (*YourDictionary*; *M-W*).

the plain architecture of the street to the privacy of the interior (see plate 28).

No portion of the inside of the house being more exposed to the weather, great pains should be taken to avoid using in its decoration materials easily damaged by rain or dust, such as carpets or wall-paper. The decoration should at once produce the impression of being weather-proof.

Marble, stone, scagliola,[2] or painted stucco are for this reason the best materials. If wood is used, it should be painted, as dust and dirt soon soil it, and unless its finish be water-proof it will require contin-ual varnishing. The decorations of the vestibule should be as perma-nent as possible in character, in order to avoid incessant small repairs.

The floor should be of stone, marble, or tiles; even a linoleum or oil-cloth[3] of sober pattern is preferable to a hard-wood floor in so exposed a situation. For the same reason, it is best to treat the walls with a decoration of stone or marble. In simpler houses the same effect may be produced at much less cost by dividing the wall-spaces into panels, with wooden mouldings applied directly to the plaster, the whole being painted in oil, either in one uniform tint or in varying shades of some cold sober color. This subdued color-scheme will pro-duce an agreeable contrast with the hall or staircase, which, being a degree nearer the centre of the house, should receive a gayer and more informal treatment than the vestibule.

The vestibule usually has two doors: an outer one opening toward the street and an inner one giving into the hall; but when the outer is entirely of wood, without glass, and must therefore be left open dur-ing the day, the vestibule is usually subdivided by an inner glass door placed a few feet from the entrance. This arrangement has the merit of keeping the house warm and of affording a shelter to the servants who, during an entertainment, are usually compelled to wait outside. The French architect always provides an antechamber for this purpose.

2. Imitation marble used for floors and columns (*M-W*).

3. Fabric treated with oil in order to make it waterproof; usually used to cover floors (*M-W*).

28. Antechamber in the Villa Cambiaso, Genoa. Built by Alessi, XVI Century.

No furniture which is easily soiled or damaged, or difficult to keep clean, is appropriate in a vestibule. In large and imposing houses marble or stone benches and tables should be used, and the ornamentation may consist of statues, vases, or busts on pedestals (see plate 29). When the decoration is simpler and wooden benches are used, they should resemble those made for French gardens, with seats of one piece of wood, or of broad thick slats; while in small vestibules, benches and chairs with cane seats are appropriate.

The excellent reproductions of Robbia ware made by Cantagalli of Florence look well against painted walls;[4] while plaster or terracotta bas-reliefs are less expensive and equally decorative, especially against a pale-blue or green background.

The lantern, the traditional form of fixture for lighting vestibules, is certainly the best in so exposed a situation; and though where electric light is used draughts need not be considered, the sense of fitness requires that a light in such a position should always have the semblance of being protected.

4. Ulisse Cantagalli (1839–1901): Italian pottery manufacturer whose factory specialized in earthenware, reminiscent of Robbia ware (*Oxford Reference*). Edith Wharton and Ogden Codman Jr. are probably referring to Florentine sculptor Luca della Robbia (1400?–1482), who developed the process for which his family became known—enameled terra-cotta pottery—passing it on to his nephew Andrea della Robbia and great-nephews Giovanni della Robbia and Girolamo della Robbia (*EB* 2019y). Wharton had recently established a group of life-sized terra-cottas as the work of Giovanni della Robbia (1469–1529), publishing her findings in the *Scribner's Magazine* essay "A Tuscan Shrine" (1895). In so doing, Wharton was correcting a misattribution by Harvard art historian Bernard Berenson.

9

Hall and Stairs

What is technically known as the staircase (in German the *Treppen-haus*) has, in our lax modern speech, come to be designated as the hall.

In Gwilt's *Encyclopedia of Architecture* the staircase is defined as "that part or subdivision of a building containing the stairs which enable people to ascend or descend from one floor to another"; while the hall is described as follows: "The first large apartment on entering a house . . . In magnificent edifices, where the hall is larger and loftier than usual, and is placed in the middle of the house, it is called a saloon; and a royal apartment consists of a hall, or chamber of guards, etc."

It is clear that, in the technical acceptance of the term, a hall is something quite different from a staircase; yet the two words were used interchangeably by so early a writer as Isaac Ware, who, in his *Complete Body of Architecture*, published in 1756, continually speaks of the staircase as the hall. This confusion of terms is difficult to explain, for in early times the staircase was as distinct from the hall as it continued to be in France and Italy, and, with rare exceptions, in England also, until the present century.

In glancing over the plans of the feudal dwellings of northern Europe it will be seen that, far from being based on any definite conception, they were made up of successive accretions about the nobleman's keep. The first room to attach itself to the keep was the "hall," a kind of microcosm in which sleeping, eating, entertaining guests and administering justice succeeded each other or went on simultaneously. In the course of time various rooms, such as the parlor, the kitchen, the offices, the muniment-room and the lady's bower,[1] were added to the primitive hall; but these were rather incidental necessities than parts of an organized scheme of planning.[†] In this agglomeration of apartments the stairs found a place where they could. Space being valuable, they were generally carried up spirally in the thickness of the wall, or in an angle-turret. Owing to enforced irregularity of plan, and perhaps to the desire to provide numerous separate means of access to the different parts of the dwelling, each castle usually contained several staircases, no one of which was more important than the others.

    It was in Italy that stairs first received attention as a feature in the general composition of the house. There, from the outset, all the conditions had been different. The domestic life of the upper classes having developed from the eleventh century onward in the comparative security of the walled town, it was natural that house-planning should be less irregular,[†] and that more regard should be given to considerations of comfort and dignity. In early Italian palaces the stairs either ascended through the open central *cortile* to an arcaded gallery on the first floor, as in the Gondi palace and the Bargello at Florence,[2] or were

---

    1. Muniment room: room used for storing and preserving important records, papers, and documents; a manuscript hidden in a muniment room factors significantly in Edith Wharton's ghost story "Mr. Jones" (*M-W*). Lady's bower: private apartment in castle or estate belonging to the resident female royal or aristocrat (*M-W*).

    † Burckhardt, in his *Geschichle der Renaissance in Italien*, justly points out that the seeming inconsequence of mediæval house-planning in northern Europe was probably due in part to the fact that the feudal castle, for purposes of defence, was generally built on an irregular site. See also Viollet-le-Duc.

    † "Der gothische Profanbau in Italien...steht im vollen Gegensatz zum Norden durch die rationelle Anlage." Burckhardt, *Geschichte der Renaissance in Italien*, p. 28. (Editor's translation: "The gothic secular building in Italy...stands wholly opposed to the north due to the rational layout." Burckhardt, *History of the Renaissance in Italy*, 28.)

    2. Courtyard surrounded by arched passageways, specifically featured in architecture of the Italian Renaissance (*EB* 1998a). Gondi Palace: Palazzo Gondi, Italian palace built at the end of the fifteenth century by Giuliano da Sangallo (1445–1516) (Gondi Palace n.d.). Bargello at Florence: ancient prison; both palace and prison feature a courtyard and a large staircase (Museums of Florence n.d.).

29. Antechamber in the Durazzo Palace, Genoa. Decorated by Torrigiani. Late XVIII Century.

carried up in straight flights between walls.[†] This was, in fact, the usual way of building stairs in Italy until the end of the fifteenth century. These enclosed stairs usually started near the vaulted entranceway leading from the street to the *cortile*. Gradually the space at the foot of the stairs, which at first was small, increased in size and in importance of decorative treatment; while the upper landing opened into an antechamber which became the centre of the principal suite of apartments. With the development of the Palladian style,[3] the whole staircase

[†] See the stairs of the Riccardi palace in Florence, of the Piccolomini palace at Pienza and of the ducal palace at Urbino.

3. Based on the style of architect Andrea Palladio (1508–80), emphasizes order, symmetry, and proportion with decorative motifs. Inigo Jones introduced the style

(provided the state apartments were not situated on the ground floor) assumed more imposing dimensions; though it was not until a much later date that the monumental staircase so often regarded as one of the chief features of the Italian Renaissance began to be built. Indeed, a detailed examination of the Italian palaces shows that even in the seventeenth and eighteenth centuries such staircases as were built by Fontana in the royal palace at Naples, by Juvarra in the Palazzo Madama at Turin and by Vanvitelli at Caserta, were seen only in royal palaces.[4] Even Morelli's staircase in the Braschi palace in Rome, magnificent as it is, hardly reaches the popular conception of the Italian state staircase[5]—a conception probably based rather upon the great open stairs of the Genoese *cortili* than upon any actually existing staircases. It is certain that until late in the seventeenth century (as Bernini's[6] Vatican staircase shows) intermural stairs were thought grand enough for the most splendid palaces of Italy (see plate 30).

---

to England in the seventeenth century. On Palladian windows, see chapter 5 (*EB* 2017d).

4. Domenico Fontana (1543–1607): who built the Royal Palace of Naples, featuring an enormous main staircase that splits into a left and right side, each with intricately designed banisters (*EB* 2019k). Palazzo Madama: built by Filippo Juvarra (1678–1736) in 1718, characterized by sharply defined, traditionally designed spaces (*EB* 2019m). Its staircase is wide and imposing, though not the focal point of the room, as it is situated against the wall; Caserta: Royal Palace at Caserta, considered crowning achievement of architect Luigi Vanvitelli (1700–1773), known as one of the last Italian baroque masterpieces (*EB* 2019aa). It is most famous for its Grand Staircase of Honour—or rather, staircases—as its two lengthy flights of steps, a left and right side, each decorated with friezes and life-size lion statues, enclose an arched hallway.

5. Palazzo Braschi, now the Museo di Roma, built by Cosimo Morelli (1732–1812); its turning staircase is surrounded by columns, arches, and elaborately carved ceilings (Ehrlich et al. 2019).

6. Gian Lorenzo Bernini (1598–1680): Italian sculptor considered by Wharton "the genius of the Baroque." Her gothic short story "The Duchess at Prayer" (1901) centers on a fictional Bernini sculpture of a penitent wife kneeling in prayer, perhaps inspired by Bernini's *Ecstasy of Saint Teresa* (1647–52). In *Italian Villas and Their Gardens*, Wharton celebrates Bernini as "the greatest Italian architect and sculptor of the seventeenth century" (1904, 254).

30. Staircase in the Parodi Palace, Genoa. XVI Century. (Showing Inter-Mural Stairs and Marble Floor.)

The spiral staircase, soon discarded by Italian architects save as a means of secret communication or for the use of servants, held its own in France throughout the Renaissance. Its structural difficulties afforded scope for the exercise of that marvellous, if sometimes super-fluous, ingenuity which distinguished the Gothic builders. The spiral staircase in the court-yard at Blois is an example of this kind of skilful

engineering and of the somewhat fatiguing use of ornament not infrequently accompanying it; while such anomalies as the elaborate out-
of-door spiral staircase enclosed within the building at Chambord are
still more in the nature of a *tour de force*—something perfect in itself,
but not essential to the organism of the whole.[7]

Viollet-le-Duc, in his dictionary of architecture, under the head-
ing *Château*, has given a sympathetic and ingenious explanation of the
tenacity with which the French aristocracy clung to the obsolete complications of Gothic house-planning and structure long after frequent
expeditions across the Alps had made them familiar with the simpler
and more rational method of the Italian architects. It may be, as he
suggests, that centuries of feudal life, with its surface of savagery and
violence and its undercurrent treachery, had fostered in the nobles of
northern Europe a desire for security and isolation that found expression in the intricate planning of their castles long after the advance of
civilization had made these precautions unnecessary. It seems more
probable, however, that the French architects of the Renaissance made
the mistake of thinking that the essence of the classic styles lay in the
choice and application of ornamental details. This exaggerated estimate of the importance of detail is very characteristic of an imperfect
culture; and the French architects who in the fifteenth century were
eagerly taking their first lessons from their contemporaries south of
the Alps, had behind them nothing like the great synthetic tradition
of the Italian masters. Certainly it was not until the Northern builders

7. Royal estate in the Loire Valley of France that showcases the evolution of
French architecture through its four wings. The spiral staircase to which the authors
refer is elaborately decorated and built into the façade of the building, facing outward
to the main courtyard; the steps are only covered by the flights above them, thus the
staircase is technically outdoors (Château Royal de Blois n.d.). Chambord: royal chateau, also in the Loire Valley, known for its fascinating double spiral staircase. The
authors refer to it as "out-of-door" because it is not enclosed in a hallway, but rather
can be seen through each floor. The two twisting ramps never converge; however,
they both reach the main floors of the chateau, as well as the tallest towers (Domaine
National de Chambord n.d.).

learned that the beauty of the old buildings was, above all, a matter of proportion, that their own style, freed from its earlier incoherencies, set out on the line of unbroken national development which it followed with such harmonious results until the end of the eighteenth century.

In Italy the staircase often gave directly upon the entranceway; in France it was always preceded by a vestibule, and the upper landing invariably led into an antechamber.

In England the relation between vestibule, hall and staircase was never so clearly established as on the Continent. The old English hall, so long the centre of feudal life, preserved its somewhat composite character after the *grand'salle*[8] of France and Italy had been broken up into the vestibule, the guard-room and the saloon. In the grandest Tudor houses the entrance-door usually opened directly into this hall. To obtain in some measure the privacy which a vestibule would have given, the end of the hall nearest the entrance-door was often cut off by a screen that supported the musicians' gallery. The corridor formed by this screen led to the staircase, usually placed behind the hall, and the gallery opened on the first landing of the stairs. This use of the screen at one end of the hall had so strong a hold upon English habits that it was never quite abandoned. Even after French architecture and house-planning had come into fashion in the eighteenth century, a house with a vestibule remained the rarest of exceptions in England; and the relative privacy afforded by the Gothic screen was then lost by substituting for the latter an open arcade, of great decorative effect, but ineffectual in shutting off the hall from the front door.

The introduction of the Palladian style by Inigo Jones transformed the long and often narrow Tudor hall into the many-storied central saloon of the Italian villa, with galleries reached by concealed staircases, and lofty domed ceiling; but it was still called the hall, it still served as a vestibule, or means of access to the rest of the house, and, curiously enough, it usually adjoined another apartment, often of the same dimensions, called a saloon. Perhaps the best way of defining the

8. French: great hall.

English hall of this period is to say that it was really an Italian saloon, but that it was used as a vestibule and called a hall.

Through all these changes the staircase remained shut off from the hall, upon which it usually opened. It was very unusual, except in small middle-class houses or suburban villas, to put the stairs in the hall, or, more correctly speaking, to make the front door open into the staircase. There are, however, several larger houses in which the stairs are built in the hall. Inigo Jones, in remodelling Castle Ashby for the Earl of Northampton, followed this plan; though this is perhaps not a good instance to cite, as it may have been difficult to find place for a separate staircase.[9] At Chevening, in Kent, built by Inigo Jones for the Earl of Sussex, the stairs are also in the hall; and the same arrangement is seen at Shobden Court, at West Wycombe, built by J. Donowell for Lord le Despencer (where the stairs are shut off by a screen) and at Hurlingham, built late in the eighteenth century by G. Byfield.[10]

This digression has been made in order to show the origin of the modern English and American practice of placing the stairs in the hall and doing away with the vestibule. The vestibule never formed part of the English house, but the stairs were usually divided from the hall in houses of any importance; and it is difficult to see whence the modern architect has derived his idea of the combined hall and staircase. The tendency to merge into one any two apartments designed for different

9. Manor in Northamptonshire. The original architectural plans from 1574 called for the house to be built into an *E* shape to celebrate Queen Elizabeth I. The steps in the central courtyard then formed the central stroke of the *E*. In 1624 Inigo Jones added a new front façade and built around the staircase. Perhaps as a nod to the castle, Wharton would name the protagonist of her ghost story "Pomegranate Seed" (1937) Charlotte Ashby (Castle Ashby n.d.).

10. Chevening House: manor in Kent; the staircase in its main hall is a tight spiral under which one can walk (Chevening House n.d.). Shobdon Court: eighteenth-century manor house since demolished; no accessible records exist where a hidden staircase is mentioned (Herefordshire Past n.d.). Hurlingham House: now an athletic club known as Hurlingham Club, neoclassic mansion expanded from a cottage; its main staircase has since been modernized, but the twist and general size of the steps is original (Hurlingham Club n.d.).

uses shows a retrogression in house-planning; and while it is fitting
that the vestibule or hall should adjoin the staircase, there is no good
reason for uniting them and there are many for keeping them apart.

The staircase in a private house is for the use of those who inhabit
it; the vestibule or hall is necessarily used by persons in no way concerned with the private life of the inmates. If the stairs, the main artery
of the house, be carried up through the vestibule, there is no security
from intrusion. Even the plan of making the vestibule precede the
staircase, though better, is not the best. In a properly planned house
the vestibule should open on a hall or antechamber of moderate size,
giving access to the rooms on the ground floor, and this antechamber
should lead into the staircase. It is only in houses where all the living-
rooms are up-stairs that the vestibule may open directly into the staircase without lessening the privacy of the house.

In Italy, where wood was little employed in domestic architecture, stairs were usually of stone. Marble came into general use in the
grander houses when, in the seventeenth century, the stairs, instead of
being carried up between walls, were often placed in an open staircase.
The balustrade was usually of stone or marble, iron being much less
used than in France.

In the latter country the mediæval stairs, especially in the houses
of the middle class, were often built of wood; but this material was
soon abandoned, and from the time of Louis XIV stairs of stone with
wrought-iron rails are a distinctive feature of French domestic architecture. The use of wrought-iron in French decoration received a strong
impulse from the genius of Jean Lamour, who, when King Stanislas of
Poland remodelled the town of Nancy early in the reign of Louis XV,
adorned its streets and public buildings with specimens of iron-work
unmatched in any other part of the world.[11] Since then French decorators have expended infinite talent in devising the beautiful stair-rails

11. Jean Lamour (1698–1771): master locksmith and ironworker under Stanislaw I of Poland (1677–1766). In 1760 Stanislaw, father-in-law of Louis XV, commissioned a French architect to expand and organize the town of Nancy in northeastern
France, which had previously been separated into two villages.

31. Staircase of the Hôtel de Ville, Nancy. Louis XV Period. Built by Héré de Corny; Stair-Rail by Jean Lamour.

and balconies which are the chief ornament of innumerable houses throughout France (see plates 31 and 32).

Stair-rails of course followed the various modifications of taste which marked the architecture of the day. In the seventeenth and early eighteenth centuries they were noted for severe richness of design. With the development of the rocaille manner their lines grew lighter and more fanciful, while the influence of Gabriel, which, toward the end of the reign of Louis XV, brought about a return to classic models, manifested itself in a simplified mode of treatment. At this period the outline of a classic baluster formed a favorite motive for the iron rail. Toward the close of the eighteenth century the designs for these rails grew thin and poor, with a predominance of upright iron bars divided at long intervals by some meagre medallion or geometrical figure. The exuberant sprays and volutes of the rococo period and the architectural lines of the Louis XVI style were alike absent from these later designs, which are chiefly marked by the negative merit of inoffensiveness.

In the old French stair-rails steel was sometimes combined with gilded iron. The famous stair-rail of the Palais Royal, designed by Coutant d'Ivry, is made of steel and iron, and the Duc d'Aumale copied this combination in the stair-rail at Chantilly.[12] There is little to recommend the substitution of steel for iron in such cases. It is impossible to keep a steel stair-rail clean and free from rust, except by painting it; and since it must be painted, iron is the more suitable material.

In France the iron rail is usually painted black, though a very dark blue is sometimes preferred. Black is the better color, as it forms a stronger contrast with the staircase walls, which are presumably neutral in tint and severe in treatment. Besides, as iron is painted, not to improve its appearance, but to prevent its rusting, the color which most resembles its own is more appropriate. In French houses of a certain importance the iron stair-rail often had a few touches of gilding, but these were sparingly applied.

12. Former royal palace in Paris that faces the Louvre; the site is important to Wharton's novel *A Son at the Front* (1923). Jules Coutant-d'Ivry (1854–1913): primarily a French politician, but his stair rail can be seen accompanying the double Grand Staircase in the palace. It is made of wrought iron that is delicately and ornately woven into gilded patterns. Chantilly: chateau in northern France that was owned by Henry d'Orléans (1822–97), the Duc d'Aumale, or the Duke of Aumale, the son of the last king of France, Louis-Philippe (1773–1850). The stair rail accompanying its winding grand staircase is made of gilded wrought-iron rails and wrought-iron spirals as its central decoration.

In England wooden stair-rails were in great favor during the Tudor and Elizabethan period. These rails were marked rather by fanciful elaboration of detail than by intrinsic merit of design, and are doubtless more beautiful now that time has given them its patina, than they were when first made.

With the Palladian style came the classic balustrade of stone or marble, or sometimes, in simpler houses, of wood. Iron rails were seldom used in England, and those to be found in some of the great London houses (as in Carlton House, Chesterfield House and Norfolk House)[13] were probably due to the French influence which made itself felt in English domestic architecture during the eighteenth century. This influence, however, was never more than sporadic; and until the decline of decorative art at the close of the eighteenth century, Italian rather than French taste gave the note to English decoration.

The interrelation of vestibule, hall and staircase having been explained, the subject of decorative detail must next be considered; but before turning to this, it should be mentioned that hereafter the space at the foot of the stairs, though properly a part of the staircase, will for the sake of convenience be called *the hall*, since in the present day it goes by that name in England and America.

In contrasting the vestibule with the hall, it was pointed out that the latter might be treated in a gayer and more informal manner than the former. It must be remembered, however, that as the vestibule is the introduction to the hall, so the hall is the introduction to the living-rooms of the house; and it follows that the hall must be as much more formal than the living-rooms as the vestibule is more formal than the hall. It is necessary to emphasize this because the tendency

13. Carlton House: estate whose main staircase was made of gilded wrought-iron, under the watchful eye of Dominique Daguerre, a French *marchand-mercier*, or a merchant of luxury items active in Paris from 1772 to his death in 1796; Chesterfield House's wrought-iron stair rail was not gilded, though its central design was made of ornate twisting flower shapes; Norfolk House's twisting stair rail was wrought iron and decorated with classic shapes. All three eighteenth-century London residences have since been demolished.

of recent English and American decoration has been to treat the hall, not as a hall, but as a living-room. Whatever superficial attractions this treatment may possess, its inappropriateness will be seen when the purpose of the hall is considered. The hall is a means of access to all the rooms on each floor; on the ground floor it usually leads to the chief living-rooms of the house as well as to the vestibule and street; in addition to this, in modern houses even of some importance it generally contains the principal stairs of the house, so that it is the centre upon which every part of the house directly or indirectly opens. This publicity is increased by the fact that the hall must be crossed by the servant who opens the front door, and by any one admitted to the house. It follows that the hall, in relation to the rooms of the house, is like a public square in relation to the private houses around it. For some reason this obvious fact has been ignored by many recent decorators, who have chosen to treat halls like rooms of the most informal character, with open fireplaces, easy-chairs for lounging and reading, tables with lamps, books and magazines, and all the appointments of a library. This disregard of the purpose of the hall, like most mistakes in household decoration, has a very natural origin. When, in the first reaction from the discomfort and formality of sixty years ago, people began, especially in England, to study the arrangement of the old Tudor and Elizabethan houses, many of these were found to contain large panelled halls opening directly upon the porch or the terrace. The mellow tones of the wood-work; the bold treatment of the stairs, shut off as they were merely by a screen; the heraldic imagery of the hooded stone chimney-piece and of the carved or stuccoed ceiling, made these halls the chief feature of the house; while the rooms opening from them were so often insufficient for the requirements of modern existence, that the life of the inmates necessarily centred in the hall. Visitors to such houses saw only the picturesqueness of the arrangement—the huge logs glowing on the hearth, the books and flowers on the old carved tables, the family portraits on the walls; and, charmed with the impression received, they ordered their architects to reproduce for them a hall which, even in the original Tudor houses, was a survival of older social conditions.

32. Staircase in the Palace of Fontainebleau. Louis XV Period.

One might think that the recent return to classic forms of architecture would have done away with the Tudor hall; but, except in a few instances, this has not been the case. In fact, in the greater number of large houses, and especially of country houses, built in America since the revival of Renaissance and Palladian architecture, a large many-storied hall communicating directly with the vestibule, and containing the principal stairs of the house, has been the distinctive feature. If there were any practical advantages in this overgrown hall, it might be regarded as one of those rational modifications in plan which mark the difference between an unreasoning imitation of a past style and the intelligent application of its principles; but the Tudor hall, in its composite character as vestibule, parlor and dining-room, is only another instance of the sacrifice of convenience to archaism.

The abnormal development of the modern staircase-hall cannot be defended on the plea sometimes advanced that it is a roofed-in adaptation of the great open *cortile* of the Genoese palace, since there is no reason for adapting a plan so useless and so unsuited to our climate and way of living. The beautiful central *cortile* of the Italian palace, with its monumental open stairs, was in no sense part of a "private house" in our interpretation of the term. It was rather a thoroughfare like a public street, since the various stories of the Italian palace were used as separate houses by different branches of the family.

In most modern houses the hall, in spite of its studied resemblance to a living-room, soon reverts to its original use as a passageway; and this fact should indicate the treatment best suited to it. In rooms where people sit, and where they are consequently at leisure to look about them, delicacy of treatment and refinement of detail are suitable; but in an anteroom or a staircase only the first impression counts, and forcible simple lines, with a vigorous massing of light and shade, are essential. These conditions point to the use of severe strongly-marked panelling, niches for vases or statues, and a stair-rail detaching itself from the background in vigorous decisive lines.[†]

The furniture of the hall should consist of benches or straight-backed chairs, and marble-topped tables and consoles. If a press[14] is used, it should be architectural in design, like the old French and Italian *armoires* painted with arabesques and architectural motives, or the English seventeenth-century presses made of some warm-toned wood like walnut and surmounted by a broken pediment with a vase or bust in the centre (see plate 33).

The walls of the staircase in large houses should be of panelled stone or marble, as in the examples given in the plates accompanying this chapter.

In small houses, where an expensive decoration is out of the question, a somewhat similar architectural effect may be obtained by the

---

[†] For a fine example of a hall-niche containing a statue, see plate 30.

14. Carved wooden cupboard, typically ornate.

use of a few plain mouldings fixed to the plaster, the whole being painted in one uniform tint, or in two contrasting colors, such as white for the mouldings, and buff, gray, or pale green for the wall. To this scheme may be added plaster medallions, as suggested for the vestibule, or garlands and other architectural motives made of staff, in imitation of the stucco ornaments of old French and Italian decorators. When such ornaments are used, they should invariably be simple and strong in design. The modern decorator is too often tempted by mere prettiness of detail to forget the general effect of his composition. In a staircase, where only the general effect is seized, prettiness does not count; and the effect produced should be strong, clear and telling.

For the same reason, a stair-carpet, if used, should be of one color, without pattern. Masses of plain color are one of the chief means of producing effect in any scheme of decoration.

When the floor of the hall is of marble or mosaic—as, if possible, it should be—the design, like that of the walls, should be clear and decided in outline (see plate 30). On the other hand, if the hall is used as an antechamber and carpeted, the carpet should be of one color, matching that on the stairs.

In many large houses the stairs are now built of stone or marble, while the floor of the landings is laid in wood, apparently owing to the idea that stone or marble floors are cold. In the tropically-heated American house not even the most sensitive person could be chilled by passing contact with a stone floor; but if it is thought to "look cold," it is better to lay a rug or a strip of carpet on the landing than to permit the proximity of two such different substances as wood and stone.

Unless the stairs are of wood, that material should never be used for the rail; nor should wooden stairs be put in a staircase of which the walls are of stone, marble, or scagliola. If the stairs are of wood, it is better to treat the walls with wood or plaster panelling. In simple staircases the best wall-decoration is a wooden dado-moulding nailed on the plaster, the dado thus formed being painted white, and the wall above it in any uniform color. Continuous pattern, such as that on paper or stuff hangings, is specially objectionable on the walls of a staircase, since it disturbs the simplicity of composition best fitted to this part of the house.

For the lighting of the hall there should be a lantern like that in the vestibule, but more elaborate in design. This mode of lighting harmonizes with the severe treatment of the walls and indicates at once that the hall is not a living-room, but a thoroughfare.[†]

If lights be required on the stairs, they should take the form of fire-gilt bronze sconces, as architectural as possible in design, without any finikin prettiness of detail. (For good examples, see the *appliques* in plates 5 and 34). It is almost impossible to obtain well-designed *appliques* of this kind in America; but the increasing interest shown in house-decoration will in time doubtless cause a demand for a better type of gas and electric fixtures. Meantime, unless imported sconces can be obtained, the plainest brass fixtures should be chosen in preference to the more elaborate models now to be found here.

Where the walls of a hall are hung with pictures, these should be few in number, and decorative in composition and coloring. No subject requiring thought and study is suitable in such a position. The mythological or architectural compositions of the Italian and French schools of the last two centuries, with their superficial graces of color and design, are for this reason well suited to the walls of halls and antechambers.

The same may be said of prints. These should not be used in a large high-studded hall; but they look well in a small entrance-way, if hung on plain-tinted walls. Here again such architectural compositions as Piranesi's, with their bold contrasts of light and shade, Marc Antonio's classic designs, or some frieze-like procession, such as Mantegna's "Triumph of Julius Cæsar," are especially appropriate;[15]

[†] In large halls the tall *torchère* of marble or bronze may be used for additional lights (see plate 32).

15. Giovanni Battista Piranesi (1720–78): Italian printmaker and architect who depicted classical and postclassical Rome with precise detail and Romantic splendor; his original etching technique created a distinct effect of chiaroscuro (*EB* 2019p).

whereas the subtle detail of the German Little Masters, the symbolism of Dürer's etchings and the graces of Marillier or Moreau le Jeune would be wasted in a situation where there is small opportunity for more than a passing glance.[16]

In most American houses, the warming of hall and stairs is so amply provided for that where there is a hall fireplace it is seldom used. In country houses, where it is sometimes necessary to have special means for heating the hall, the open fireplace is of more service; but it is not really suited to such a situation. The hearth suggests an idea of intimacy and repose that has no place in a thoroughfare like the hall; and, aside from this question of fitness, there is a practical objection to placing an open chimney-piece in a position where it is exposed to continual draughts from the front door and from the rooms giving upon the hall.

The best way of heating a hall is by means of a faience[17] stove—not the oblong block composed of shiny white or brown tiles seen in Swiss and German *pensions*, but one of the fine old stoves of architectural design still used on the Continent for heating the vestibule and dining-room. In Europe, increased attention has of late been given

---

Marcantonio Raimondi (1480–1534): Renaissance engraver who reproduced works of Raphael, Michelangelo, and the like (*EB* 2019bb). *Triumph of Caesar* (or *The Triumphs of Caesar*), made by Italian artist Andrea Mantegna, a series of nine paintings gifted to Giovanni de' Medici and hung in the Palazzo di San Sebastiano in Mantua (Web Gallery of Art n.d.).

16. Little Masters, also known as Kleinmeister: a group of sixteenth-century Nurnberg engravers whose finished works depicted subjects appealing to the masses and were small, portable, and flawless in technique (*EB* 2019w). These masters were all influenced by Albrecht Dürer (1471–1528): painter and printmaker, regarded as the greatest German Renaissance artist (Ruhmer 2019). Moreau le Jeune: Jean-Michel Moreau le Jeune (1741–1814), known best as an engraver, provided drawings for Diderot's *Encyclopedie*, as well as illustrations for Voltaire and Rousseau (Getty n.d.).

17. Glazed earthenware specifically made in France, Germany, Spain, or Scandinavia (*EB* 2012f).

33. French Armoire, Louis XIV Period. Museum of Decorative Arts, Paris.

to the design and coloring of these stoves; and if better known here, they would form an important feature in the decoration of our halls. Admirable models may be studied in many old French and German houses and on the borders of Switzerland and Italy; while the museum at Parma contains several fine examples of the rocaille period.

10

The Drawing-Room, Boudoir, and Morning-Room

The "with-drawing-room" of mediæval England, to which the lady and her maidens retired from the boisterous festivities of the hall, seems at first to have been merely a part of the bedchamber in which the lord and lady slept. In time it came to be screened off from the sleeping-room; then, in the king's palaces, it became a separate room for the use of the queen and her damsels; and so, in due course, reached the nobleman's castle, and established itself as a permanent part of English house-planning.

In France the evolution of the *salon* seems to have proceeded on somewhat different lines. During the middle ages and the early Renaissance period, the more public part of the nobleman's life was enacted in the hall, or *grand'salle*, while the social and domestic side of existence was transferred to the bedroom. This was soon divided into two rooms, as in England. In France, however, both these rooms contained beds; the inner being the real sleeping-chamber, while in the outer room, which was used not only for administering justice and receiving visits of state, but for informal entertainments and the social side of family life, the bedstead represented the lord's *lit de parade*,[1] traditionally associated with state ceremonial and feudal privileges.

The custom of having a state bedroom in which no one slept (*chambre de parade*, as it was called) was so firmly established that

1. French: state bed.

34. Sala della Maddalena, Royal Palace, Genoa. XVIII Century.
(Italian Drawing-Room in Rocaille Style.)

even in the engravings of Abraham Bosse, representing French life
in the reign of Louis XIII, the fashionable apartments in which card-
parties, suppers, and other entertainments are taking place, invariably contain a bed.

In large establishments the *chambre de parade* was never used as
a sleeping-chamber except by visitors of distinction; but in small
houses the lady slept in the room which served as her boudoir and

drawing-room. The Renaissance, it is true, had introduced from Italy the *cabinet* opening off the lady's chamber,[2] as in the palaces of Urbino and Mantua; but these rooms were at first seen only in kings' palaces, and were, moreover, too small to serve any social purpose. The *cabinet* of Catherine de' Medici at Blois is a characteristic example.[3]

Meanwhile, the gallery had relieved the *grand'salle* of some of its numerous uses; and these two apartments seem to have satisfied all the requirements of society during the Renaissance in France.

In the seventeenth century the introduction of the two-storied Italian saloon produced a state apartment called a *salon*; and this, towards the beginning of the eighteenth century, was divided into two smaller rooms: one, the *salon de compagnie*, remaining a part of the gala suite used exclusively for entertaining (see plate 34), while the other—the *salon de famille*—became a family apartment like the English drawing-room.

The distinction between the *salon de compagnie* and the *salon de famille* had by this time also established itself in England, where the state drawing-room retained its Italian name of *salone*, or saloon, while the living-apartment preserved, in abbreviated form, the mediæval designation of the lady's with-drawing-room.

Pains have been taken to trace as clearly as possible the mixed ancestry of the modern drawing-room, in order to show that it is the result of two distinct influences—that of the gala apartment and that of the family sitting-room. This twofold origin has curiously affected

2. French: closet or bureau. In this case, the authors are most likely referring to a room attached to a main bedroom, comparable to today's walk-in closet. Oftentimes, these rooms had small cabinets built into the walls. Women's private closets of this sort factor meaningfully into the plot of a number of Edith Wharton short stories (e.g., "The Lady's Maid's Bell," 1902).

3. A small room in what was originally Catherine de' Medici's bedchamber at the Chateau de Blois that contains 237 small cabinets that are built into the walls and adorned with decorative woodwork. None of the cabinets have knobs or handles, which led to the rumor that the hidden cabinets held a private apothecary—the contents of which she used to poison political enemies. However, it is much more likely these cabinets held small works of art or important records (Black 2019).

the development of the drawing-room. In houses of average size, where there are but two living-rooms—the master's library, or "den," and the lady's drawing-room—it is obvious that the latter ought to be used as a *salon de famille*, or meeting-place for the whole family; and it is usually regarded as such in England, where common sense generally prevails in matters of material comfort and convenience, and where the drawing-room is often furnished with a simplicity which would astonish those who associate the name with white-and-gold walls and uncomfortable furniture.

In modern American houses both traditional influences are seen. Sometimes, as in England, the drawing-room is treated as a family apartment, and provided with books, lamps, easy-chairs and writing-tables. In other houses it is still considered sacred to gilding and discomfort, the best room in the house, and the convenience of all its inmates, being sacrificed to a vague feeling that no drawing-room is worthy of the name unless it is uninhabitable. This is an instance of the *salon de compagnie* having usurped the rightful place of the *salon de famille*; or rather, if the bourgeois descent of the American house be considered, it may be more truly defined as a remnant of the "best parlor" superstition.[4]

Whatever the genealogy of the American drawing-room, it must be owned that it too often fails to fulfil its purpose as a family apartment. It is curious to note the amount of thought and money frequently spent on the one room in the house used by no one, or occupied at most for an hour after a "company" dinner.

To this drawing-room, from which the inmates of the house instinctively flee as soon as their social duties are discharged, many necessities are often sacrificed. The library, or den, where the members of the family sit, may be furnished with shabby odds and ends;

4. Edith Wharton and Ogden Codman Jr. express their dismay with a bourgeois proclivity for considering a drawing room too special for the residents to inhabit. (For a discussion of the mixed ancestry of the parlor, which originated from the gala apartment and family sitting room, see Grier 1988).

35. Console in the Petit Trianon, Versailles. Late Louis XV Style. Bust of Louis XVI, by Pajou.

but the drawing-room must have its gilt chairs covered with brocade, its *vitrines* full of modern Saxe, its guipure curtains and velvet carpet.[5]

The *salon de compagnie* is out of place in the average house. Such a room is needed only where the dinners or other entertainments given are so large as to make it impossible to use the ordinary living-rooms of the house. In the grandest houses of Europe the gala-rooms are never thrown open except for general entertainments, or to receive

5. Vitrine: any glass display case or cabinet (*M-W*). Modern Saxe: specific type of china or porcelain that would be held in a vitrine. Guipure curtains: dressing made of heavy lace fabric from France consisting of thick embroidered pieces held together by large connecting stitches and thick thread (Dictionary.com).

guests of exalted rank, and the spectacle of a dozen people languishing after dinner in the gilded wilderness of a state saloon is practically unknown.

The purpose for which the *salon de compagnie* is used necessitates its being furnished in the same formal manner as other gala apartments. Circulation must not be impeded by a multiplicity of small pieces of furniture holding lamps or other fragile objects, while at least half of the chairs should be so light and easily moved that groups may be formed and broken up at will. The walls should be brilliantly decorated, without needless elaboration of detail, since it is unlikely that the temporary occupants of such a room will have time or inclination to study its treatment closely. The chief requisite is a gay first impression. To produce this, the wall-decoration should be light in color, and the furniture should consist of a few strongly marked pieces, such as handsome cabinets and consoles, bronze or marble statues, and vases and candelabra of imposing proportions. Almost all modern furniture is too weak in design and too finikin in detail to look well in a gala drawing-room.[†] (For examples of drawing-room furniture, see plates 6, 9, 34, and 35.)

Beautiful pictures or rare prints produce little effect on the walls of a gala room, just as an accumulation of small objects of art, such as enamels, ivories and miniatures, are wasted upon its tables and cabinets. Such treasures are for rooms in which people spend their days, not for those in which they assemble for an hour's entertainment.

But the *salon de compagnie*, being merely a modified form of the great Italian saloon, is a part of the gala suite,[6] and any detailed discussion of the decorative treatment most suitable to it would result in a repetition of what is said in the chapter on Gala Rooms.

[†] Much of the old furniture which appears to us unnecessarily stiff and monumental was expressly designed to be placed against the walls in rooms used for general entertainments, where smaller and more delicately made pieces would have been easily damaged, and would, moreover, have produced no effect.

6. Rooms in a house used exclusively for entertaining. As Wharton and Codman explain in the next chapter, these should be separate from the living quarters.

36. Salon, Palace of Fontainebleau.

The lighting of the company drawing-room—to borrow its French designation—should be evenly diffused, without the separate centres of illumination needful in a family living-room. The proper light is that of wax candles. Nothing has done more to vulgarize interior decoration than the general use of gas and of electricity in the living-rooms of modern houses. Electric light especially, with its harsh white glare, which no expedients have as yet overcome, has taken from our drawing-rooms all air of privacy and distinction. In passageways and offices, electricity is of great service; but were it not that all "modern improvements" are thought equally applicable to every condition of life, it would be difficult to account for the adoption of a mode of lighting which makes the *salon* look like a railway-station, the dining-room like a restaurant. That such light is not needful in a drawing-room is shown by the fact that electric bulbs are usually covered by shades of some deep color, in order that the glare may be made as inoffensive as possible.

The light in a gala apartment should be neither vivid nor concentrated: the soft, evenly diffused brightness of wax candles is best fitted to bring out those subtle modellings of light and shade to which old furniture and objects of art owe half their expressiveness.

The treatment of the *salon de compagnie* naturally differs from that of the family drawing-room: the latter is essentially a room in which people should be made comfortable. There must be a well-appointed writing-table; the chairs must be conveniently grouped about various tables, each with its lamp;—in short, the furniture should be so disposed that people are not forced to take refuge in their bedrooms for lack of fitting arrangements in the drawing-room.

The old French cabinet-makers excelled in the designing and making of furniture for the *salon de famille*. The term "French furniture" suggests to the Anglo-Saxon mind the stiff appointments of the gala room—heavy gilt consoles, straight-backed arm-chairs covered with tapestry, and monumental marble-topped tables. Admirable furniture of this kind was made in France; but in the grand style the Italian cabinet-makers competed successfully with the French; whereas the latter stood alone in the production of the simpler and more comfortable furniture adapted to the family living-room. Among those who have not studied the subject there is a general impression that eighteenth-century furniture, however beautiful in design and execution, was not comfortable in the modern sense. This is owing to the fact that the popular idea of "old furniture" is based on the appointments of gala rooms in palaces: visitors to Versailles or Fontainebleau[7] are more likely to notice the massive gilt consoles and benches in the state saloons than the simple easy-chairs and work-tables of the *petits appartements*. A visit to the Garde Meuble or to the Musée des Arts

7. A royal chateau in southeastern Paris that served as a sovereign residence for eight centuries (Château de Fontainebleau n.d.).

Décoratifs of Paris,[8] or the inspection of any collection of French eighteenth-century furniture, will show the versatility and common sense of the old French cabinet-makers. They produced an infinite variety of small *meubles*,[9] in which beauty of design and workmanship were joined to simplicity and convenience.

The old arm-chair, or *bergère*, is a good example of this combination. The modern upholsterer pads and puffs his seats[10] as though they were to form the furniture of a lunatic's cell; and then, having expanded them to such dimensions that they cannot be moved without effort, perches their dropsical bodies on four little casters. Any one who compares such an arm-chair to the eighteenth-century *bergère*, with its strong tapering legs, its snugly-fitting back and cushioned seat, must admit that the latter is more convenient and more beautiful (see plates 8 and 37).

The same may be said of the old French tables—from desks, card and work-tables, to the small *guéridon*[11] just large enough to hold a book and candlestick. All these tables were simple and practical in design: even in the Louis XV period, when more variety of outline and ornament was permitted, the strong structural lines were carefully maintained, and it is unusual to see an old table that does not stand firmly on its legs and appear capable of supporting as much weight as its size will permit (see Louis XV writing-table in plate 46).

The French tables, cabinets and commodes used in the family apartments were usually of inlaid wood, with little ornamentation save the design of the marquetry—elaborate mounts of chiselled bronze

---

8. Garde-Meuble de la Couronne: eighteenth-century department that took responsibility for all furniture and decorations in royal palaces; has since been renamed the Mobilier National (*M-W*). Musée des Arts Décoratifs: Parisian museum specializing in furniture and decorative objects (MAD Paris n.d.).

9. French: furniture.

10. The authors' fundamental distrust of modern house decorating is particularly palpable here and would inform Wharton's description of the newly moneyed Simon Rosedale of *The House of Mirth*, his "smart London clothes fitting him like upholstery."

11. French: pedestal table.

37. Room in the Palace of Fontainebleau. Louis XV Panelling, Louis XVI Furniture.

being reserved for the furniture of gala rooms (see plate 10). Old French marquetry was exquisitely delicate in color and design, while Italian inlaying of the same period, though coarser, was admirable in composition. Old Italian furniture of the seventeenth and eighteenth centuries was always either inlaid or carved and painted in gay colors: chiselled mounts are virtually unknown in Italy.

The furniture of the eighteenth century in England, while not comparable in design to the best French models, was well made and dignified; and its angularity of outline is not out of place against the somewhat cold and formal background of an Adam room.

English marquetry suffered from the poverty of ornament marking the wall-decoration of the period. There was a certain timidity

about the decorative compositions of the school of Adam and Sheraton, and in their scanty repertoire the laurel-wreath, the velarium and
the cornucopia reappear with tiresome frequency.

The use to which the family drawing-room is put should indicate the character of its decoration. Since it is a room in which many
hours of the day are spent, and in which people are at leisure, it should
contain what is best worth looking at in the way of pictures, prints,
and other objects of art; while there should be nothing about its decoration so striking or eccentric as to become tiresome when continually seen. A fanciful style may be pleasing in apartments used only for
stated purposes, such as the saloon or gallery; but in a living-room,
decoration should be subordinate to the individual, forming merely a
harmonious but unobtrusive background (see plates 36 and 37). Such
a setting also brings out the full decorative value of all the drawing-
room accessories—screens, andirons, *appliques*, and door and window-
fastenings. A study of any old French interior will show how much
these details contributed to the general effect of the room.

Those who really care for books are seldom content to restrict
them to the library, for nothing adds more to the charm of a drawing-
room[12] than a well-designed bookcase: an expanse of beautiful bindings is as decorative as a fine tapestry.

The boudoir is, properly speaking, a part of the bedroom suite,
and as such is described in the chapter on the Bedroom. Sometimes,
however, a small sitting-room adjoins the family drawing-room, and
this, if given up to the mistress of the house, is virtually the boudoir.

The modern boudoir is a very different apartment from its
eighteenth-century prototype. Though it may preserve the delicate decorations and furniture suggested by its name, such a room is now generally used for the prosaic purpose of interviewing servants, going over
accounts and similar occupations. The appointments should therefore

12. In Wharton's *The Age of Innocence* (1920), set in Gilded Age New York, Ellen
Olenska's drawing room would put this theory into practice, sharply contrasting the
more conventional room decorated by May Welland.

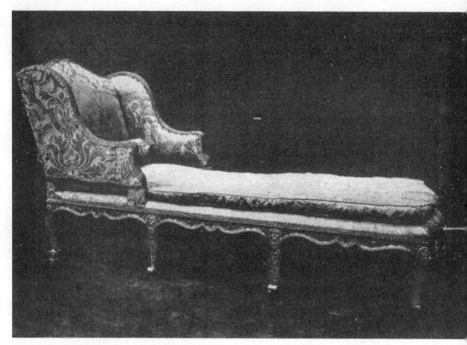

38. Lit de Repos, Early Louis XV Period.

comprise a writing-desk, with pigeon-holes, drawers, and cupboards, and a comfortable lounge, or *lit de repos*,[13] for resting and reading.

The *lit de repos*, which, except in France, has been replaced by the clumsy upholstered lounge, was one of the most useful pieces of eighteenth-century furniture (see plate 38). As its name implies, it is shaped somewhat like a bed, or rather like a cradle that stands on four legs instead of swinging. It is made of carved wood, sometimes upholstered, but often seated with cane (see plate 39). In the latter case it is fitted with a mattress and with a pillow-like cushion covered with some material in keeping with the hangings of the room. Sometimes the *duchesse*,[14] or upholstered *bergère* with removable foot-rest in the shape of a square bench, is preferred to the *lit de repos*; but the latter is the more elegant and graceful, and it is strange that it should have

13. French: daybed (Metropolitan Museum of Art n.d.).
14. French: chaise longue with arms (*M-W*).

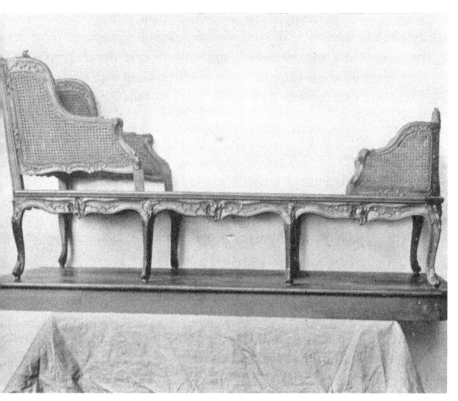

39. Lit de Repos, Louis XV Period.

been discarded in favor of the modern lounge, which is not only ugly, but far less comfortable.

As the boudoir is generally a small room, it is peculiarly suited to the more delicate styles of painting or stucco ornamentation described in the third chapter. A study of boudoir-decoration in the last century, especially in France, will show the admirable sense of proportion regulating the treatment of these little rooms (see plate 40). Their adornment was naturally studied with special care by the painters and decorators of an age in which women played so important a part.

It is sometimes thought that the eighteenth-century boudoir was always decorated and furnished in a very elaborate manner. This idea originates in the fact, already pointed out, that the rooms usually seen by tourists are those in royal palaces, or in such princely houses as are thrown open to the public on account of their exceptional magnificence. The same type of boudoir is continually reproduced in books on architecture and decoration; and what is really a small private sitting-room for the lady of the house, corresponding with her husband's "den," has thus come to be regarded as one of the luxuries of a great establishment.

The prints of Eisen,[15] Marillier, Moreau le Jeune, and other book-illustrators of the eighteenth century show that the boudoir in the average private house was, in fact, a simple room, gay and graceful in decoration, but as a rule neither rich nor elaborate (see plate 41). As it usually adjoined the bedroom, it was decorated in the same manner, and even when its appointments were expensive all appearance of costliness was avoided.[†]

The boudoir is the room in which small objects of art—prints, mezzotints and *gouaches*[16]—show to the best advantage. No detail is wasted, and all manner of delicate effects in wood-carving, marquetry, and other ornamentation, such as would be lost upon the walls and furniture of a larger room, here acquire their full value. One or two well-chosen prints hung on a background of plain color will give more pleasure than a medley of photographs, colored photogravures,[17] and other decorations of the cotillon-favor type. Not only do mediocre ornaments become tiresome when seen day after day, but the mere crowding of furniture and gimcracks[18] into a small room intended for work and repose will soon be found fatiguing.

15. Eisen (1790–1848): Japanese printmaker and illustrator best known for his portraits of *bijin*—beautiful women (Ronin Gallery n.d.).

[†] The ornate boudoir seen in many XVIIIth-century prints is that of the *femme galante.*

16. Mezzotint: method of engraving in which the surface of the metal plate is pricked with small holes that can hold ink; process can produce a large yet subtle range of tones; also known as "black manner." Gouache: painting technique in which white pigment is added to watercolors to produce opacity (*EB* 2018k).

17. Image, colored by hand, produced from the negative of a photograph and etched into a metal plate (Dictionary.com).

18. Ostentatious object of little use or cheap material (*M-W*).

40. Painted Wall-Panel and Door, Château of Chantilly. Louis XV.
(Example of Chinoiserie Decoration.)

Many English houses, especially in the country, contain a useful room called the "morning-room," which is well defined by Robert Kerr,[19] in *The English Gentleman's House,* as "the drawing-room in

19. Robert Kerr (1823–1904): British architect, writer, and cofounder of the
Architectural Association. Revised the third edition of Fergusson's *History of the
Modern Styles of Architecture* in 1891.

Sa triſte amante abandonnee
Pleure ſes maux et ſes plaiſirs.

41. French Boudoir, Louis XVI Period. (From a Print by Le Bouteux.)

ordinary." It is, in fact, a kind of undress drawing-room, where the family may gather informally at all hours of the day. The out-of-door life led in England makes it specially necessary to provide a sitting-room which people are not afraid to enter in muddy boots and wet clothes. Even if the drawing-room be not, as Mr. Kerr quaintly puts it, "preserved"—that is, used exclusively for company—it is still likely to contain the best furniture in the house; and though that "best" is not too fine for every-day use, yet in a large family an informal, wet-weather room of this kind is almost indispensable.

No matter how elaborately the rest of the house is furnished, the appointments of the morning-room should be plain, comfortable, and capable of resisting hard usage. It is a good plan to cover the floor with a straw matting, and common sense at once suggests the furniture best suited to such a room: two or three good-sized tables with lamps, a comfortable sofa, and chairs covered with chintz, leather, or one of the bright-colored horse-hairs now manufactured in France.

11

Gala Rooms

Ball-Room, Saloon, Music-Room, Gallery

European architects have always considered it essential that those rooms which are used exclusively for entertaining—gala rooms, as they are called—should be quite separate from the family apartments—either occupying an entire floor (the Italian *piano nobile*) or being so situated that it is not necessary to open them except for general entertainments.

In many large houses lately built in America, with ball and music rooms and a hall simulating the two-storied Italian saloon, this distinction has been disregarded, and living and gala rooms have been confounded in an agglomeration of apartments where the family, for lack of a smaller suite, sit under gilded ceilings and cut-glass chandeliers, in about as much comfort and privacy as are afforded by the public "parlors" of one of our new twenty-story hotels. This confusion of two essentially different types of room, designed for essentially different phases of life, has been caused by the fact that the architect, when called upon to build a grand house, has simply enlarged, instead of altering, the *maison bourgeoise*[1] that has hitherto been the accepted model of the American gentleman's house; for it must not

---

1. French: literally "middle-class house." It is a comfortable home as opposed to the *maison de maître*, an elegant bourgeois mansion of eighteenth- or nineteenth-century origins that would originally have been the home of a squire or other minor landowner. The *maison bourgeoise* is similar to the *maison de maître* in its elegant appearance, but does not have quite the same standing. But whereas the latter is

be forgotten that the modern American dwelling descends from the English middle-class house, not from the aristocratic country-seat or town residence. The English nobleman's town house was like the French *hôtel*, with gates, porter's lodge, and court-yard surrounded by stables and offices; and the planning of the country-seat was even more elaborate.

A glance at any collection of old English house-plans, such as Campbell's *Vitruvius Britannicus*,[2] will show the purely middle-class ancestry of the American house, and the consequent futility of attempting, by the mere enlargement of each room, to turn it into a gentleman's seat or town residence. The kind of life which makes gala rooms necessary exacts a different method of planning; and until this is more generally understood the treatment of such rooms in American houses will never be altogether satisfactory.

Gala rooms are meant for general entertainments, never for any assemblage small or informal enough to be conveniently accommodated in the ordinary living-rooms of the house; therefore to fulfil their purpose they must be large, very high-studded, and not over-crowded with furniture, while the walls and ceiling—the only parts of a crowded room that can be seen—must be decorated with greater elaboration than would be pleasing or appropriate in other rooms. All these conditions unfit the gala room for any use save that for which it is designed. Nothing can be more cheerless than the state of a handful of people sitting after dinner in an immense ball-room with gilded ceiling, bare floors and a few pieces of monumental furniture ranged round the walls; yet in any house which is simply an enlargement of the ordinary private dwelling the hostess is often compelled to use the ball-room or saloon as a drawing-room.

---

usually near some type of agricultural or industrial building to aid in supervision, the *maison bourgeoise* is normally near a garden or park.

2. Colen Campbell (1676–1729): eighteenth-century Scottish architect whose designs set precedents for the British Palladianism era. *Vitruvius Britannicus*: Campbell's most influential book, named after the Roman architect Marcus Vitruvius Pollio, published in three volumes in 1712, 1718, and 1725 ("Campbell, Colen" 2011).

A gala room is never meant to be seen except when crowded: the crowd takes the place of furniture. Occupied by a small number of people, such a room looks out of proportion, stiff and empty. The hostess feels this, and tries, by setting chairs and tables askew, and introducing palms, screens and knick-knacks, to produce an effect of informality. As a result the room dwarfs the furniture, loses the air of state, and gains little in real comfort while it becomes necessary, when a party is given, to remove the furniture and disarrange the house, thus undoing the chief *raison d'être* of such apartments.

The Italians, inheriting the grandiose traditions of the Augustan age,[3] have always excelled in the treatment of rooms demanding the "grand manner." Their unfailing sense that house-decoration is interior architecture, and must clearly proclaim its architectural affiliations, has been of special service in this respect. It is rare in Italy to see a large room inadequately treated. Sometimes the "grand manner"—the mimic *terribilità*[4]—may be carried too far to suit Anglo-Saxon taste—it is hard to say for what form of entertainment such a room as Giulio Romano's Sala dei Giganti in the Palazzo del T would form a pleasing or appropriate background—but apart from such occasional aberrations, the Italian decorators showed a wonderful sense of fitness in the treatment of state apartments. To small dribbles of ornament they preferred bold forcible mouldings, coarse but clear-cut free-hand ornamentation in stucco, and either a classic severity of treatment or the turbulent bravura style of the saloon of the Villa Rotonda and of Tiepolo's Cleopatra frescoes in the Palazzo Labia at Venice.[5]

---

3. Either the prolific period of sophisticated literary pursuits of Roman writers from 43 BCE to 18 CE or a similar "golden age" of eighteenth-century English literature when Jonathan Swift and Alexander Pope were active. The authors, in this context, seem to reference the former (*EB* 2017a).

4. Italian: terribleness. Also, a quality that expresses or evokes intensity, terror, and awe. Associated with Michelangelo (*M-W*).

5. Villa Rotonda: Renaissance villa in northern Italy designed by Andrea Palladio and built in 1550. Its design, especially its large central hall with a low, circular dome, was often copied by eighteenth-century English architects. Also known as Villa Capra. Palazzo Labia: baroque palace in Venice commissioned by the Labia

42. Salon à l'italienne. (From a Picture by Coypel.)

The saloon and gallery are the two gala rooms borrowed from Italy by northern Europe. The saloon has already been described in the chapter on Hall and Stairs. It was a two-storied apartment, usually

family, known for its frescoed ballroom painted by Tiepolo. On Tiepolo's Cleopatra frescoes, see chapter 3, note 6.

with clerestory,[6] domed ceiling, and a gallery to which access was obtained by concealed staircases (see plates 42 and 43). This gallery was often treated as an arcade or loggia, and in many old Italian prints and pictures there are representations of these saloons, with groups of gaily dressed people looking down from the gallery upon the throngs crowding the floor. The saloon was used in Italy as a ball-room or gambling-room—gaming being the chief social amusement of the eighteenth century.

In England and France the saloon was rarely two stories high, though there are some exceptions, as for example the saloon at Vaux-le-Vicomte. The cooler climate rendered a clerestory less necessary, and there was never the same passion for grandiose effects as in Italy. The saloon in northern Europe was always a stately and high-studded room, generally vaulted or domed, and often circular in plan; but it seldom reached such imposing dimensions as its Italian prototype, and when more than one story high was known by the distinctive designation of *un salon à l'italienne*.

The gallery was probably the first feature in domestic house-planning to be borrowed from Italy by northern Europe. It is seen in almost all the early Renaissance châteaux of France; and as soon as the influence of such men as John of Padua and John Shute[7] asserted itself in England, the gallery became one of the principal apartments of the Elizabethan mansion. There are several reasons for the popularity of the gallery. In the cold rainy autumns and winters north of the Alps

6. High section of wall that contains windows above eye level. The purpose is to admit light, fresh air, or both.

7. John of Padua (active between 1543 and 1557): an elusive figure of the English Renaissance employed at the courts of Henry VIII and his successor, Edward VI, during a period in which numerous foreign architects and artisans arrived in England, bringing with them the new concepts and evolutions of the Italian Renaissance as it spread across Europe. John Shute (d. 1563): English writer and painter, authored the first English treatise on architecture, *The First and Chief Groundes of Architecture* (1563), based on his study of Italian architecture, especially in relation to proportion, for which Lord Dudley (1532–88) sent him to Italy in 1550 (*Grove Encyclopedia of Northern Renaissance Art* 2009).

it was invaluable as a sheltered place for exercise and games; it was well adapted to display the pictures, statuary and bric-à-brac which, in emulation of Italian collectors, the Northern nobles were beginning to acquire; and it showed off to advantage the long line of ancestral portraits and the tapestries representing a succession of episodes from the *Æneid*,[8] the *Orlando Innamorato*,[9] or some of the interminable epics that formed the light reading of the sixteenth century. Then, too, the gallery served for the processions which were a part of the social ceremonial in great houses: the march to the chapel or banquet-hall, the escorting of a royal guest to the state bedroom, and other like pageants.

In France and England the gallery seems for a long time to have been used as a saloon and ball-room, whereas in Italy it was, as a rule, reserved for the display of the art-treasures of the house, no Italian palace worthy of the name being without its gallery of antiquities or of marbles.

In modern houses the ball-room and music-room are the two principal gala apartments. A music-room need not be a gala room in the sense of being used only for large entertainments; but since it is outside the circle of every-day use, and more or less associated with entertaining, it seems best to include it in this chapter.

Many houses of average size have a room large enough for informal entertainments. Such a room, especially in country houses, should be decorated in a gay simple manner in harmony with the rest of the house and with the uses to which the room is to be put. Rooms of this

8. Epic composed by the Roman poet Virgil between 30 and 19 BCE. Drawing from Homer's *Iliad* and *Odyssey*, it recounts various stories of the legendary Trojan Aeneas (*EB* 2018b).

9. 1487 poem composed by Italian poet Matteo Maria Boiardo (1441–94) that evokes the Matter of France, which focuses on the Carolingian cycle of literature based on the history and legends connected to Charlemagne. Literally "Orlando in Love," concerns the falling in and out of love of several characters (especially Orlando/Roland) with the princess Angelica (*Concise Oxford Companion to English Literature* 2013).

43. Ball-Room, Royal Palace, Genoa. Late XVIII Century. (Example of Stucco Decoration.)

kind may be treated with a white dado, surmounted by walls painted in a pale tint, with boldly modelled garlands and attributes in stucco, also painted white (see plate 13). If these stucco decorations are used to frame a series of pictures, such as fruit and flower-pieces or decorative subjects, the effect is especially attractive. Large painted panels with eighteenth-century *genre* subjects or pastoral scenes, set in simple white panelling, are also very decorative. A coved ceiling is best suited to rooms of this comparatively simple character, while in state ball-rooms the dome increases the general appearance of splendor.

A panelling of mirrors forms a brilliant ball-room decoration, and charming effects are produced by painting these mirrors with birds, butterflies, and garlands of flowers, in the manner of the famous Italian mirror-painter, Mario dei Fiori—"Mario of the Flowers"[10]—as he was called in recognition of his special gift. There is a beautiful room by this artist in the Borghese Palace[11] in Rome, and many Italian palaces contain examples of this peculiarly brilliant style of decoration, which might be revived to advantage by modern painters.

In ball-rooms of great size and importance, where the walls demand a more architectural treatment, the use of an order naturally suggests itself. Pilasters of marble, separated by marble niches containing statues, form a severe but splendid decoration; and if white and colored marbles are combined, and the whole is surmounted by a domed ceiling frescoed in bright colors, the effect is extremely brilliant.

In Italy the architectural decoration of large rooms was often entirely painted (see plate 44), the plaster walls being covered with a fanciful piling-up of statues, porticoes and balustrades, while figures in Oriental costume, or in the masks and particolored dress of the *Comédie Italienne*,[12] leaned from simulated loggias or wandered through marble colonnades.

The Italian decorator held any audacity permissible in a room used only by a throng of people, whose mood and dress made them ready to

10. Mario Nuzzi (1603–73): Roman painter whose training is linked to Tommaso Salini, who may have been his uncle. His early specialization in flower paintings led him to become that genre's most outstanding proponent in his time. His widespread success is clear in the number of his works listed in the inventories of numerous Roman palaces. Judging from the number of still lifes and floral scenes in Edith Wharton's private art collection, she likely would have greatly admired the work of *Mario of the Flowers*.

11. Feudal palace built between 1590 and 1607 by Martino Longhi the Elder and Flaminio Ponzio as the main seat of the Borghese family. Known as "Il Cembalo," or "the harpsichord," for its shape (*Hutchinson Unabridged Encyclopedia* 2018).

12. Italian-language theater and opera performed in France. The first official use of the term was in 1680, when it was given to the commedia dell'arte troupe at the Hôtel de Bourgogne, to distinguish it from the French troupe, the Comédie Française, which was founded that year. Over time French phrases, songs, whole scenes, and eventually plays were incorporated into the Comédie Italienne's performances.

accept the fairy-tales on the walls as a fitting background to their own masquerading. Modern travellers, walking through these old Italian saloons in the harsh light of day, while cobwebs hang from the audacious architecture, and the cracks in the plaster look like wounds in the cheeks of simpering nymphs and shepherdesses, should remember that such apartments were meant to be seen by the soft light of wax candles in crystal chandeliers, with fantastically dressed dancers thronging the marble floor.

Such a ball-room, if reproduced in the present day, would be far more effective than the conventional white-and-gold room which, though unobjectionable when well decorated, lacks the imaginative charm, the personal note, given by the painter's touch.

Under Louis XIV many French apartments of state were panelled with colored marbles, with an application of attributes or trophies, and other ornamental motives in fire-gilt bronze: a sumptuous mode of treatment according well with a domed and frescoed ceiling. Tapestry was also much used, and forms an admirable decoration, provided the color-scheme is light and the design animated. Seventeenth and eighteenth-century tapestries are the most suitable, as the scale of color is brighter and the compositions are gayer than in the earlier hangings.

Modern dancers prefer a polished wooden floor, and it is perhaps smoother and more elastic than any other surface; but in beauty and decorative value it cannot be compared with a floor of inlaid marble, and as all the dancing in Italian palaces is still done on such floors, the preference for wood is probably the result of habit. In a ball-room of any importance, especially where marble is used on the walls, the floor should always be of the same substance (see floors in plates 29, 30, and 55).

Gala apartments, as distinguished from living-rooms, should be lit from the ceiling, never from the walls. No ball-room or saloon is complete without its chandeliers: they are one of the characteristic features of a gala room (see plates 5, 19, 34, 43, 45, 50). For a ball-room, where all should be light and brilliant, rock-crystal or cut-glass

44. Saloon in the Villa Vertemati. XVI Century. (Example of frescoed Walls and Carved Wooden Ceiling.)

chandeliers are most suitable: reflected in a long line of mirrors, they are an invaluable factor in any scheme of gala decoration.[13]

The old French decorators relied upon the reflection of mirrors for producing an effect of distance in the treatment of gala rooms. Above the mantel, there was always a mirror with another of the same shape and size directly opposite; and the glittering perspective thus produced gave to the scene an air of fantastic unreality. The gala suite being so planned that all the rooms adjoined each other, the effect

13. The authors' suggestions on ballroom decoration offer an especially helpful context for reading Julius and Regina Beaufort's ballroom in Wharton's *The Age of Innocence*.

45. Sala dello Zodiaco, Ducal Palace, Mantua. XVIII Century. (Example of Stucco Decoration.)

of distance was further enhanced by placing the openings in line, so that on entering the suite it was possible to look down its whole length. The importance of preserving this long vista, or *enfilade*,[14] as the French call it, is dwelt on by all old writers on house-decoration. If a ball-room be properly lit and decorated, it is never necessary to dress it up with any sort of temporary ornamentation: the true mark of the well-decorated ball-room is to look always ready for a ball.

The only chair seen in most modern ball-rooms is the folding camp-seat hired by the hundred when entertainments are given; but

14. Suite of rooms formally aligned with each other, much like a row of columns; a common feature in grand European architecture from the baroque period onward.

there is no reason why a ball-room should be even temporarily disfigured by these makeshifts, which look their worst when an effort is made to conceal their cheap construction under a little gilding and satin. In all old ball-rooms, benches and *tabourets* (small seats without backs) were ranged in a continuous line along the walls. These seats, handsomely designed, and covered with tapestry, velvet, or embroidered silk slips, were a part of the permanent decoration of the room. On ordinary occasions they would be sufficient for a modern ball-room; and when larger entertainments made it needful to provide additional seats, these might be copied from the seventeenth-century *perroquets*, examples of which may be found in the various French works on the history of furniture. These *perroquets*, or folding chairs without arms, made of natural walnut or gilded, with seats of tapestry, velvet or decorated leather, would form an excellent substitute for the modern cotillon seat.

The first rule to be observed in the decoration of the music-room is the avoidance of all stuff hangings, draperies, and substances likely to deaden sound. The treatment chosen for the room must of course depend on its size and its relation to the other rooms in the house. While a music-room should be more subdued in color than a ball-room, sombre tints and heavy ornament are obviously inappropriate: the effect aimed at should be one of lightness and serenity in form and color. However small and simple the music-room may be, it should always appear as though there were space overhead for the notes to escape; and some form of vaulting or doming is therefore more suitable than a flat ceiling.

While plain panelling, if well designed, is never out of keeping, the walls of a music-room are specially suited to a somewhat fanciful style of decoration. In a ball-room, splendor and brilliancy of effect are more needful than a studied delicacy; but where people are seated, and everything in the room is consequently subjected to close and prolonged scrutiny, sprightliness of composition should be combined with variety of detail, the decoration being neither so confused and intricate as to distract attention, nor so conventional as to be dismissed with a glance on entering the room.

The early Renaissance compositions in which stucco low-reliefs blossom into painted arabesques and tendrils, are peculiarly adapted to a small music-room; while those who prefer a more architectural treatment may find admirable examples in some of the Italian eighteenth-century rooms decorated with free-hand stucco ornament, or in the sculptured wood-panelling of the same period in France. At Remiremont[15] in the Vosges, formerly the residence of a noble order of canonesses, the abbess's *hôtel* contains an octagonal music-room of exceptional beauty, the panelled walls being carved with skilfully combined musical instruments and flower-garlands.

In larger apartments a fanciful style of fresco-painting might be employed, as in the rooms painted by Tiepolo in the Villa Valmarana, near Vicenza, or in the staircase of the Palazzo Sina, at Venice, decorated by Longhi[16] with the episodes of an eighteenth-century carnival. Whatever the design chosen, it should never resemble the formal treatment suited to ball-room and saloon: the decoration should sound a note distinctly suggestive of the purpose for which the music-room is used.

It is difficult to understand why modern music-rooms have so long been disfigured by the clumsy lines of grand and upright pianos, since the cases of both might be modified without affecting the construction of the instrument.[17] Of the two, the grand piano would be the

15. Town in the Grand Est region, formally known as Alsace-Lorraine, of eastern France. The order of nuns mentioned by the authors attained considerable power after settling in the region in 910, the abbess becoming a princess of the Holy Roman Empire. The abbess's palace is now used as the town hall (*EB* 2020u).

16. Pietro Longhi (1702–85): Italian painter of the rococo style; known for scenes of Venetian social and domestic life, often depicting Venice's bourgeoisie and upper class (*EB* 2021i). Villa Valmarana: eighteenth-century villa in Vicenza known for its frescoes by Tiepolo (Villa Valmarana ai Nani n.d.). Palazzo Sina: in chapter 7 of *Italian Backgrounds* Wharton praises Longhi's frescoes in "the Palazzo Grassi (now Sina)" on the Grand Canal, Venice; she describes it as a "fine palace, built about 1740 by Massari, the architect of the Gesuati" (Wharton 1905).

17. The original statement, visible in the typed manuscript, was much more critical in tone: "It is difficult to understand why this hideous monster, and its equally

46. French Table (Transition between Louis XIV and Louis XV Periods.)

easier to remodel: if its elephantine supports were replaced by slender fluted legs, and its case and sounding-board were painted, or inlaid with marquetry, it would resemble the charming old clavecin[18] which preceded the pianoforte.

Fewer changes are possible in the "upright"; but a marked improvement could be produced by straightening its legs and substituting right angles for the weak curves of the lid. The case itself might be made of plainly panelled mahogany, with a few good ormolu ornaments; or of inlaid wood, with a design of musical instruments and similar "attributes"; or it might be decorated with flower-garlands and arabesques painted either on the natural wood or on a gilt or colored background.

---

mis-shapen junior, the 'upright,' have so long been allowed to disfigure the modern house."

18. French: harpsicord; altered form of *clavessin* (1611), from medieval Latin *clavicymbalum*, from *clavis* (key) (Robert 1978, 324).

47. Library of Louis XVI, Palace of Versailles. (Louis XV Writing-Table with Bust.)

Designers should also study the lines of those two long-neglected pieces of furniture, the music-stool and music-stand. The latter should be designed to match the piano, and painted or inlaid like its case. The revolving mushroom that now serves as a music-stool is a modern invention: the old stools were substantial circular seats resting on four fluted legs. The manuals of the eighteenth-century cabinet-makers contain countless models of these piano-seats, which might well be reproduced by modern designers: there seems no practical reason why the accessories of the piano should be less decorative than those of the harpsichord.

12

The Library, Smoking-Room, and "Den"

In the days when furniture was defined as "that which may be carried about," the natural bookcase was a chest with a strong lock. These chests, packed with precious manuscripts, followed the prince or noble from one castle to another, and were even carried after him into camp. Before the invention of printing, when twenty or thirty books formed an exceptionally large library, and many great personages were content with the possession of one volume, such ambulant bookcases were sufficient for the requirements of the most eager bibliophile. Occasionally the volumes were kept in a small press or cupboard, and placed in a chest only when their owner travelled; but the bookcase, as now known, did not take shape until much later, for when books multiplied with the introduction of printing, it became customary to fit up for their reception little rooms called *cabinets*. In the famous *cabinet* of Catherine de' Medici at Blois the walls are lined with book-shelves concealed behind sliding panels—a contrivance rendered doubly necessary by the general insecurity of property, and by the fact that the books of that period, whether in manuscript or printed, were made sumptuous as church jewelry by the art of painter and goldsmith.

Long after the establishment of the printing-press, books, except in the hands of the scholar, continued to be a kind of curiosity, like other objects of art: less an intellectual need than a treasure upon which rich men prided themselves. It was not until the middle of the seventeenth century that the taste for books became a taste for reading. France led the way in this new fashion, which was assiduously cultivated in those Parisian *salons* of which Madame de Rambouillet's is the recognized type. The possession of a library, hitherto the privilege of kings, of wealthy monasteries, or of some distinguished patron of letters like Grolier, Maioli, or de Thou,[1] now came to be regarded as a necessity of every gentleman's establishment. Beautiful bindings were still highly valued, and some of the most wonderful work produced in France belongs to the seventeenth and eighteenth centuries; but as people began to buy books for the sake of what they contained, less exaggerated importance was attached to their exterior, so that bindings, though perfect as taste and skill could make them, were seldom as extravagantly enriched as in the two preceding centuries. Up to a certain point this change was not to be regretted: the mediæval book, with its gold or ivory bas-reliefs bordered with precious stones, and its massive jewelled clasps, was more like a monstrance or reliquary than anything meant for less ceremonious use. It remained for the Italian printers and binders of the sixteenth century, and for their French imitators, to adapt the form of the book to its purpose, changing, as it were, a jewelled idol to a human companion.

The substitution of the octavo for the folio, and certain modifications in binding which made it possible to stand books upright instead of laying one above the other with edges outward, gradually gave to the library a more modern aspect. In France, by the middle of the seventeenth century, the library had come to be a recognized feature in private houses. The Renaissance *cabinet* continued to be the common receptacle for books; but as the shelves were no longer concealed,

---

1. Catherine de Vivonne, marquise de Rambouillet (1588–1655): famous and well-respected literary and society hostess in Paris (Credit: Joel Goldfield). Jean Grolier de Servières, viscount d'Aguisy (c. 1489/90–1565): French bibliophile known for his library of three thousand volumes bound in expensive leather and decorated with intricate designs. A patron of one of the first printing companies, Grolier helped expand the bookbinding trade in France (*EB* 2020m). Thomas Mahieu (Maioli): sixteenth-century French book collector and secretary to Catherine de' Medici from 1549–1560 (British Museum n.d.). Jacques-Auguste de Thou (1553–1617): French bibliophile, statesman, and historian known for producing several unbiased, historical accounts of his era (*EB* 2020l).

48. Small Library at Audley End, England. XVIII Century.

bindings now contributed to the decoration of the room. Movable book-cases were not unknown, but these seem to have been merely presses in which wooden door-panels were replaced by glass or by a lattice-work of brass wire. The typical French bookcase *à deux corps*—that is, made in two separate parts, the lower a cupboard to contain prints and folios, the upper with shelves and glazed or latticed doors—was introduced later, and is still the best model for a movable book-case. In rooms of any importance, however, the French architect always preferred to build his book-shelves into niches formed in the thickness of the wall, thus utilizing the books as part of his scheme of decoration.

There is no doubt that this is not only the most practical, but the most decorative, way of housing any collection of books large enough to be so employed. To adorn the walls of a library, and then conceal their ornamentation by expensive bookcases, is a waste, or rather a misapplication, of effects—always a sin against æsthetic principles.

The importance of bookbindings as an element in house-decoration has already been touched upon; but since a taste for good bindings has come to be regarded as a collector's fad, like accumulating snuff-boxes or *baisers-de-paix*,[2] it seems needful to point out how obvious and valuable a means of decoration is lost by disregarding the outward appearance of books. To be decorative, a bookcase need not contain the productions of the master-binders—old volumes by Eve and Derôme, or the work of Roger Payne and Sanderson[3]—unsurpassed as they are in color-value. Ordinary bindings of half morocco or vellum[4] form an expanse of warm lustrous color; such bindings are comparatively inexpensive; yet people will often hesitate to pay for a good edition bound in plain levant half the amount they are ready to throw away upon a piece of modern Saxe[5] or a silver photograph-frame.

The question of binding leads incidentally to that of editions, though the latter is hardly within the scope of this book. People who have begun to notice the outside of their books naturally come to

2. French: (plural) "kiss of peace." A small plaque, often in gilded or silvered bronze, presented during a Catholic mass for the kiss of the faithful. These plaques are usually engraved with a scene from the life of Christ (Commission Diocésaine d'Art Sacré de Paris n.d.).

3. Nicolas Eve and Nicolas Derôme, among France's master bookbinders; Derôme (1731–90) is said to have started the practice of dentelle bindings, or bindings with decorative tool work resembling lace (Campbell 2008). Roger Payne (1738–97): English bookbinder known for his excellent and finely detailed tooling (SMU Bridwell Library n.d.). Thomas James Cobden-Sanderson (1840–1922): English artist and bookbinder associated with the Arts and Crafts movement (Campbell 2014).

4. Traditionally goatskin leather from Morocco used for bookbinding since the seventeenth century, though sheepskin and lambskin were also used. Vellum: writing material made from the skin of young animals, usually calves (Ward 2008).

5. Also called Meissen porcelain, Dresden porcelain, and *porcelaine de Saxe*, the first true porcelain to be produced in Europe, beginning in 1710 and continuing to the present day. It was fabricated in the Meissen factory in Dresden, Saxony, part of what is now Germany, which dominated the industry until 1756, when they were surpassed by French Sèvres porcelain (*EB* 2020x).

appreciate paper and type; and thus learn that the modern book is too often merely the cheapest possible vehicle for putting words into print. The last few years have brought about some improvement; and it is now not unusual for a publisher, in bringing out a book at the ordinary rates, to produce also a small edition in large-paper copies. These large-paper books, though as yet far from perfect in type and make-up, are superior to the average "commercial article"; and, apart from their artistic merit, are in themselves a good investment, since the value of such editions increases steadily year by year. Those who cannot afford both edition and binding will do better to buy large-paper books or current first editions in boards, than "handsomely bound" volumes unworthy in type and paper. The plain paper or buckram covers of a good publisher are, in fact, more decorative, because more artistic, than showy tree-calf[6] or "antique morocco."

The same principle applies to the library itself: plain shelves filled with good editions in good bindings are more truly decorative than ornate bookcases lined with tawdry books.

It has already been pointed out that the plan of building book-shelves into the walls is the most decorative and the most practical (see plate 48). The best examples of this treatment are found in France. The walls of the rooms thus decorated were usually of panelled wood, either in natural oak or walnut, as in the beautiful library of the old university at Nancy, or else painted in two contrasting colors, such as gray and white. When not set in recesses, the shelves formed a sort of continuous lining around the walls, as in the library of Louis XVI in the palace at Versailles (see plate 47), or in that of the Duc de Choiseul at Chanteloup,[7] now set up in one of the rooms of the public library at Tours.

6. Stiff fabric, usually cotton or linen, used in bookbinding. Tree calf: calfskin treated with chemicals to produce a tree-like design for book bindings; the authors clearly disapprove of this style (M-W).

7. Étienne-François, Duc de Choiseul (1719–85): under the title Count de Stainville, began his career in the French military during the War of Austrian Succession (1740–48). Gained admittance to King Louis XV's circle of nobles after the

In either case, instead of being detached pieces of furniture, the bookcases formed an organic part of the wall-decoration. Any study of old French works on house-decoration and furniture will show how seldom the detached bookcase was used in French libraries: but few models are to be found, and these were probably designed for use in the boudoir or study, rather than in the library proper (see bookcase in plate 5).

In England, where private libraries were fewer and less extensive, the movable bookcase was much used, and examples of built-in shelves are proportionately rarer. The hand-books of the old English cabinet-makers contain innumerable models of handsome bookcases, with glazed doors set with diamond-shaped panes in wooden mouldings, and the familiar broken pediment surmounted by a bust or an urn. It was natural that where books were few, small bookcases should be preferred to a room lined with shelves; and in the seventeenth century, according to John Evelyn,[8] the "three nations of Great Britain" contained fewer books than Paris.

Almost all the old bookcases had one feature in common: that is, the lower cupboard with solid doors. The bookcase proper rested upon this projecting cupboard, thus raising the books above the level of the furniture. The prevalent fashion of low book-shelves, starting from the floor, and not extending much higher than the dado-moulding, has probably been brought about by the other recent fashion of low-studded rooms. Architects are beginning to rediscover the forgotten

war and was named Duke of Choiseul in 1758, the same year Louis XV designated him secretary of state for foreign affairs. Choiseul would dominate the domestic and foreign politics of France during his time serving the king (*EB* 2024a). Châteaux de Chanteloup: eighteenth-century French château with elaborate gardens, compared by contemporaries to Versailles; located in the Loire Valley on the south bank of the Loire River. From 1761 to 1785 Chanteloup belonged to the Duke of Choiseul.

8. John Evelyn (1620–1706): English country gentleman who wrote about thirty books concerning the fine arts, forestry, and religion. Evelyn served on a variety of commissions under King Charles II after the monarchy was restored in 1660 and became a lifelong member of the Royal Society. His *Diary*, begun at age eleven and continued for over fifty years, is a rich source of information on the politics, culture, and religious practices of seventeenth-century England (*EB* 2020o).

fact that the stud of a room should be regulated by the dimensions of its floor-space; so that in the newer houses the dwarf bookcase is no longer a necessity. It is certainly less convenient than the tall old-fashioned press; for not only must one kneel to reach the lower shelves, but the books are hidden, and access to them is obstructed, by their being on a level with the furniture.

The general decoration of the library should be of such character as to form a background or setting to the books, rather than to distract attention from them. The richly adorned room in which books are but a minor incident is, in fact, no library at all. There is no reason why the decorations of a library should not be splendid; but in that case the books must be splendid too, and sufficient in number to dominate all the accessory decorations of the room.

When there are books enough, it is best to use them as part of the decorative treatment of the walls, panelling any intervening spaces in a severe and dignified style; otherwise movable bookcases may be placed against the more important wall-spaces, the walls being decorated with wooden panelling or with mouldings and stucco ornaments; but in this case composition and color-scheme must be so subdued as to throw the bookcases and their contents into marked relief. It does not follow that because books are the chief feature of the library, other ornaments should be excluded; but they should be used with discrimination, and so chosen as to harmonize with the spirit of the room. Nowhere is the modern litter of knick-knacks and photographs more inappropriate than in the library. The tables should be large, substantial, and clear of everything but lamps, books and papers—one table at least being given over to the filing of books and newspapers. The library writing-table is seldom large enough, or sufficiently free from odds and ends in the shape of photograph-frames, silver boxes, and flower-vases, to give free play to the elbows. A large solid table of the kind called *bureau-ministre*[9] (see the table in plate 47) is well adapted to

9. French: literally "minister's desk," traditionally a substantial wooden one with drawers.

49. Writing-Chair, Louis XV Period.

the library; and in front of it should stand a comfortable writing-chair such as that represented in plate 49.

The housing of a great private library is one of the most interesting problems of interior architecture. Such a room, combining monumental dimensions with the rich color-values and impressive effect produced by tiers of fine bindings, affords unequalled opportunity for the exercise of the architect's skill. The two-storied room with gallery and stairs and domed or vaulted ceiling is the finest setting for a great collection. Space may of course be gained by means of a series of bookcases projecting into the room and forming deep bays along each of the walls; but this arrangement is seldom necessary save in a public library, and however skilfully handled must necessarily diminish the architectural effect of the room. In America the great private library is still so much a thing of the future that its treatment need not be discussed in detail. Few of the large houses lately built in the United States contain a library in the serious meaning of the term; but it is to be hoped that the next generation of architects will have wider opportunities in this direction.[10]

The smoking-room proper, with its *mise en scène* of Turkish divans, narghilehs,[11] brass coffee-trays, and other Oriental properties, is no longer considered a necessity in the modern house; and the room which would formerly have been used for this special purpose now comes rather under the head of the master's lounging-room, or "den"—since the latter word seems to have attained the dignity of a technical term.

Whatever extravagances the upholsterer may have committed in other parts of the house, it is usually conceded that common sense should regulate the furnishing of the den. Fragile chairs, lace-petticoat lamp-shades and irrelevant bric-à-brac are consequently excluded; and the master's sense of comfort often expresses itself in a set of "office" furniture—a roller-top desk,[12] a revolving chair, and others of the puffy type already described as the accepted model of a luxurious seat. Thus freed from the superfluous, the den is likely to

10. Although Edith Wharton did not always follow her own decorating advice (e.g., she did paper some of her walls), her Massachusetts estate, The Mount, constructed after the publication of this book, boasts a library "in the serious meaning of the term."

11. Divan: long couch low to the ground with no arms used for sitting or reclining (*M-W*). Narghileh: hookah (Reverso n.d.).

12. Desk, usually for writing, with various drawers and cubbies for storing paper, pens, and letters with a top that can be lowered to hide clutter (Dutch Crafters 2016).

be the most comfortable room in the house; and the natural infer-
ence is that a room, in order to be comfortable, must be ugly. One can
picture the derision of the man who is told that he might, without the
smallest sacrifice of comfort or convenience, transact his business at a
Louis XVI writing-table, seated in a Louis XVI chair!—yet the hand-
somest desks of the last century—the fine old *bureaux à la Kaunitz* or
à cylindre[13]—were the prototypes of the modern "roller-top"; and the
cane or leather-seated writing-chair, with rounded back and five slim
strong legs, was far more comfortable than the amorphous revolving
seat. Convenience was not sacrificed to beauty in either desk or chair;
but both the old pieces, being designed by skilled cabinet-makers, were
as decorative as they were useful. There seems, in fact, no reason why
the modern den should not resemble the financiers' *bureaux* seen in so
many old prints: rooms of dignified plainness, but where each line of
wall-panelling and furniture was as carefully studied and intelligently
adapted to its ends as though intended for a drawing-room or boudoir.

Reference has been made to the way in which, even in small houses,
a room may be sacrificed to a supposed "effect," or to some inherited
tradition as to its former use. Thus the family drawing-room is too
often made uninhabitable from some vague feeling that a "drawing-
room" is not worthy of its name unless too fine to sit in; while the
small front room on the ground floor—in the average American house
the only corner given over to the master—is thrown into the hall,
either that the house may appear larger and handsomer, or from sheer
inability to make so small a room habitable.

There is no reason why even a ten-by-twelve or an eight-by-
fourteen foot room should not be made comfortable; and the following
suggestions are intended to indicate the lines on which an appropriate
scheme of decoration might be carried out.

In most town houses the small room down-stairs is built with an
opening in the longitudinal wall, close to the front door, while there is

---

13. French: Kaunitz or cylinder desk. Predecessor to the rolltop desk, sometimes
referred to as a Kaunitz desk after Prince Kaunitz, who is generally believed to have
invented it. First used by Louis XV.

50. Dining-Room, Palace of Compiègne. Louis XVI Period. (Over-Doors and Over-Mantel Painted in Grisaille, by Sauvage.)

usually another entrance at the back of the room, facing the window; one at least of these openings being, as a rule, of exaggerated width. In such cases the door in the side of the room should be walled up: this gives privacy and provides enough additional wall-space for a good-sized piece of furniture.

The best way of obtaining an effect of size is to panel the walls by means of clear-cut architectural mouldings: a few strong vertical lines will give dignity to the room and height to the ceiling. The walls should be free from pattern and light in color, since dark walls necessitate much artificial light, and have the disadvantage of making a room look small.

The ceiling, if not plain, must be ornamented with the lightest tracery, and supported by a cornice correspondingly simple in design.

Heavy ceiling-mouldings are obviously out of place in a small room, and a plain expanse of plaster is always preferable to misapplied ornament.

A single curtain made of some flexible material, such as corduroy or thin unlined damask, and so hung that it may be readily drawn back during the day, is sufficient for the window; while in a corner near this window may be placed an easy-chair and a small solidly made table, large enough to hold a lamp and a book or two.

These rooms, in some recently built town houses, contain chimneys set in an angle of the wall: a misplaced attempt at quaintness, making it inconvenient to sit near the hearth, and seriously interfering with the general arrangement of the room. When the chimney occupies the centre of the longitudinal wall there is space, even in a very narrow room, for a group of chairs about the fireplace—provided, as we are now supposing, the opening in the parallel wall has been closed. A book-case or some other high piece of furniture may be placed on each side of the mantel, and there will be space opposite for a sofa and a good-sized writing-table. If the pieces of furniture chosen are in scale with the dimensions of the room, and are placed against the wall, instead of being set sideways, with the usual easel or palm-tree behind them, it is surprising to see how much a small room may contain without appearing to be overcrowded.

13

The Dining-Room

The dining-room, as we know it, is a comparatively recent innovation in house-planning. In the early middle ages the noble and his retainers ate in the hall; then the *grand'salle*, built for ceremonial uses, began to serve as a banqueting-room, while the meals eaten in private were served in the lord's chamber. As house-planning adapted itself to the growing complexity of life, the mediæval bedroom developed into a private suite of living-rooms, preceded by an antechamber; and this antechamber, or one of the small adjoining cabinets, was used as the family dining-room, the banqueting-hall being still reserved for state entertainments.

The plan of dining at haphazard in any of the family living-rooms persisted on the Continent until the beginning of the eighteenth century: even then it was comparatively rare, in France, to see a room set apart for the purpose of dining. In small *hôtels* and apartments, people continued to dine in the antechamber; where there were two antechambers, the inner was used for that purpose; and it was only in grand houses, or in the luxurious establishments of the *femmes galantes*,[1] that dining-rooms were to be found. Even in such cases the room described as a *salle à manger*[2] was often only a central antechamber or saloon into which the living-rooms opened; indeed, Madame du Barry's sumptuous dining-room at Luciennes[3] was a vestibule giving directly upon the peristyle of the villa.

1. French: courtesans (*WordSense Dictionary*; *M-W*). A term raised by Edith Wharton and Ogden Codman in an original footnote to chapter ten.

2. French: dining room.

3. Also called Pavillon de Louveciennes. Palace given to Madame du Barry by Louis XV in 1769, decorated and refurbished by Charles-Nicolas Ledoux (1736–1806) (Campbell 1995; Goncourt 1914).

In England the act of dining seems to have been taken more seriously, while the rambling outgrowths of the Elizabethan residence included a greater variety of rooms than could be contained in any but the largest houses built on more symmetrical lines. Accordingly, in old English house-plans we find rooms designated as "dining-parlors"; many houses, in fact, contained two or three, each with a different exposure, so that they might be used at different seasons. These rooms can hardly be said to represent our modern dining-room, since they were not planned in connection with kitchen and offices, and were probably used as living-rooms when not needed for dining. Still, it was from the Elizabethan dining-parlor that the modern dining-room really developed; and so recently has it been specialized into a room used only for eating, that a generation ago old-fashioned people in England and America habitually used their dining-rooms to sit in. On the Continent the incongruous uses of the rooms in which people dined made it necessary that the furniture should be easily removed. In the middle ages, people dined at long tables composed of boards resting on trestles, while the seats were narrow wooden benches or stools, so constructed that they could easily be carried away when the meal was over. With the sixteenth century, the *table-à-tréteaux*[4] gave way to various folding tables with legs, and the wooden stools were later replaced by folding seats without arms, called *perroquets*. In the middle ages, when banquets were given in the *grand'salle*, the plate was displayed on movable shelves covered with a velvet slip, or on elaborately carved dressers; but on ordinary occasions little silver was set out in French dining-rooms, and the great English side-board,[5] with

4. French: trestle table, or a table supported by a braced frame (Reverso n.d.; *M-W*).

5. Substantial piece of dining room furniture, usually with shortened legs and set against a wall, used to display plates, decanters, side dishes, and other objects associated with dining. It was first used in the Middle Ages to display valuable utensils, and by the nineteenth century the sideboard was routinely used in dining room décor. At the height of her career, Edith Wharton was (disparagingly) described by critic Vernon Parrington as being "finished as a Sheraton sideboard" (Parrington 2010, 293–95; *EB* 2024d).

51. Dining-Room Fountain, Palace of Fontainebleau. Louis XV Period.

its array of urns, trays and wine-coolers, was unknown in France. In the common antechamber dining-room, whatever was needed for the table was kept in a press or cupboard with solid wooden doors; changes of service being carried on by means of serving-tables, or *servantes*— narrow marble-topped consoles ranged against the walls of the room.

For examples of dining-rooms, as we understand the term, one must look to the grand French houses of the eighteenth century (see plate 50) and to the same class of dwellings in England. In France such dining-rooms were usually intended for gala entertainments, the family being still served in antechamber or cabinet; but English houses of the same period generally contain a family dining-room and another intended for state.

The dining-room of Madame du Barry at Luciennes, already referred to, was a magnificent example of the great dining-saloon. The ceiling was a painted Olympus; the white marble walls were subdivided by Corinthian[6] pilasters with plinths and capitals of gilt bronze, surmounted by a frieze of bas-reliefs framed in gold; four marble niches contained statues by Pajou, Lecomte, and Moineau;[7] and the general brilliancy of effect was increased by crystal chandeliers, hung in the intercolumniations against a background of looking-glass.

Such a room, the banqueting-hall of the official mistress, represents the *courtisane's*[8] ideal of magnificence: decorations as splendid, but more sober and less theatrical, marked the dining-rooms of the aristocracy, as at Choisy, Gaillon and Rambouillet.[9]

6. One of the three orders of ancient Greek architecture. The lightest and most ornate of the orders, it is known for its large capitals stylized with acanthus leaves (*M-W*).

7. Félix Lecomte (1737–1817): French sculptor active in the second half of the eighteenth century; Edmond de Goncourt's book *Madame du Barry* cites a sculptor named Moineau.

8. French: courtesan.

9. Château de Choisy, also Château de Choisy-le-Roi: property located near Paris and bought in 1680 by La Grande Mademoiselle, Anne-Marie-Louise d'Orléans (1627–93), who had it demolished and rebuilt to her taste. After belonging to Le Grand Dauphin (1661–1711) and later Marie Anne de Bourbon (1666–1739), Louis XV purchased it in 1739 as a refuge for himself and Madame de Pompadour (1721–64), who was gifted the property in 1746. Its decoration was simple, especially in contrast to Versailles. During the French Revolution, it was confiscated by the new regime and its furniture sold off, causing the château to fall into disrepair; all that remains is its two pavilions (Schmidt 2013). Château de Gaillon: first a medieval fortress in Normandy, rebuilt in 1502 by Georges I d'Amboise, cardinal-archbishop of Rouen and minister of Louis XII in the Renaissance style. Considered the first Renaissance château in France, it is best known for its gardens, redesigned in 1692 by

The state dining-rooms of the eighteenth century were often treated with an order, niches with statues being placed between the pilasters. Sometimes one of these niches contained a fountain serving as a wine-cooler—a survival of the stone or metal wall-fountains in which dishes were washed in the mediæval dining-room. Many of these earlier fountains had been merely fixed to the wall; but those of the eighteenth century, though varying greatly in design, were almost always an organic part of the wall-decoration (see plate 51). Sometimes, in apartments of importance, they formed the pedestal of a life-size group or statue, as in the dining-room of Madame de Pompadour;[10] while in smaller rooms they consisted of a semicircular basin of marble projecting from the wall and surmounted by groups of cupids, dolphins or classic attributes. The banqueting-gallery of Trianon-sous-Bois[11] contains in one of its longitudinal walls two wide

---

André Le Nôtre, and its excellent fountain in the center of the courtyard (Campbell 2009). Rambouillet: Château de Rambouillet, estate in northern France dating before the fourteenth century but restored after the Hundred Years' War (1337–1453). A French courtier and financier, Fleuriau d'Amernonville, bought the property in 1699 and had built a series of garden canals and pools that partially survive today. It was bought in 1783 by Louis XVI, who had built La Laiterie de la Reine, designed by Jacques-Jean Thévenin, for Marie-Antoinette. This garden building is considered among the finest of other eighteenth-century French designs (Taylor 2006).

10. Jeanne-Antoinette Poisson, marquise de Pompadour (1721–64): mistress of Louis XV and patron of literature and art. Her daughter, Alexandrine, by husband Charles-Guillaume Le Normant d'Étoiles, was a favorite among Parisian society, gaining special notice of Louis XV. When Louis XV's wife suddenly died, he quickly adopted Madame d'Étoiles as his mistress, who subsequently procured a legal separation from her husband and was named marquise de Pompadour. Historians had for some time ascribed considerable political influence to Madame de Pompadour but more recent analysis shows the king had relative autonomy. Collaborated with the king and her brother on the building and decorating of several high-profile buildings, including the palace of Compiègne, the Petit Trianon Palace at Versailles, and Château de Bellevue. Her twenty years at the side of Louis XV is considered the pinnacle of French taste (Mitford n.d.).

11. Wing of the Grand Trianon, baroque style château of the Palace of Versailles, which was commissioned by Louis XIV in 1670, designed by Jules Hardouin-Mansart

niches with long marble basins; and Mariette's edition of d'Aviler's *Cours d'Architecture*[12] gives the elevation of a recessed buffet flanked by small niches containing fountains. The following description, accompanying d'Aviler's plate, is quoted here as an instance of the manner in which elaborate compositions were worked out by the old decorators: "The second antechamber, being sometimes used as a dining-room, is a suitable place for the buffet represented. This buffet, which may be incrusted with marble or stone, or panelled with wood-work, consists in a recess occupying one of the side walls of the room. The recess contains a shelf of marble or stone, supported on brackets and surmounting a small stone basin which serves as a wine-cooler. Above the shelf is an attic flanked by volutes, and over this attic may be placed a picture, generally a flower or fruit-piece, or the representation of a concert, or some such agreeable scene; while in the accompanying plate the attic is crowned by a bust of Comus,[13] wreathed with vines by two little satyrs—the group detaching itself against a trellised

---

(1646–1708), and completed 1687. The Trianon-sous-Bois wing was built in 1708, again by Hardouin-Mansart, as the palace had grown too small for Louis XIV's family. Simple and elegant, the Trianon-sous-Bois wing embodies the prevailing style of eighteenth-century architecture (Château de Versailles n.d.).

    12. Pierre-Jean Mariette (1694–1774): French print dealer, publisher, collector, and writer. Son of Jean Mariette (1660–1742), author of *L'Architecture française*, published in five volumes in 1727. An expert drawer and printer, Pierre-Jean Mariette was also extremely knowledgeable on art history. In his later life, Mariette focused on becoming a historian and connoisseur, and amassed an impressive collection of high-quality drawings and engravings. The Mariette family owned and operated a printing and publishing business and were engravers, collectors, and writers, spanning four generations during the seventeenth and eighteenth centuries (Walsh 2003). *Cours d'Architecture*: volume on architecture first published in 1691 by Augustin-Charles d'Aviler (1653–1701), French architect and writer. A wide success, *Cours d'Architecture* features many plates illustrating various types of buildings as well as an exhaustive glossary of architectural terms. D'Aviler worked closely with Jules Hardouin-Mansart on the Château de Versailles for about eight years and continued to have a prolific career as an architect (Skliar-Piguet 2003).

    13. Greek god of festivities and revelry, son of Dionysus, appearing in late antiquity (Theoi Greek Mythology n.d.).

52. Dining-Chair, Louis XIV Period.

background enlivened with birds. The composition is completed by
two lateral niches for fountains, adorned with masks, tritons and dolphins of gilded lead."

These built-in sideboards and fountains were practically the only
feature distinguishing the old dining-rooms from other gala apartments. At a period when all rooms were painted, panelled, or hung

53. Dining-Chair, Louis XVI Period.

with tapestry, no special style of decoration was thought needful for the dining-room; though tapestry was seldom used, for the practical reason that stuff hangings are always objectionable in a room intended for eating.

Towards the end of the seventeenth century, when comfortable seats began to be made, an admirably designed dining-room chair replaced the earlier benches and *perroquets*. The eighteenth century dining-chair is now often confounded with the light *chaise volante*[14] used in drawing-rooms, and cabinet-makers frequently sell the latter as copies of old dining-chairs. These were in fact much heavier and more comfortable, and whether cane-seated or upholstered, were invariably made with wide deep seats, so that the long banquets of the day might be endured without constraint or fatigue; while the backs were low and narrow, in order not to interfere with the service of the table. (See plates 52 and 53. Plates 46 and 50 also contain good examples of dining-chairs.) In England the state dining-room was decorated much as it was in France: the family dining-room was simply a plain parlor, with wide mahogany sideboards or tall glazed cupboards for the display of plate and china. The solid English dining-chairs of mahogany, if less graceful than those used on the Continent, are equally well adapted to their purpose.

The foregoing indications may serve to suggest the lines upon which dining-room decoration might be carried out in the present day. The avoidance of all stuff hangings and heavy curtains is of great importance: it will be observed that even window-curtains were seldom used in old dining-rooms, such care being given to the decorative detail of window and embrasure that they needed no additional ornament in the way of drapery. A bare floor of stone or marble is best suited to the dining-room; but where the floor is covered, it should be with a rug, not with a nailed-down carpet.

The dining-room should be lit by wax candles in side *appliques* or in a chandelier; and since anything tending to produce heat and to exhaust air is especially objectionable in a room used for eating, the walls should be sufficiently light in color to make little artificial light necessary. In the dining-rooms of the last century, in England as well

14. French: literally "flying chair"; in the context of a drawing room, possibly a wingback chair (Château de Versailles n.d.).

as on the Continent, the color-scheme was usually regulated by this principle: the dark dining-room panelled with mahogany or hung with sombre leather is an invention of our own times. It has already been said that the old family dining-room was merely a panelled parlor. Sometimes the panels were of light unvarnished oak, but oftener they were painted in white or in some pale tint easily lit by wax candles. The walls were often hung with fruit or flower-pieces, or with pictures of fish and game: a somewhat obvious form of adornment which it has long been the fashion to ridicule, but which was not without decorative value and appropriateness. Pictures representing life and action often grow tiresome when looked at over and over again, day after day: a fact which the old decorators probably had in mind when they hung what the French call *natures mortes*[15] in the dining-room.

Concerning the state dining-room that forms a part of many modern houses little remains to be said beyond the descriptions already given of the various gala apartments. It is obvious that the banqueting-hall should be less brilliant than a ball-room and less fanciful in decoration than a music-room: a severer and more restful treatment naturally suggests itself, but beyond this no special indications are required.

The old dining-rooms were usually heated by porcelain stoves. Such a stove, of fine architectural design, set in a niche corresponding with that which contains the fountain, is of great decorative value in the composition of the room; and as it has the advantage of giving out less concentrated heat than an open fire, it is specially well suited to a small or narrow dining-room, where some of the guests must necessarily sit close to the hearth.

Most houses which have banquet-halls contain also a smaller apartment called a breakfast-room; but as this generally corresponds in size and usage with the ordinary family dining-room, the same style of decoration is applicable to both. However ornate the banquet-hall may be, the breakfast-room must of course be simple and free from gilding:

---

15. French: (plural) still life. Painting or drawing including one or more inanimate objects (*M-W*).

the more elaborate the decorations of the larger room, the more restful such a contrast will be found.

Of the dinner-table, as we now know it, little need be said. The ingenious but ugly extension-table[16] with a central support, now used all over the world, is an English invention. There seems no reason why the general design should not be improved without interfering with the mechanism of this table; but of course it can never be so satisfactory to the eye as one of the old round or square tables, with four or six tapering legs, such as were used in eighteenth-century dining-rooms before the induction of the "extension."

16. Table whose length can be extended with a leaf. As evident in the dining room at The Mount, Wharton's historic home, a round table is preferable as it does not allow for a head of table per se (*M-W*).

14

Bedrooms

The history of the bedroom has been incidentally touched upon in tracing the development of the drawing-room from the mediæval hall. It was shown that early in the middle ages the sleeping-chamber, which had been one of the first outgrowths of the hall, was divided into the *chambre de parade*,[1] or incipient drawing-room, and the *chambre au giste*, or actual sleeping-room.

The increasing development of social life in the sixteenth century brought about a further change; the state bedroom being set aside for entertainments of ceremony, while the sleeping-chamber was used as the family living-room and as the scene of suppers, card-parties, and informal receptions—or sometimes actually as the kitchen. Indeed, so varied were the uses to which the *chambre au giste* was put, that in France especially it can hardly be said to have offered a refuge from the promiscuity of the hall.

As a rule, the bedrooms of the Renaissance and of the seventeenth century were very richly furnished. The fashion of raising the bed on a dais separated from the rest of the room by columns and a balustrade was introduced in France in the time of Louis XIV. This innovation gave rise to the habit of dividing the decoration of the room into two parts; the walls being usually panelled or painted, while the "alcove," as it was called, was hung in tapestry, velvet, or some rich stuff in keeping with the heavy curtains that completely enveloped the bedstead.

1. French: the authors distinguish between the "state bedroom in which no one slept" (as they define *chambre de parade* in chapter 10) and the actual sleeping chamber.

54. Bedroom, Palace of Fontainebleau. Louis XIV Period (Louis XVI Bed and Chair, Modern Sofa.)

This use of stuff hangings about the bed, so contrary to our ideas of bedroom hygiene, was due to the difficulty of heating the large high-studded rooms of the period, and also, it must be owned, to the prevalent dread of fresh air as of something essentially unwholesome and pernicious.[2]

2. The miasma theory of diseases was the predominant way in which people explained sickness, believing unpleasant odors made a person ill. This theory was defended by many nineteenth-century physicians who associated epidemics in urban areas with filthy conditions that contributed to noxious smells. Increased efforts in public sanitation during this era both reduced bad odors and the frequency of disease, further "proof" of the miasma theory. Before the emergence of scientific germ theory, many Americans additionally believed in "bad air" and "good air," apart from

In the early middle ages people usually slept on the floor; though it would seem that occasionally, to avoid cold or dampness, the mattress was laid on cords stretched upon a low wooden framework. In the fourteenth century the use of such frameworks became more general, and the bed was often enclosed in curtains hung from a tester resting on four posts. Bed-hangings and coverlet were often magnificently embroidered; but in order that it might not be necessary to transport from place to place the unwieldy bedstead and tester, these were made in the rudest manner, without attempt at carving or adornment. In course of time this primitive framework developed into the sumptuous four-post bedstead of the Renaissance, with elaborately carved cornice and *colonnes torses*[3] enriched with gilding. Thenceforward more wealth and skill were expended upon the bedstead than upon any other article of furniture. Gilding, carving, and inlaying of silver, ivory or mother-of-pearl, combined to adorn the framework, and embroidery made the coverlet and hangings resplendent as church vestments. This magnificence is explained by the fact that it was customary for the lady of the house to lie in bed while receiving company. In many old prints representing suppers, card-parties, or afternoon visits, the hostess is thus seen, with elaborately dressed head and stiff brocade gown, while her friends are grouped about the bedside in equally rich attire. This curious custom persisted until late in the eighteenth century and under such conditions it was natural that the old cabinet-makers should vie with each other in producing a variety

---

odors. Nighttime air was traditionally considered bad for being cold and possibly damp, but in the advent of germ theory, the nineteenth century saw an increase in ventilation (especially by fireplace) of the bedrooms, which would preclude the use of heavy bed hangings. Additionally, since the metabolic process of respiration was discovered in the late eighteenth century, many were afraid bed-curtains would prevent oxygen from entering one's sleeping space, causing the person to breathe in their released carbon dioxide, potentially resulting in death. This belief was held into the 1870s and 1880s. See Henry James's *Daisy Miller* and Edith Wharton's "Roman Fever" for literary examples (Magner 2009; Mey 1991, 458).

    3. French: twisted columns.

of ornate and fanciful bedsteads. It would be useless to enumerate here the modifications in design marking the different periods of decoration: those who are interested in the subject will find it treated in detail in the various French works on furniture.

It was natural that while the bedroom was used as a *salon* it should be decorated with more elaboration than would otherwise have been fitting; but two causes combined to simplify its treatment in the eighteenth century. One of these was the new fashion of *petits appartements*. With artists so keenly alive to proportion as the old French designers, it was inevitable that such a change in dimensions should bring about a corresponding change in decoration. The bedrooms of the eighteenth century, though sometimes elaborate in detail, had none of the pompous richness of the great Renaissance or Louis XIV room (see plate 54). The pretentious dais with its screen of columns was replaced by a niche containing the bed; plain wood-panelling succeeded to tapestry and embroidered hangings; and the heavy carved ceiling with its mythological centre-picture made way for light traceries on plaster.

The other change in the decoration of French bedrooms was due to the substitution of linen or cotton bed and window-hangings for the sumptuous velvets and brocades of the seventeenth century. This change has usually been ascribed to the importation of linens and cottons from the East; and no doubt the novelty of these gay *indiennes*[4] stimulated the taste for simple hangings. The old inventories, however, show that, in addition to the imported India hangings, plain white linen curtains with a colored border were much used; and it is probably the change in the size of rooms that first led to the adoption of thin washable hangings. The curtains and bed-draperies of damask or brocatelle,[5] so well suited to the high-studded rooms of the seventeenth century, would have been out of place in the small apartments of the Regency. In studying the history of decoration, it will generally be found that the supposed vagaries of house-furnishing were

4. From the French for "Indian." A light cotton fabric with designs, printed or painted, inspired by Indian textiles (*M-W*).

5. Stiff fabric with patterns in high relief (*M-W*).

actually based on some practical requirement; and in this instance the old decorators were doubtless guided rather by common sense than by caprice. The adoption of these washable materials certainly introduced a style of bedroom-furnishing answering to all the requirements of recent hygiene;[6] for not only were windows and bedsteads hung with unlined cotton or linen, but chairs and sofas were covered with removable *housses*,[7] or slip-covers; while the painted wall-panelling and bare brick or parquet floors came far nearer to the modern sanitary ideal than do the papered walls and nailed-down carpets still seen in many bedrooms. This simple form of decoration had the additional charm of variety; for it was not unusual to have several complete sets of curtains and slip-covers, embroidered to match, and changed with the seasons. The hangings and covers of the queen's bedroom at Versailles were changed four times a year.

Although bedrooms are still "done" in chintz, and though of late especially there has been a reaction from the satin-damask bedroom with its dust-collecting upholstery and knick-knacks, the modern habit of lining chintz curtains and of tufting chairs has done away with the chief advantages of the simpler style of treatment. There is something illogical in using washable stuffs in such a way that they cannot be washed, especially in view of the fact that the heavily lined curtains, which might be useful to exclude light and cold, are in nine cases out of ten so hung by the upholsterer that they cannot possibly be drawn

---

6. Advances in technology and medicine throughout the nineteenth century brought about the development of the germ theory of disease. By the 1840s, scientists had theorized that the air contained small microbes that contributed to disease and putrefaction. This is aligned somewhat with miasma theory, the difference being that germ theory hypothesized (correctly) that it was not the air itself, but something in it, that makes people sick. In 1876 scientist Robert Koch discovered the organism that causes anthrax, and soon afterward identified the bacteria of tuberculosis and cholera. At the time of this publication, the filtration of bacteria to prevent illness was becoming more widely accepted and practiced; and in 1896, one year before publication, scientist Martinus Willem Beijerinck correctly theorized the existence of filterable viruses (Hardy 2003).

7. French: covers.

at night. Besides, the patterns of modern chintzes have so little in common with the *toiles imprimées*[8] of the seventeenth and eighteenth centuries that they scarcely serve the same decorative purpose, and it is therefore needful to give some account of the old French bedroom hangings, as well as of the manner in which they were employed.

The liking for *cotonnades*[9] showed itself in France early in the seventeenth century. Before this, cotton materials had been imported from the East; but in the seventeenth century a manufactory was established in France, and until about 1800 cotton and linen curtains and furniture-coverings remained in fashion. This taste was encouraged by the importation of the *toiles des Indes*,[10] printed cottons of gay color and fanciful design, much sought after in France, especially after the government, in order to protect native industry, had restricted the privilege of importing them to the *Compagnie des Indes*.[11] It was not until Oberkampf established his manufactory at Jouy[12] in 1760 that

8. French: printed canvas.

9. French: (plural) *cotonnade*. Pure or blended woven cotton fabrics with checks or stripes (TLFi n.d.).

10. French: Indian fabrics.

11. French: Company of the Indies, also known as the French East India Company from 1664 to 1719 and Company of the Indies from 1720 to 1789, referring to the various French trading companies of the seventeenth and eighteenth centuries to supervise French trading in India, East Africa, and territories in the Indian Ocean and the East Indies. Due to competition from the Dutch East India Company and the British East India Company, the Compagnie des Indes failed to be as successful and lucrative, and was dissolved during the French Revolution, in 1794. (Year cited on same Petit Robert page, also verified in facsimile of French legal documents [Ménard et Desenne 1826, 397].) (*EB* 2013a).

12. Christophe-Philippe Oberkampf (1738–1815): German-born French textile manufacturer and industrialist. Born to a family in the textile trade, he began his career as an engraver and colorist in Paris in 1758. In 1760 he opened his own workshop for printed fabrics in Jouy-en-Josas, a village near Versailles. This workshop soon became one of the most successful textile factories in France, owing its success to its products' fine quality and Oberkampf's incorporation of the latest scientific advancements, such as copperplate printing and later roller printing. The year 1783 became an important year for Jouy: the factory was named Manufacture Royale and

the French *toiles* began to replace those of foreign manufacture. Hitherto the cottons made in France had been stamped merely in outline, the colors being filled in by hand; but Oberkampf invented a method of printing in colors, thereby making France the leading market for such stuffs.

The earliest printed cottons having been imported from India and China, it was natural that the style of the Oriental designers should influence their European imitators. Europe had, in fact, been prompt to recognize the singular beauty of Chinese art, and in France the passion for *chinoiseries*, first aroused by Mazarin's[13] collection of Oriental objects of art, continued unabated until the general decline of taste at the end of the eighteenth century. Nowhere, perhaps, was the influence of Chinese art more beneficial to European designers than in the composition of stuff-patterns. The fantastic gaiety and variety of Chinese designs, in which the human figure so largely predominates, gave fresh animation to European compositions, while the absence of perspective and modelling preserved that conventionalism so essential in pattern-designing. The voluminous acanthus-leaves, the fleur-de-lys, arabesques[14] and massive scroll-work so suitable to the Genoese velvets and Lyons silks[15] of the sixteenth and seventeenth centuries,

---

started a successful twenty-eight-year collaboration with Jean-Baptiste Huet I, who introduced the monochrome neoclassical and genre scene prints that would become synonymous with Jouy (Browne 2003).

13. Jules Mazarin (1602–61): also known as Giulio Raimondo Mazzarino or Mazarini, minister of France during the early rule of Louis XIV. Born in Italy to a family with ties to the Colonna house, Mazarin completed a Jesuit education in Rome and studied law in Madrid, later becoming secretary to Cardinal Richelieu. Mazarin's lifelong goal was to negotiate peace between Spain and France (Dethan 2020).

14. Decorative and architectural motif of *Acanthus spinosus*, a common plant of the Mediterranean with jagged leaves; seen often on capitals of the Corinthian column, especially in the Temple of Olympian Zeus in Athens (*EB* 2016a). Fleur-de-lys, or fleur-de-lis: French for "lily flower." Before the Middle Ages, a Roman Catholic symbol for purity, associated with the Virgin Mary. In French heraldry, a symbol of the French crown in use since the fifth century (*EB* 2017c).

15. Material produced in Genoa, known for its superior quality, especially its black velvet which was particularly luxurious (Watt 2011). Lyon silk: Lyon became

would have been far too magnificent for the cotton stuffs that were beginning to replace those splendid tissues. On a thin material a heavy architectural pattern was obviously inappropriate; besides, it would have been out of scale with the smaller rooms and lighter style of decoration then coming into fashion.

The French designer, while influenced by Chinese compositions, was too artistic to be satisfied with literal reproductions of his Oriental models. Absorbing the spirit of the Chinese designs, he either blent mandarins and pagodas[16] with Italian grottoes, French landscapes, and classical masks and trophies, in one of those delightful inventions which are the fairy-tales of decorative art, or applied the principles of Oriental design to purely European subjects. In comparing the printed cottons of the seventeenth and eighteenth centuries with modern chintzes, it will be seen that the latter are either covered with monotonous repetitions of a geometrical figure, or with realistic reproductions of some natural object. Many wall-papers and chintzes of the present day represent loose branches of flowers scattered on a plain surface, with no more relation to each other or to their background than so many real flowers fixed at random against the wall. This literal rendering of natural objects with deceptive accuracy, always condemned by the best artists, is especially inappropriate when brought in close contact with the highly conventionalized forms of architectural composition. In this respect, the endlessly repeated geometrical figure is obviously less objectionable; yet the geometrical design, as produced to-day, has one defect in common with the other—that is, lack of imagination. Modern draughtsmen[17] in eliminating from their work that fanciful element (always strictly subordinated to some general scheme of composition) which marked the designs of the last two

---

the center of silk production in France after a reorganization of the industry in the seventeenth century by Jean-Baptiste Colbert (1619–83), superintendent of finance under Louis XIV (Watt 2003).

16. Tower, often a temple or memorial, of several stories common in eastern Asia that at each story has a roof with tips curved upward (M-W).

17. British spelling of *draftsmen*, makers of plans and sketches (M-W).

centuries, have deprived themselves of the individuality and freshness that might have saved their patterns from monotony.

This rejection of the fanciful in composition is probably due to the excessive use of pattern in modern decoration. Where much pattern is used, it must be as monotonous as possible, or it will become unbearable. The old decorators used few lines, and permitted themselves more freedom in design; or rather they remembered, what is now too often forgotten, that in the decoration of a room furniture and objects of art help to make design, and in consequence they were chiefly concerned with providing plain spaces of background to throw into relief the contents of the room. Of late there has been so marked a return to plain panelled or painted walls that the pattern-designer will soon be encouraged to give freer rein to his fancy. In a room where walls and floor are of uniform tint, there is no reason why the design of curtains and chair-coverings should consist of long straight rows of buttercups or crocuses, endlessly repeated.

It must not be thought that the old designs were unconventional. Nature, in passing through the medium of the imagination, is necessarily transposed and in a manner conventionalized; and it is this transposition, this deliberate selection of certain characteristics to the exclusion of others, that distinguishes the work of art from a cast or a photograph. But the reduction of natural objects to geometrical forms is only one of the results of artistic selection. The Italian fresco-painters—the recognized masters of wall-decoration in the flat—always used the naturalistic method, but subject to certain restrictions in composition or color. This applies also to the Chinese designers, and to the humbler European pattern-makers who on more modest lines followed the same sound artistic traditions. In studying the *toiles peintes*[18] manufactured in Europe previous to the present century, it will be seen that where the design included the human figure or landscape naturalistically treated (as in the fables of Æsop and La Fontaine,

18. French: painted fabric or canvases.

or the history of Don Quixote),[19] the pattern was either printed entirely in one color, or so fantastically colored that by no possibility could it pass for an attempt at a literal rendering of nature. Besides, in all such compositions (and here the Chinese influence is seen) perspective was studiously avoided, and the little superimposed groups or scenes were either connected by some decorative arabesque, or so designed that by their outline they formed a recurring pattern. On the other hand, when the design was obviously conventional a variety of colors was freely used. The introduction of the human figure, animals, architecture and landscape into stuff-patterns undoubtedly gave to the old designs an animation lacking in those of the present day; and a return to the *pays bleu* of the Chinese artist would be a gain to modern decoration.

Of the various ways in which a bedroom may be planned, none is so luxurious and practical as the French method of subdividing it into a suite composed of two or more small rooms. Where space is not restricted there should in fact be four rooms, preceded by an ante-chamber separating the suite from the main corridor of the house. The small sitting-room or boudoir opens into this antechamber; and next comes the bedroom, beyond which are the dressing and bath rooms. In French suites of this kind there are usually but two means of entrance from the main corridor: one for the use of the occupant, leading into the antechamber, the other opening into the bath-room,

19. Aesop: traditionally understood to be a Greek slave who lived around 600 BCE to whom various fables are attributed, most notably "The Fox and the Grapes" and "The City Mouse and the Country Mouse." These fables feature animals that behave like people, showcasing common human vices and virtues in a comedic way (Alexander 2006). La Fontaine: Jean de La Fontaine (1621–95), French poet known for his *Fables*, twelve books published in three collections based on Aesop's fables and, later, East Asian tradition (Sykes 2020). *Don Quixote*: novel by Miguel de Cervantes (1547–1616) published in two parts in 1602 and 1615. Cervantes intended his novel to be a parody of the chivalric romances, recounting the adventures of the knight Don Quixote and his squire Sancho Panza (*EB* 2020i).

55. Bath-Room, Pitti Palace, Florence. Late XVIII Century. Decorated by Cacialli.

to give access to the servants. This arrangement, besides giving greater privacy, preserves much valuable wall-space, which would be sacrificed in America to the supposed necessity of making every room in a house open upon one of the main passageways.

The plan of the bedroom suite can of course be carried out only in large houses; but even where there is no lack of space, such an arrangement is seldom adopted by American architects; and most of the more important houses recently built contain immense bedrooms, instead of a series of suites. To enumerate the practical advantages of the suite over the single large room hardly comes within the scope of this book; but as the uses to which a bedroom is put fall into certain natural sub-divisions, it will be more convenient to consider it as a suite.

Since bedrooms are no longer used as *salons*, there is no reason for decorating them in an elaborate manner; and, however magnificent the other apartments, it is evident that in this part of the house simplicity is most fitting. Now that people have been taught the unhealthiness of sleeping in a room with stuff hangings, heavy window-draperies and tufted furniture, the old fashion of painted walls and bare floors natu-rally commends itself; and as the bedroom suite is but the subdivision of one large room, it is obviously better that the same style of decora-tion should be used throughout.

For this reason, plain panelled walls and chintz or cotton hangings are more appropriate to the boudoir than silk and gilding. If the walls are without pattern, a figured chintz may be chosen for curtains and furniture; while those who prefer plain tints should use unbleached cotton, trimmed with bands of color, or some colored linen with applications of gimp or embroidery. It is a good plan to cover all the chairs and sofas in the bedroom suite with slips matching the window-curtains; but where this is done, the furniture should, if possible, be designed for the purpose, since the lines of modern upholstered chairs are not suited to slips. The habit of designing furniture for slip-covers originated in the middle ages. At a time when the necessity of trans-porting furniture was added to the other difficulties of travel, it was usual to have common carpenter-built benches and tables, that might be left behind without risk, and to cover these with richly embroidered slips. The custom persisted long after furniture had ceased to be a part of luggage, and the benches and *tabourets*[20] now seen in many Euro-

20. In the late seventeenth century, tabourets (also taborets) were upholstered stools for the more privileged ladies of Louis XIV's court to sit upon in the royal presence. In the following century tabourets became fashionable as household furni-ture, particularly in France and England.

pean palaces are covered merely with embroidered slips. Even when a set of furniture was upholstered with silk, it was usual, in the eighteenth century, to provide embroidered cotton covers for use in summer, while curtains of the same stuff were substituted for the heavier hangings used in winter. Old inventories frequently mention these *tentures d'été*,[21] which are well adapted to our hot summer climate.

The boudoir should contain a writing-table, a lounge or *lit de repos*, and one or two comfortable arm-chairs, while in a bedroom forming part of a suite only the bedstead and its accessories should be placed.

The pieces of furniture needed in a well-appointed dressing-room are the toilet-table, wash-stand, clothes-press and cheval-glass,[22] with the addition, if space permits, of one or two commodes or chiffonniers.[23] The designing of modern furniture of this kind is seldom satisfactory; yet many who are careful to choose simple, substantial pieces for the other rooms of the house, submit to the pretentious "bedroom suit" of bird's-eye maple or mahogany, with its wearisome irrelevance of line and its excess of cheap ornament. Any study of old bedroom furniture will make clear the inferiority of the modern manufacturer's designs. Nowhere is the old sense of proportion and fitness seen to better advantage than in the simple, admirably composed commodes and clothes-presses of the eighteenth-century bedroom.

The bath-room walls and floor should, of course, be water-proof. In the average bath-room, a tiled floor and a high wainscoting of tiles are now usually seen; and the detached enamel or porcelain bath has in most cases replaced the built-in metal tub. The bath-rooms in the larger houses recently built are, in general, lined with marble; but though the use of this substance gives opportunity for fine architectural effects, few modern bath-rooms can in this respect be compared with those seen in the great houses of Europe. The chief fault of the American bath-room is that, however splendid the materials used, the treatment is seldom architectural. A glance at the beautiful bath-room

21. French: summer wall hangings.
22. Full-length mirror on a frame that can be tilted (*M-W*).
23. Tall chest of drawers, sometimes with a mirror on top (*M-W*).

in the Pitti Palace at Florence[24] (see plate 55) will show how much effect may be produced in a small space by carefully studied composition. A mere closet is here transformed into a stately room, by that regard for harmony of parts which distinguishes interior architecture from mere decoration.[25] A bath-room lined with precious marbles, with bath and wash-stand ranged along the wall, regardless of their relation to the composition of the whole, is no better architecturally than the tiled bath-room seen in ordinary houses: design, not substance, is needed to make the one superior to the other.

24. Renaissance palace in Florence built for Luca Pitti in 1457, left unfinished by the family's dwindling fortune. Its design has been traditionally attributed to Filippo Brunelleschi (1377–1446), but his death in 1446 makes this nearly impossible; the design has also been attributed to Leon Battista Alberti (1404–72). The Medici family, rivals of the Pitti, bought the palace in 1550 and commissioned Bartolommeo Ammannati (1511–92) to enlarge it, the palace now becoming the main Medici residence; various alterations and additions were made into the nineteenth century. Pitti Palace was opened as a public gallery in 1833 after the fall of the Medici dynasty. The nouveau riche Elmer Moffatt of *The Custom of the Country* erects a mansion on Fifth Avenue as "an exact copy of the Pitti Palace" (Chilvers 2015).

25. One of the more eloquent iterations of the book's central concern.

15

The School-Room and Nurseries

One of the most important and interesting problems in the planning and decoration of a house is that which has to do with the arrangement of the children's rooms.[1]

There is, of course, little opportunity for actual decoration in school-room or nursery; and it is only by stretching a point that a book dealing merely with the practical application of æsthetics may be made to include a chapter bordering on pedagogy.[2] It must be remembered, however, that any application of principles presupposes some acquaintance with the principles themselves; and from this standpoint there is a certain relevance in studying the means by which the child's surroundings may be made to develop his sense of beauty.

The room where the child's lessons are studied is, in more senses than one, that in which he receives his education. His whole view of what he is set to learn, and of the necessity and advantage of learning anything at all, is tinged, more often than people think, by the appearance of the room in which his studying is done. The æsthetic sensibilities wake early in some children, and these, if able to analyze their emotions, could testify to what suffering they have been subjected by the habit of sending to school-room and nurseries whatever

1. This chapter elicited considerable criticism from reviewers as many of the recommendations were not thought practical. Some questioned the credibility of the authors, neither of whom had children.

2. In this case, having to do with the education of children (M-W).

furniture is too ugly or threadbare to be used in any other part of the house.

In the minds of such children, curious and lasting associations are early established between the appearance of certain rooms and the daily occupations connected with them; and the aspect of the school-room too often aggravates instead of mitigating the weariness of lesson-learning.

There are, of course, many children not naturally sensitive to artistic influences, and the parents of such children often think that no special care need be spent on their surroundings—a curious misconception of the purpose of all æsthetic training. To teach a child to appreciate any form of beauty is to develop his intelligence, and thereby to enlarge his capacity for wholesome enjoyment. It is, therefore, never idle to cultivate a child's taste; and those who have no pronounced natural bent toward the beautiful in any form need more guidance and encouragement than the child born with a sense of beauty. The latter will at most be momentarily offended by the sight of ugly objects; while they may forever blunt the taste and narrow the views of the child whose sluggish imagination needs the constant stimulus of beautiful surroundings.

If art is really a factor in civilization, it seems obvious that the feeling for beauty needs as careful cultivation as the other civic virtues. To teach a child to distinguish between a good and a bad painting, a well or an ill-modelled statue, need not hinder his growth in other directions, and will at least develop those habits of observation and comparison that are the base of all sound judgments. It is in this sense that the study of art is of service to those who have no special aptitude for any of its forms: its indirect action in shaping æsthetic criteria constitutes its chief value as an element of culture.

The habit of regarding "art" as a thing apart from life is fatal to the development of taste. Parents may conscientiously send their children to galleries and museums, but unless the child can find some point of contact between its own surroundings and the contents of the galleries, the interest excited by the pictures and statues will be short-lived and ineffectual. Children are not reached by abstract ideas, and a picture hanging on a museum wall is little better than an abstraction to the child's vivid but restricted imagination. Besides, if the home surroundings are tasteless, the unawakened sense of form will not be roused by a hurried walk through a museum. The child's mind must be prepared by daily lessons in beauty to understand the masterpieces of art. A child brought up on foolish story-books could hardly be expected to enjoy *The Knight's Tale* or the *Morte d'Arthur*[3] without some slight initiation into the nature and meaning of good literature; and to pass from a house full of ugly furniture, badly designed wall-papers and worthless knick-knacks to a hurried contemplation of the Venus of Milo or of a model of the Parthenon[4] is not likely to produce the desired results.

The daily intercourse with poor pictures, trashy "ornaments," and badly designed furniture may, indeed, be fittingly compared with a mental diet of silly and ungrammatical story-books. Most parents nowadays recognize the harmfulness of such a *régime*,[5] and are careful to feed their children on more stimulating fare. Skilful compilers

3. The authors cite these works of the medieval period as representative of "good literature." "A Knight's Tale," one of the twenty-four stories included in Geoffrey Chaucer's *The Canterbury Tales*, is a romance based on Giovanni Boccaccio's *Teseida*, adapted to fit the character of the Knight (*EB* 2018o). The *Morte d'Arthur*, by Sir Thomas Malory, was the first English-language prose version of the legend of King Arthur (ca. 1470) (*EB* 2018i).

4. Edith Wharton and Ogden Codman Jr. reference these works as prime examples of artistic masterpieces that require an appreciation of beauty from viewers. *Venus de Milo* is an ancient marble statue thought to represent Aphrodite, the Greek goddess of love and beauty (*EB* 2015b). It was carved by Alexandros of Antioch between 130 and 100 BCE. In 1820 it was found in pieces on the Aegean island of Melos and presented to King Louis XVIII of France, who then donated it to the Louvre Museum in Paris, where it remains today, though the arms of the reconstructed statue were never found. The Parthenon is the iconic temple that dominates the hill of the Acropolis in Athens. It was erected in the mid-fifth century BCE and dedicated to the Greek goddess Athena (*EB* 2020s).

5. Also commonly written *regime*, meaning "a regular pattern or occurrence or action," much like a routine (*M-W*).

have placed Mallory and Chaucer,[6] Cervantes and Froissart,[7] within reach of the childish understanding, thus laying the foundations for a lasting appreciation of good literature. No greater service can be rendered to children than in teaching them to know the best and to want it; but while this is now generally conceded with regard to books, the child's eager eyes are left to fare as best they may on chromos[8] from the illustrated papers and on carefully hoarded rubbish from the Christmas tree.

The mention of the Christmas tree suggests another obstacle to the early development of taste. Many children, besides being surrounded by ugly furniture and bad pictures, are overwhelmed at Christmas, and on every other anniversary, by presents not always selected with a view to the formation of taste. The question of presents is one of the most embarrassing problems in the artistic education of children. As long as they are in the toy age no great harm is done: it is when they are considered old enough to appreciate "something pretty for their rooms" that the season of danger begins. Parents themselves are often the worst offenders in this respect, and the sooner they begin to give their children presents which, if not beautiful, are at least useful, the

6. Sir Thomas Mallory (also spelled Malory) and Geoffrey Chaucer, the medieval writers whose works were just mentioned. The specifics of Mallory's identity are still uncertain, but he is credited as the author of *Le Morte D'Arthur* (*EB* 2019kk). More biographical details are known about Chaucer (1342–1400), whose *Canterbury Tales* (1387–1400) is recognized as one of the greatest works in the English language.

7. Miguel de Cervantes (1547–1616): Spanish novelist, playwright, and author of *Don Quixote*, glossed above (*EB* 2021g). Jean Froissart (1333–1400): French medieval poet and court historian. He authored *Chronicles*, documenting the feudal times of fourteenth century Europe, as well as providing an exposition of chivalric and courtly ideals, following suit with the popular genre of the age (*EB* 2019u).

8. Short for chromolithograph, a colored picture printed by lithography, especially in the late nineteenth and early twentieth centuries (*M-W*). A chromo called *Rock of Ages* figures significantly in Wharton's early novella of 1870s working-class New York, *Bunner Sisters*, written in the 1890s but not published until 1916. The authors reference newspaper chromos in chapter 15.

sooner will the example be followed by relatives and friends. The selection of such presents, while it might necessitate a little more trouble,
need not lead to greater expense. Good things do not always cost more
than bad.[9] A good print may often be bought for the same price as a
poor one, and the money spent on a china "ornament," in the shape of
a yellow Leghorn hat[10] with a kitten climbing out of it, would probably purchase a good reproduction of one of the Tanagra statuettes,[11]
a plaster cast of some French or Italian bust, or one of Cantagalli's
copies of the Robbia bas-reliefs[12]—any of which would reveal a world
of unsuspected beauty to many a child imprisoned in a circle of *articles
de Paris.*[13]

The children of the rich are usually the worst sufferers in such
cases, since the presents received by those whose parents and relations are not "well off" have the saving merit of usefulness. It is the
superfluous gimcrack[14]—the "ornament"—which is most objectionable, and the more expensive such articles are the more likely are

9. A simply stated version of one of the most important premises of this book.

10. With the image of a kitten climbing out of a hat it is likely Wharton and
Codman allude to Miss Kate Fearing Strong (later Mrs. Arthur Welman), who
attended Alva Vanderbilt's 1883 costume ball wearing a hat featuring a taxidermied
cat. (For image, see Museum of the City of New York n.d.). Leghorn: popular hat
style of the time, made out of leghorn straw, which is a fine, plaited straw of Italian
wheat. The hats typically have a flat brim or crown (*M-W*).

11. Referred to in the following chapter as Tanagra figurines, small terra-cotta
figures that date to the third century BCE and were found in Boeotia, east-central
Greece. They were crafted using molds and covered in white coating before being
painted. Young, well-dressed women in various sitting and standing poses are the
most popular subjects for the figurines. In Oscar Wilde's novel *The Picture of Dorian
Gray* (1891), Dorian compares his love interest Sybil to "the delicate grace of the
Tanagra figurine."

12. See chapter 8, note 4.

13. French: "goods from Paris"; in this context, the dreaded knickknacks or sou-
venirs that fail to contribute to the artistic and intellectual development of a child's
mind.

14. A showy object of little use or value.

they to do harm. Rich children suffer from the quantity as well as the quality of the presents they receive. Appetite is surfeited,[15] curiosity blunted, by the mass of offerings poured in with every anniversary. It would be better if, in such cases, friends and family could unite in giving to each child one thing worth having—a good edition, a first-state etching or engraving, or some like object fitted to give pleasure at the time and lasting enjoyment through life. Parents often make the mistake of thinking that such presents are too "serious"—that children do not care for good bindings, fine engravings, or reproductions of sculpture. As a matter of fact, children are quick to appreciate beauty when pointed out and explained to them, and an intelligent child feels peculiar pride in being the owner of some object which grown-up people would be glad to possess. If the selection of such presents is made with a reasonable regard for the child's tastes and understanding—if the book chosen is a good edition, well bound, of the *Morte d'Arthur* or of *Chaucer*—if the print represents some Tuscan Nativity, with a joyous dance of angels on the thatched roof, or a group of splendid horsemen and strange animals from the wondrous fairy-tale of the Riccardi chapel[16]—the present will give as much immediate pleasure as a "juvenile" book or picture, while its intrinsic beauty and significance may become important factors in the child's æsthetic development. The possession of something valuable, that may not be knocked about, but must be handled with care and restored to its place after being looked at, will also cultivate in the child that habit of carefulness and order which may be defined as good manners toward inanimate objects.

15. Overindulged. The noun surfeit means excess or, more specifically, disgust caused by excess (*M-W*).

16. The Palazzo Medici-Riccardi in Florence was built between 1444 and 1459; its private chapel was decorated by Benozzo Gozzoli, and so the *Procession of the Magi* extends across the east, south, and west walls of the main room, while the *Adoration of the Child* decorates the chancel with the angels painted on the side walls. The paintings tell a religious story, or a "wondrous fairy-tale" (*EB* 2021h).

Children suffer not only from the number of presents they receive, but from that over-crowding of modern rooms that so often makes it necessary to use the school-room and nurseries as an outlet for the overflow of the house. To the children's quarters come one by one the countless objects "too good to throw away" but too ugly to be tolerated by grown-up eyes—the bead-work cushions that have "associations," the mildewed Landseer prints[17] of foaming, dying animals, the sheep-faced Madonna and Apostles in bituminous draperies,[18] commemorating a paternal visit to Rome in the days when people bought copies of the "Old Masters."[19]

Those who wish to train their children's taste must resolutely clear the school-room of all such stumbling-blocks. Ugly furniture cannot always be replaced; but it is at least possible to remove unsuitable pictures and knick-knacks.

It is essential that the school-room should be cheerful. Dark colors, besides necessitating the use of much artificial light, are depressing to children and consequently out of place in the school-room: white woodwork, and walls tinted in some bright color, form the best background for both work and play.

Perhaps the most interesting way of decorating the school-room is that which might be described as the rotation system. To carry out this plan—which requires the coöperation of the children's teacher—the walls must be tinted in some light color, such as turquoise-blue or pale green, and cleared of all miscellaneous adornments. These should then

17. Sir Edwin Landseer (1802–73) was a British painter and sculptor best known for his painting of animals, which at first were inspired by anatomical knowledge, and the subjects were healthy (*EB* 2020j). However, over time the depictions were marred, such as Landseer's *Shoeing* from 1844, depicting a human placing a horse-shoe upon a horse's hoof, rather than the animal roaming free.

18. Unfavorable comparison to bituminous coal; in this context a displeasing picture of the Virgin Mary and Apostles marked by dark draperies. Wharton and Codman recommend more cheerful hues for the schoolroom (*M-W*).

19. Wharton and Codman advise procuring newly accessible reproductions of works of the canonical painters of the sixteenth, seventeenth, or early eighteenth centuries (*M-W*).

be replaced by a few carefully-chosen prints, photographs and plaster casts, representing objects connected with the children's studies. Let it, for instance, be supposed that the studies in hand include natural history, botany, and the history of France and England during the sixteenth century. These subjects might be respectively illustrated by some of the clever Japanese outline drawings of plants and animals,[20] by Holbein's portrait of Henry VIII,[21] Clouet's of Charles IX and of Elizabeth of Austria,[22] Dürer's etchings of Luther and Erasmus,[23] and views of some of the principal buildings erected in France and England during the sixteenth century.[24]

The prints and casts shown at one time should be sufficiently inexpensive and few in number to be changed as the child's lessons proceed, thus forming a kind of continuous commentary upon the various branches of study.

This plan of course necessitates more trouble and expense than the ordinary one of giving to the walls of the school-room a permanent

20. Probable reference to the Japanese art style, ukiyo-e, popular during the Tokugawa period (1603–1867). The name translates to "pictures of the floating world" and wood-block prints became popular, which developed an outlined form that depicted elements of nature, beauty, and spirituality (*EB* 2013b).

21. Hans Holbein the Younger (1497–1543) was a German painter, renowned for the realism of his portraits, particularly of the court of King Henry VIII of England (*EB* 2021d). Wharton's short story "After Holbein," which refers to his *Dance of Death* series, was first published in 1928 and later collected in her volume *Certain People* (1930).

22. François Clouet (1515–72): French painter who famously captured in his portraits the court of the royal house of Valois; official painter to Charles XI, finishing his most popular portrait of the French king in the 1560s; Elizabeth of Austria, his wife, queen of France, from 1570 to 1574, when King Charles IX died (*Britannica Academic* n.d.).

23. See chapter 9, note 16, on "German Little Masters." Erasmus (1460s–1536): Dutch scholar of the Northern Renaissance and first editor of the New Testament (*EB* 2021b). The Protestant Reformation deeply affected Albrecht Dürer, inspiring his portrait of Martin Luther (1483–1546) (*EB* 2020a).

24. Wharton and Codman cite French and English Renaissance architecture, along with Italian, as the source for the "best models" to emulate (*EB* 2020v).

decoration: an arrangement which may also be made interesting and suggestive, if the child's requirements are considered. When casts and pictures are intended to remain in place, it is a good idea to choose them at the outset with a view to the course of studies likely to be followed. In this way, each object may serve in turn to illustrate some phase of history or art: even this plan will be found to have a vivifying effect upon the dry bones of "lessons."

In a room decorated in this fashion, the prints or photographs selected might represent the foremost examples of Greek, Gothic, Renaissance and eighteenth-century architecture, together with several famous paintings of different periods and schools; sculpture being illustrated by casts of the Disk-thrower,[25] of one of Robbia's friezes of child-musicians,[26] of Donatello's Saint George,[27] and Pigalle's "Child with the Bird."[28]

Parents who do not care to plan the adornment of the school-room on such definite lines should at least be careful to choose appropriate casts and pictures. It is generally conceded that nothing painful should be put before a child's eyes; but the deleterious effects of namby-pamby[29] prettiness are too often disregarded. Anything "sweet" is considered appropriate for the school-room or nursery; whereas it is essential to the child's artistic training that only the sweetness which proceeds *de forte*[30] should be held up for admiration. It is easy to find among the world's masterpieces many pictures interesting to children. Vandyck's

25. Bronze Greek sculpture *Discobolus* (discus thrower) by Myron, active in Athens in the mid-fifth century BCE. The sculpture survives in numerous Roman marble copies as well as copies of lesser value.

26. See chapter 8, note 4.

27. Famous marble sculpture by Italian Renaissance artist Donatello (1386–1466). The original sculpture was completed in 1419 (*EB* 2020w).

28. French sculptor Jean-Baptiste Pigalle's *Child with a Bird Cage*. One of several smaller, sentimental sculptures of children in the rococo style, completed in 1750 (*EB* 2021e).

29. Lacking in character or substance; insipid, weak. In this case, overly sentimental or effeminate (*M-W*).

30. French: in such a way.

"Children of Charles I";[31] Bronzino's solemn portraits of Medici babies;[32] Drouais' picture of the Comte d'Artois holding his little sister on the back of a goat;[33] the wan little princes of Velasquez;[34] the ruddy beggar-boys of Murillo[35]—these are but a few of the subjects that at once suggest themselves. Then, again, there are the wonder-books of those greatest of all story-tellers, the Italian fresco-painters—Benozzo Gozzoli, Pinturicchio, Carpaccio[36]—incorrigible gossips every one, lingering over the minor episodes and trivial details of their stories with the desultory slowness dear to childish listeners. In sculpture, the range of choice is no less extended. The choristers of Robbia,[37] the lean little St. Johns of Donatello and his school[38]—Verrocchio's fierce

31. Anthony van Dyck (1599–1641): Flemish painter who in his later years was appointed "principalle Paynter in ordinary of the Majesties" by King Charles I of England and specialized in portraits of English society; frequently painted Charles I and his children (*EB* 2020b).

32. Agnolo Bronzino (1503–72): Florentine painter and court artist for the Medici family (Gáldy 2013).

33. François-Hubert Drouais (1727–75): French court painter. Wharton and Codman reference his 1763 portrait *Charles-Philippe of France and his Sister, Marie-Adelaide Clotilde, as Children*, in which the children are portrayed in court clothes, representative of the fact that royal children were expected to behave and dress like adults.

34. Diego Velázquez (1599–1660): Spanish master painter of the seventeenth century; perhaps a reference to the oil portrait of Philip Prospero, son of Philip IV of Spain, and his second wife, Mariana of Austria, as an infant.

35. Bartolomé Esteban Murillo (1618–82): the most popular baroque painter of seventeenth-century Spain, completed the oil painting *The Young Beggar* (1645–50), depicting a barefooted young boy, eyes cast downward in despair (*EB* 2020f).

36. Benozzo Gozzoli (1421–97): early Italian Renaissance painter; his masterpiece was a fresco cycle in the chapel of the Medici-Riccardi Palace, Florence (*EB* 2020g). Pinturicchio (1454–1513): Italian Renaissance painter known for his decorative frescoes; his most important work was the decoration of the suite of six rooms in the Vatican known as the Borgia Apartments (*EB* 2020t). Vittore Carpaccio (1460–1525/26): known as the greatest early Renaissance narrative painter; one of his best-known works is *Dream of St. Ursula* (see chapter 5, note 8) (*EB* 2019nn).

37. Likely *Cantoria* (Children Signing in Choir) by Luca della Robbia.

38. Possibly a nod to the large stucco roundels with scenes from the life of Saint John the Evangelist, below the dome of the old sacristy of San Lorenzo in Florence.

young David,[39] and the Capitol "Boy with the Goose"[40]—these may alternate with fragments of the Parthenon frieze, busts of great men, and studies of animals, from the Assyrian lions[41] to those of Canova and Barye.[42]

Above all, the walls should not be overcrowded. The importance of preserving in the school-room bare wall-spaces of uniform tint has hitherto been little considered; but teachers are beginning to understand the value of these spaces in communicating to the child's brain a sense of repose which diminishes mental and physical restlessness.

The furniture of the school-room should of course be plain and substantial. Well-designed furniture of this kind is seldom made by modern manufacturers, and those who can afford the slight extra expense should commission a good cabinet-maker to reproduce some of the simple models which may be found in the manuals of old French and English designers. It is of special importance to provide a large, solid writing-table: children are too often subjected to the needless constraint and fatigue of writing at narrow unsteady desks, too small to hold even the books in use during the lesson.

A well-designed bookcase with glass doors is a valuable factor in the training of children. It teaches a respect for books by showing that they are thought worthy of care; and a child is less likely to knock

39. Andrea del Verrocchio (1435–88): fifteenth-century Florentine sculptor and painter and mentor to Leonardo da Vinci; earliest surviving figurative sculpture is a small bronze statue of David, generally dated before 1476 (*EB* 2021a).

40. Possibly a reference to a copy of a marble statue that had been part of the Louvre's collection until 1884. The Roman writer Pliny mentions a sculptor called Boethos who made a group of a boy and goose.

41. Perhaps a reference to the royal Lion Hunt of Ashurbanipal, shown on a famous group of Assyrian palace reliefs from the North Palace of Nineveh now displayed at the British Museum; widely regarded as the supreme masterpieces of Assyrian art.

42. The Canova Lions were sculpted in marble by Antonio Canova (1757–1822) in 1792 for the tomb of Pope Clement XIII (*EB* 2020d). Antoine-Louis Barye (1795–1875): French sculptor who received a number of commissions for wild animal sculptures in the 1850s, one being *Lion Devouring a Gavial* (*EB* 2020c).

about and damage a book which must be taken from and restored to such a bookcase, than one which, after being used, is thrust back on an open shelf. Children's books, if they have any literary value, should be bound in some bright-colored morocco: dingy backs of calf or black cloth are not likely to attract the youthful eye, and the better a book is bound the more carefully it will be handled. Even lesson-books, when they become shabby, should have a covering of some bright-colored cloth stitched over the boards.

The general rules laid down for the decoration of the school-room may, with some obvious modifications, be applied to the treatment of nursery and of children's rooms. These, like the school-room, should have painted walls and a floor of hard wood with a removable rug or a square of matting. In a house containing both school-room and nursery, the decoration of the latter room will of course be adapted to the tastes of the younger children. Mothers often say, in answer to suggestions as to the decoration of the nursery, that little children "like something bright"—as though this precluded every form of art above the newspaper chromo and the Christmas card! It is easy to produce an effect of brightness by means of white wood-work and walls hung with good colored prints, with large photographs of old Flemish or Italian pictures—say, for example, Bellini's baby-angels playing on musical instruments[43]—and with a few of the Japanese plant and animal drawings already referred to. All these subjects would interest and amuse even very young children; and there is no reason why a gay Japanese screen, with boldly drawn birds and flowers, should not afford as much entertainment as one composed of a heterogeneous collection of Christmas cards, chromos, and story-book pictures, put together without any attempt at color-harmony or composition.

Children's rooms should be as free as possible from all superfluous draperies. The windows may be hung with either shades or curtains: it is needless to have both. If curtains are preferred, they should be of

43. Possibly a reference to *Music-Making Angels* (1480) by the early Renaissance painter Giovanni Bellini (1430–1516), featured on the *San Giobbe Altarpiece* (*EB* 2021c; see also Powers 2004).

chintz, or of some washable cotton or linen. The reproductions of the old *toiles de Jouy*,[44] with pictures from Æsop and La Fontaine, or from some familiar myth or story, are specially suited to children's rooms; while another source of interest and amusement may be provided by facing the fireplace with blue and white Dutch tiles representing the finding of Moses, the story of David and Goliath,[45] or some such familiar episode.

As children grow older, and are allotted separate bedrooms, these should be furnished and decorated on the same principles and with the same care as the school-room. Pieces of furniture for these bedrooms would make far more suitable and interesting presents than the costly odds and ends so often given without definite intention. In the arrangement of the child's own room the expression of individual taste should be encouraged and the child allowed to choose the pictures and casts with which the walls are hung. The responsibility of such selection will do much to develop the incipient faculties of observation and comparison.

To sum up, then: the child's visible surroundings form the basis of the best, because of the most unconscious, cultivation: and not of æsthetic cultivation only, since, as has been pointed out, the development of any artistic taste, if the child's general training is of the right sort, indirectly broadens the whole view of life.

44. French: fabrics of Jouy. Cotton or linen printed with designs of landscapes and figures; created in the eighteenth-century factory Jouy-en-Josas, near Versailles in France (*EB* 2017g).

45. Flat, square, decorative tiles from the Netherlands often used on the faces of fireplaces (Harris 2006). While different colors may have been available, the Delft blue were most popular. Sometimes popular artwork would be printed onto the tiles as well, such as the painting that depicts the "finding of Moses" or the other popular biblical story of David and Goliath (*EB* 2024c).

16

Bric-à-Brac

It is perhaps not uninstructive to note that we have no English word to describe the class of household ornaments which French speech has provided with at least three designations, each indicating a delicate and almost imperceptible gradation of quality. In place of bric-à-brac, bibelots, *objets d'art*,[1] we have only knick-knacks—defined by Stormonth as "articles of small value."

This definition of the knick-knack fairly indicates the general level of our artistic competence. It has already been said that cheapness is not necessarily synonymous with trashiness; but hitherto this assertion has been made with regard to furniture and to the other necessary appointments of the house. With knick-knacks the case is different. An artistic age will of course produce any number of inexpensive trifles fit to become, like the Tanagra figurines, the museum treasures of later centuries; but it is hardly necessary to point out that modern shop-windows are not overflowing with such immortal toys. The few objects of art produced in the present day are the work of distinguished artists. Even allowing for what Symonds[2] calls the

---

1. Small, decorative trinkets (*M-W*). *Objets d'art* translates literally from the French to "art objects" or "works of art" (*M-W*). However, in the context of this chapter, it most commonly refers to decorative knickknacks.

2. John Addington Symonds (1840–93): English essayist, poet and biographer. The quotation is taken from his book *Renaissance in Italy* (1875). In chapter 9 of *The Age of Innocence* the reader learns that Newland Archer reads many of the books on Italian art history read by Edith Wharton: "His boyhood had been saturated with Ruskin, and he had read all the latest books: John Addington Symonds, Vernon Lee's

"vicissitudes of taste," it seems improbable that our commercial knick-knack will ever be classed as a work of art.

It is clear that the weary man must have a chair to sit on, the hungry man a table to dine at; nor would the most sensitive judgment condemn him for buying ugly ones, were no others to be had; but objects of art are a counsel of perfection. It is quite possible to go without them; and the proof is that many do go without them who honestly think to possess them in abundance. This is said, not with any intention of turning to ridicule the natural desire to "make a room look pretty," but merely with the purpose of inquiring whether such an object is ever furthered by the indiscriminate amassing of "ornaments." Decorators know how much the simplicity and dignity of a good room are diminished by crowding it with useless trifles.[3] Their absence improves even bad rooms, or makes them at least less multitudinously bad. It is surprising to note how the removal of an accumulation of knick-knacks will free the architectural lines and restore the furniture to its rightful relation with the walls.

Though a room must depend for its main beauty on design and furniture, it is obvious that there are many details of luxurious living not included in these essentials. In what, then, shall the ornamentation of rooms consist? Supposing walls and furniture to be satisfactory, how put the minor touches that give to a room the charm of completeness? To arrive at an answer, one must first consider the different kinds of minor embellishment. These may be divided into two classes: the object of art *per se*, such as the bust, the picture, or the vase; and, on the other hand, those articles, useful in themselves—lamps, clocks, fire-screens, bookbindings, candelabra—which art has only to touch to make them the best ornaments any room can contain. In past times such articles took the place of bibelots. Few purely ornamental objects

---

'Euphorion,' the essays of P. G. Hamerton, and a wonderful new volume called 'The Renaissance' by Walter Pater" (*EB* 2020n).

3. This piece of decorating advice is astonishingly resonant for twenty-first-century devotees of Marie Kondo's bestselling book, *The Life-Changing Magic of Tidying Up* (2014).

56. Bronze Andiron. Venetian School, XVI Century.

were to be seen, save in the cabinets of collectors; but when Botticelli[4] decorated the panels of linen chests, and Cellini[5] chiselled book-clasps and drinking-cups, there could be no thought of the vicious distinction between the useful and the beautiful. One of the first obligations of art is to make all useful things beautiful: were this neglected principle applied to the manufacture of household accessories, the modern room would have no need of knick-knacks.

Before proceeding further, it is necessary to know what constitutes an object of art. It was said at the outset that, though cheapness and trashiness are not always synonymous, they are apt to be so in the case of the modern knick-knack. To buy, and even to make, it may cost a great deal of money; but artistically it is cheap, if not worthless; and too often its artistic value is in inverse ratio to its price. The one-dollar china pug is less harmful than an expensive onyx lamp-stand[6] with moulded bronze mountings dipped in liquid gilding.[7] It is one of the misfortunes of the present time that the most preposterously bad things often possess the powerful allurement of being expensive. One might think it an advantage that they are not within every one's reach; but, as a matter of fact, it is their very unattainableness which, by making them more desirable, leads to the production of that worst curse of modern civilization—cheap copies of costly horrors.

An ornament is of course not an object of art because it is expensive—though it must be owned that objects of art are seldom cheap.

4. Sandro Botticelli (1445–1510): Italian painter in the Florentine Renaissance. Perhaps best known for his *Birth of Venus* (1484–86) and *Primavera* (1482); mentored by Filippo Lippi, an admired Florentine master (*EB* 2021j).

5. Benvenuto Cellini (1500–1571): Florentine sculptor, goldsmith, and writer; Wharton mentions Cellini in her essay "The Vice of Reading" (1903) and her story "The Daunt Diana" (1909) (*EB* 2020h).

6. Striped, semiprecious variety of the silica mineral, with black and white alternating bands (*EB* 2018l).

7. Art of decorating the whole, or parts, of wood, metal, plaster, glass, or other objects with gold, in leaf or powder form. Gilded is of course not golden, a fact that inspired Mark Twain to name the post–Civil War period "the Gilded Age" (*EB* 2016b).

Good workmanship, as distinct from designing, almost always commands a higher price than bad; and good artistic workmanship having become so rare that there is practically no increase in the existing quantity of objects of art, it is evident that these are more likely to grow than to diminish in value. Still, as has been said, costliness is no test of merit in an age when large prices are paid for bad things. Perhaps the most convenient way of defining the real object of art is to describe it as *any ornamental object which adequately expresses an artistic conception.* This definition at least clears the ground of the mass of showy rubbish forming the stock-in-trade of the average "antiquity" dealer.

Good objects of art give to a room its crowning touch of distinction. Their intrinsic beauty is hardly more valuable than their suggestion of a mellower civilization—of days when rich men were patrons of "the arts of elegance," and when collecting beautiful objects was one of the obligations of a noble leisure. The qualities implied in the ownership of such bibelots are the mark of their unattainableness. The man who wishes to possess objects of art must have not only the means to acquire them, but the skill to choose them—a skill made up of cultivation and judgment, combined with that feeling for beauty that no amount of study can give, but that study alone can quicken and render profitable.

Only time and experience can acquaint one with those minor peculiarities marking the successive "manners" of a master, or even with the technical *nuances* which at once enable the collector to affix a date to his Sèvres[8] or to his maiolica.[9] Such knowledge is acquired at the cost of great pains and of frequent mistakes; but no one should venture to buy works of art who cannot at least draw such obvious

---

8. Type of porcelain. French hard-paste porcelain, as well as soft-paste porcelain made at the royal factory of Sèvres, near Versailles from 1756 through the present. Sèvres became the leading porcelain factory in Europe after the decline of Meissen (*EB* 2020x).

9. Also majolica, tin-glazed earthenware produced from the fifteenth century in Italy. Centers included Faenza, Deruta, Urbino, and Florence. Introduced to Italy by Moorish Spain by way of the island of Maiolica (*EB* 2018j).

distinctions as those between old and new Saxe, between an old Italian and a modern French bronze, or between Chinese peach-bloom porcelain of the Khang-hi period[10] and the Japanese imitations to be found in every "Oriental emporium."

Supposing the amateur to have acquired this proficiency, he is still apt to buy too many things, or things out of proportion with the rooms for which they are intended. The scoffers at style—those who assume that to conform to any known laws of decoration is to sink one's individuality—often justify their view by the assertion that it is ridiculous to be tied down, in the choice of bibelots, to any given period or manner—as though Mazarin's great collection[11] had comprised only seventeenth-century works of art, or the Colonnas, the Gonzagas, and the Malatestas[12] had drawn all their treasures from contemporary sources!

10. Likely a reference to art under the reign of the Kangxi emperor, one of the longest-reigning world rulers and one of the most important emperors in Chinese history, celebrated for having built the foundation for the glorious age of the Qing dynasty at the height of its power and influence. The Qing dynasty was founded in 1644 with the conquest of China by the Manchus, who overthrew the weakened Ming dynasty, which had ruled China since 1368.

11. Cardinal Mazarin (1602–61): first minister of France after Cardinal Richelieu's death in 1662, was a lover of the arts who acquired an impressive collection for his Paris mansion, which serves today as the Bibliothèque Nationale, or the national library (*EB* 2020p).

12. Three noble Italian families. Colonna family: Roman family descended from the tenth century counts of Tusculum; gained power and wealth through papal favor (*EB* 2007a). In the mid-fifteenth century the family fortunes were challenged by conflict with the popes before their eventual return to peace with the papacy from the late sixteenth century onward. The Gonzaga dynasty ruled Mantua from 1328 to 1707 and Montferrat from 1536 to 1707. Beginning with Giovan Francesco II (d. 1444), the family began the tradition of raising patrons of literature and the arts. He founded the first school inspired by humanistic principles in 1423 in one of the family's villas (*EB* 2012g). The Malatesta family ruled Rimini in the European Middle Ages. Dante recorded the story of Gianciotto Malatesta (d. 1304), who killed his wife, Francesca da Polenta, and his brother Paolo for adultery. Additionally, Sigismondo Pandolfo Malatesta (1417–68) is regarded as the prototype of the Italian Renaissance prince, with a reputation as a patron of writers and artists (*EB* 2007b).

As a matter of fact, the great amateurs of the past were never fettered by such absurd restrictions. All famous patrons of art have encouraged the talent of their day; but the passion for collecting antiquities is at least as old as the Roman Empire, and Græco-Roman sculptors had to make archaistic statues to please the popular fancy, just as our artists paint pre-Raphaelite[13] pictures to attract the disciples of Ruskin and William Morris.[14] Since the Roman Empire, there has probably been no period when a taste for the best of all ages did not exist.[†] Julius II, while Michel Angelo [sic] and Raphael worked under his orders, was

13. The Pre-Raphaelite Brotherhood was formed in 1848 by three Royal Academy students: Dante Gabriel Rossetti, William Holman Hunt, and John Everett Millais. Inspired by Italian art of the fourteenth and fifteenth centuries, their name speaks to their wish to retreat to the style of Italian art before the time of Raphael. The brotherhood produced significant works of religious and medieval subjects aiming to revive the unadorned directness of fifteenth-century Florentine and Sienese painting. Though the collective quickly disbanded and the artists ventured into more secular topics, the Pre-Raphaelites enjoyed a revival after the 1882 death of Rossetti. Among the more famous Pre-Raphaelite works are Millais's *Ophelia* (1851–52) and Rossetti's *Beata Beatrix* (1864–70), for which Elizabeth Siddall modeled. On Wharton's career-long engagement with Rossetti and the Pre-Raphaelites, see Orlando 2007a.

14. On John Ruskin, see chapter 1, note 6. Ruskin's medievalist enthusiasm led him to support the Pre-Raphaelite Brotherhood, who rejected neoclassicism particularly in the example of Sir Joshua Reynolds. Ruskin published an enthusiastic pamphlet about them in 1851 (*EB* 2021f). Additionally, his writings on the social and moral basis of architecture, particularly in *The Stones of Venice*, inspired William Morris (1834–96), an English craftsman, poet, and early socialist. By "the disciples" of Ruskin and Morris, Edith Wharton and Ogden Codman Jr. likely refer to Oscar Wilde (1854–1900) and the (primarily male) artists associated with 1890s decadence (*EB* 2020y).

[†] "A little study would probably show that the Ptolemaic era in Egypt was a renaissance of the Theban age, in architecture as in other respects, while the golden period of Augustus in Rome was largely a Greek revival. Perhaps it would even be discovered that all ages of healthy human prosperity are more or less revivals, and have been marked by a retrospective tendency." *The Architecture of the Renaissance in Italy*, by W. J. Anderson. London, Batsford, 1896.

gathering antiques for the Belvedere cortile;[15] under Louis XIV, Greek marbles, Roman bronzes, cabinets of Chinese lacquer and tables of Florentine mosaic were mingled without thought of discord against Lebrun's tapestries or Bérain's arabesques;[16] and Marie-Antoinette's collection united Oriental porcelains with goldsmiths' work of the Italian Renaissance.

Taste attaches but two conditions to the use of objects of art: that they shall be in scale with the room, and that the room shall not be overcrowded with them. There are two ways of being in scale: there is the scale of proportion, and what might be called the scale of appropriateness. The former is a matter of actual measurement, while the latter is regulated solely by the nicer standard of good taste. Even in the matter of actual measurement, the niceties of proportion are not always clear to an unpractised eye. It is easy to see that the Ludovisi Juno[17] would be out of scale in a boudoir, but the discrepancy, in diminishing, naturally becomes less obvious. Again, a vase or a bust may not be out of scale with the wall-space behind it, but may appear to crush the furniture upon which it stands; and since everything a room contains should be regarded as a factor in its general composition, the relation of bric-à-brac to furniture is no less to be studied than the relation of

15. Pope Julius II, originally Giuliano della Rovere (1443–1513), was the greatest art patron of the papal line. He is most important for his close friendship with Michelangelo (1475–1564). He commissioned Michelangelo's *Moses* and paintings in the Sistine Chapel. He also was a patron of Raphael, commissioning his frescoes in the Vatican. Julius II added many buildings to Rome and laid the groundwork in the Vatican Museum for the world's greatest collection of antiques. He was also a collector of statues and initiated the construction of the Belvedere cortile (courtyard)—or the Cortile del Belvedere—where he housed his collection (*EB* 2020q).

16. During the reign of Louis XIV, Charles Le Brun personally created or supervised the production of most of the paintings, sculptures, and decorative objects commissioned by the government. On Jean Bérain, see chapter 7, note 17. Bérain satisfied the king's appetite for splendor and grand entertainments with installments such as assorted animals integrated into florid arabesques.

17. Head and neck sculpted from Greek marble dating to the first century. The head looks calmly ahead, and the hair is parted in the middle and pulled back. The bust had long been identified as an image of Juno or Hera, a Roman goddess.

bric-à-brac to wall-spaces. Much of course depends upon the effect intended; and this can be greatly modified by careful adjustment of the contents of the room. A ceiling may be made to look less high by the use of wide, low pieces of furniture, with massive busts and vases; while a low-studded room may be heightened by tall, narrow commodes[18] and cabinets, with objects of art upon the same general lines.

It is of no less importance to observe the scale of appropriateness. A bronze Pallas Athene[19] or a cowled mediæval *pleureur*[20] would be obviously out of harmony with the spirit of a boudoir; while the delicate graces of old Saxe or Chelsea would become futile in library or study.

Another kind of appropriateness must be considered in the relation of objects of art to each other: not only must they be in scale as regards character and dimensions, but also—and this, though more important, is perhaps less often considered—as regards quality. The habit of mixing good, bad, and indifferent in furniture is often excused by necessity: people must use what they have. But there is no necessity for having bad bric-à-brac. Trashy "ornaments" do not make a room more comfortable; as a general rule, they distinctly diminish its comfort; and they have the further disadvantage of destroying the effect of any good piece of work. Vulgarity is always noisier than good breeding, and it is instructive to note how a modern commercial bronze will "talk down" a delicate Renaissance statuette or bust, and a piece of Deck or Minton china[21] efface the color-values of blue-and-

18. Chests of drawers (*M-W*).

19. (Also spelled Athena): the city protectress; goddess of war, handicraft, and practical reason in Greek mythology (*EB* 2020e).

20. French: one who cries; a mourner. In the fifteenth century, figures began to appear, particularly on French tombs, dressed in large coats or cowls. Professional *pleureurs* were compensated. The width and shape of the mourning clothes distinguished the figures from monks.

21. Joseph-Théodore Deck (1823–91): French ceramicist and potter; set up his own Paris studio in 1856, most celebrated for his Iznik-style ceramics. Minton china: cream-colored and blue printed earthenware maiolica, bone china, and Parian porcelain produced at a Staffordshire factory in England founded by Thomas Minton in 1793, who also popularized the Willow pattern (*EB* 2011c).

white or the soft tints of old Sèvres. Even those who set down a preference for old furniture as an affectation will hardly maintain that new
knick-knacks are as good as old bibelots; but only those who have some
slight acquaintance with the subject know how wide is the distance,
in conception and execution, between the old object of art and its
unworthy successor. Yet the explanation is simple. In former times, as
the greatest painters occupied themselves with wall-decoration, so the
greatest sculptors and modellers produced the delicate statuettes and
the incomparable bronze mountings for vases and furniture adorning
the apartments of their day. A glance into the window of the average
furniture shop probably convinces the most unobservant that modern
bronze mountings are not usually designed by great artists; and there
is the same change in the methods of execution. The bronze formerly
chiselled is now moulded; the iron once wrought is cast; the patina[22]
given to bronze by a chemical process making it a part of the texture
of the metal is now simply applied as a surface wash; and this deterioration in processes has done more than anything else to vulgarize
modern ornament.

It may be argued that even in the golden age of art few could have
walls decorated by great painters, or furniture-mountings modelled by
great sculptors; but it is here that the superiority of the old method is
shown. Below the great painter and sculptor came the trained designer
who, formed in the same school as his superiors, did not attempt a
poor copy of their masterpieces, but did the same kind of work on
simpler lines; just as below the skilled artificer stood the plain artisan whose work was executed more rudely, but by the same genuine
processes. This explains the supposed affectation of those who "like
things just because they are old." Old bric-à-brac and furniture are,
indeed, almost always worthy of liking, since they are made on good
lines by a good process.

22. Film, usually green, that is formed naturally on copper and bronze by long
exposure or oxidization. It can also be artificially created with the use of acids, as
patina is often valued aesthetically for its color (M-W).

Two causes connected with the change in processes have contributed to the debasement of bibelots: the substitution of machine for hand-work has made possible the unlimited reproduction of works of art; and the resulting demand for cheap knick-knacks has given employment to a multitude of untrained designers having nothing in common with the *virtuoso* of former times.

It is an open question how much the mere possibility of unlimited reproduction detracts from the intrinsic value of an object of art. To the art-lover, as distinguished from the collector, uniqueness *per se* can give no value to an inartistic object; but the distinction, the personal quality, of a beautiful object is certainly enhanced when it is known to be alone of its kind—as in the case of the old bronzes made *à cire perdue*.[23] It must, however, be noted that in some cases—as in that of bronze-casting—the method which permits reproduction is distinctly inferior to that used when but one object is to be produced.

In writing on objects of art, it is difficult to escape the charge of saying on one page that reproductions are objectionable, and on the next that they are better than poor "originals." The United States customs laws have drawn a rough distinction between an original work and its reproductions, defining the former as a work of art and the latter as articles of commerce; but it does not follow that an article of commerce may not be an adequate representation of a work of art. The technical differences incidental to the various forms of reproduction make any general conclusion impossible. In the case of bronzes, for instance, it has been pointed out that the *cire perdue* process is superior to that by means of which reproductions may be made; nor is this the only cause of inferiority in bronze reproductions. The nature of bronze-casting makes it needful that the final touches should be given to bust or statue after it emerges from the mould. Upon these touches,

---

23. French, literally "with lost wax (casting)," process used in metal casting that consists of making a wax model, coating it with a refractory to form a mold, heating it until the wax melts out of the small holes left in the mold and then pouring metal into the space left vacant (*M-W*).

given by the master's chisel, the expressiveness and significance of the work chiefly depend; and multiplied reproductions, in lacking this individual stamp, must lack precisely that which distinguishes the work of art from the commercial article.

Perhaps the safest general rule is to say that the less the reproduction suggests an attempt at artistic interpretation—the more literal and mechanical is its rendering of the original—the better it fulfils its purpose. Thus, plaster-casts of sculpture are more satisfactory than bronze or marble copies; and a good photograph of a painting is superior to the average reproduction in oils or water-color.

The deterioration in gilding is one of the most striking examples of the modern disregard of quality and execution. In former times gilding was regarded as one of the crowning touches of magnificence in decoration, was little used except where great splendor of effect was desired, and was then applied by means of a difficult and costly process. To-day, after a period of reaction during which all gilding was avoided, it is again unsparingly used, under the mistaken impression that it is one of the chief characteristics of the French styles now once more in demand. The result is a plague of liquid gilding. Even in France, where good gilding is still done, the great demand for cheap gilt furniture and ornaments has led to the general use of the inferior process. The prevalence of liquid gilding, and the application of gold to furniture and decoration not adapted to such treatment, doubtless explain the aversion of many persons to any use of gilding in decoration.

In former times the expense of good gilding was no obstacle to its use, since it was employed only in gala rooms, where the whole treatment was on the same scale of costliness: it would never have occurred to the owner of an average-sized house to drench his walls and furniture in gilding, since the excessive use of gold in decoration was held to be quite unsuited to such a purpose. Nothing more surely preserves any form of ornament from vulgarization than a general sense of fitness.

Much of the beauty and propriety of old decoration was due to the fact that the merit of a work of art was held to consist, not in substance, but in design and execution. It was never thought that a badly designed bust or vase could be saved from mediocrity by being made of an expensive material. Suitability of substance always enhances a work of art; mere costliness never. The chryselephantine Zeus of Olympia[24] was doubtless admirably suited to the splendor of its surroundings; but in a different setting it would have been as beautiful in marble. In plastic art everything depends on form and execution, and the skilful handling of a substance deliberately chosen for its resistance (where another might have been used with equal fitness) is rather a *tour de force* than an artistic achievement.

These last generalizations are intended to show, not only that there is an intrinsic value in almost all old bibelots, but also that the general excellence of design and execution in past times has handed down to us many unimportant trifles in the way of furniture and household appliances worthy of being regarded as minor objects of art. In Italy especially, where every artisan seems to have had the gift of the *plasticatore*[25] in his finger-tips, and no substance was thought too poor to express a good design, there are still to be found many bits of old workmanship—clocks, *appliques*, terra-cottas, and carved picture-frames with touches of gilding—that may be characterized in the terms applied by the builder of Buckingham House[26] to his collection of pictures: "Some good, *none disagreeable*." Still, no accumulation of such trifles, even where none is disagreeable, will give to a room the same distinction as the presence of a few really fine works of art. Any one who has the patience to put up with that look of bareness so displeasing to some will do better to buy each year one superior piece rather than a dozen of middling quality.[27]

24. Statue of Zeus at Olympia, Greece, one of the Seven Wonders of the World; created by the Greek sculptor Phidias around 430 BCE (*EB* 2015a). Chryselephantine: overlaid with gold and ivory (*M-W*).

25. Italian for plasticator; in this context, Wharton and Codman essentialize the artistic gift with which the Italian artisan is endowed (*M-W*).

26. William Winde and John Fitch are credited with building the structure that became known as Buckingham House, completed around 1705.

27. The same (highly intelligent) investment advice is dispensed today on the subject of material acquisitions, including clothing.

Even the buyer who need consult only his own pleasure must remember that his very freedom from the ordinary restrictions lays him open to temptation. It is no longer likely that any collector will be embarrassed by a superfluity of treasures; but he may put too many things into one room, and no amount of individual merit in the objects themselves will, from the decorator's standpoint, quite warrant this mistake. Any work of art regardless of its intrinsic merit, must justify its presence in a room by being *more valuable than the space it occupies*—more valuable, that is, to the general scheme of decoration.

Those who call this view arbitrary or pedantic should consider, first, the importance of plain surfaces in decoration, and secondly the tendency of overcrowding to minimize the effect of each separate object, however striking in itself. Eye and mind are limited in their receptivity to a certain number of simultaneous impressions, and the Oriental habit of displaying only one or two objects of art at a time shows a more delicate sense of these limitations than the Western passion for multiplying effects.

To sum up, then, a room should depend for its adornment on general harmony of parts, and on the artistic quality of such necessities as lamps, screens, bindings, and furniture. Whoever goes beyond these essentials should limit himself in the choice of ornaments to the "labors of the master-artist's hand."[28]

28. A nod to one of Wharton's favorite writers, George Eliot, whose poem "A Minor Prophet" was published 1884. The stanza begins: "The faith that life on earth is being shaped / To glorious ends, that order, justice, love, / Mean man's completeness, mean effect as sure / As roundness in the dew-drop—that great faith / Is but the rushing and expanding stream / Of thought, of feeling, fed by all the past." The line in question reads: "At labors of the master-artist's hand / Which, trembling, touches to a finer end, / Trembling before an image seen within." Here Wharton and Codman align themselves with the principles of William Morris's design philosophy (Eliot 1884).

Conclusion

In the preceding pages an attempt has been made to show that in the treatment of rooms we have passed from the golden age of architecture to the gilded age of decoration.

Any argument in support of a special claim necessitates certain apparent injustices, sets up certain provisional limitations, and can therefore be judged with fairness only by those who make due allowance for these conditions. In the discussion of æsthetics such impartiality can seldom be expected. Not unnaturally, people resent any attempt to dogmatize on matters so generally thought to lie within the domain of individual judgment. Many hold that in questions of taste *Gefühl ist alles*;[1] while those who believe that beyond the oscillations of fashion certain fixed laws may be discerned have as yet agreed upon no formula defining their belief. In short, our civilization has not yet developed any artistic creed so generally recognized that it may be invoked on both sides of an argument without risk of misunderstanding.

This is true at least of those forms of art that minister only to the æsthetic sense. With architecture and its allied branches the case is different. Here beauty depends on fitness, and the practical requirements of life are the ultimate test of fitness.

If, therefore, it can be proved that the old practice was based upon a clearer perception of these requirements than is shown by modern decorators, it may be claimed not unreasonably that the old

1. German: "feeling is everything."

methods are better than the new. It seems, however, that the distinction between the various offices of art is no longer clearly recognized. The merit of house-decoration is now seldom measured by the standard of practical fitness; and those who would set up such a standard are suspected of proclaiming individual preferences under the guise of general principles.

In this book, an endeavor has been made to draw no conclusion unwarranted by the premises; but whatever may be thought of the soundness of some of the deductions, they must be regarded, not as a criticism of individual work, but simply of certain tendencies in modern architecture. It must be remembered, too, that the book is merely a sketch, intended to indicate the lines along which further study may profitably advance.

It may seem inconsequent that an elementary work should include much apparently unimportant detail. To pass in a single chapter from a discussion of abstract architectural laws to the combination of colors in a bedroom carpet seems to show lack of plan; yet the transition is logically justified. In the composition of a whole there is no negligible quantity: if the decoration of a room is planned on certain definite principles, whatever contributes line or color becomes a factor in the composition. The relation of proportion to decoration is like that of anatomy to sculpture: underneath are the everlasting laws. It was the recognition of this principle that kept the work of the old architect-decorators (for the two were one) free from the superfluous, free from the intemperate accumulation that marks so many modern rooms. Where each detail had its determinate part, no superficial accessories were needed to make up a whole: a great draughtsman represents with a few strokes what lesser artists can express only by a multiplicity of lines.

The supreme excellence is simplicity. Moderation, fitness, relevance—these are the qualities that give permanence to the work of the great architects. *Tout ce qui n'est pas nécessaire est nuisible.*[2] There is

2. French: "everything that is not necessary is harmful."

a sense in which works of art may be said to endure by virtue of that which is left out of them, and it is this "tact of omission" that characterizes the master-hand.

Modern civilization has been called a varnished barbarism: a definition that might well be applied to the superficial graces of much modern decoration. Only a return to architectural principles can raise the decoration of houses to the level of the past. Vasari said of the Farnesina palace[3] that it was not built, but really born—*non murato ma veramente nato;*[4] and this phrase is but the expression of an ever-present sense—the sense of interrelation of parts, of unity of the whole.

There is no absolute perfection, there is no communicable ideal; but much that is empiric, much that is confused and extravagant, will give way before the application of principles based on common sense and regulated by the laws of harmony and proportion.

3. Giorgio Vasari (1511–74): Italian painter, architect, and writer best known for his biographies of Italian Renaissance artists (*EB* 2020k). Farnesina palace in Rome: one of the most charming buildings of the High Renaissance; constructed, or "born," between 1509 and 1511 by Baldassare Peruzzi.

4. Italian: "not so much built, as born," from Giorgio Vasari's *Le vite de' più eccellenti pittori, scultori* (Quinlan-McGrath and Palladius 1990, 105).

Works Cited

Index

Works Cited

Alexander, Christine. 2006. "Aesop's Fables." In *The Oxford Companion to the Brontës*, edited by Christine Alexander and Margaret Smith. Oxford: Oxford Univ. Press. https://www.oxfordreference.com/view/10.1093/acref/9780198662181.001.0001/acref-9780198662181-e-0013.

American Heritage Dictionary. s.v. "Arras." https://www.ahdictionary.com/word/search.html?q=Arras.

Armbruster, Elif. 2019. "Dwelling in American Realism." In *The Oxford Handbook of American Realism*, edited by Keith Newlin, 411–25. New York: Oxford Univ. Press, 2019.

Archives Nationales. n.d. "The Hôtel de Soubise and the Hôtel de Rohan." Accessed August 8, 2019. http://www.archives-nationales.culture.gouv.fr/en/web/guest/hotels-de-soubise-et-de-rohan.

Bachelard, Gaston. 2014. *The Poetics of Space.* Translated by Maria Jolas. New York: Penguin.

Bayley, John Barrington. 1997. "*The Decoration of Houses* as a Practical Handbook." In *The Decoration of Houses by Edith Wharton and Ogden Codman, Jr.: The Revised and Expanded Classical America Edition*, 243–55. New York: W. W. Norton.

Benstock, Shari. 1994. *No Gifts from Chance: A Biography of Edith Wharton.* New York: Charles Scribner's Sons.

Berry, Walter. 1898. "The Decoration of Houses." *Bookman*, April 1898, 161–63.

Black, Annetta. 2019. "Catherine de Medici's Chamber of Secrets." *Atlas Obscura*, October 19, 2019. https://www.atlasobscura.com/places/catherine-de-medicis-chamber-secrets.

Bourdin, Philippe. 2013. "Le Thé à L'Anglaise." Last modified March 5, 2014. https://www.histoire-image.org/fr/etudes/anglaise.

Brander, Laurence. 2019. "William Makepeace Thackeray." In *Encyclopedia Britannica*, last updated February 7, 2024. https://www.britannica.com /biography/William-Makepeace-Thackeray.

British Museum. n.d. "Thomas Mahieu (Maioli)." Accessed January 20, 2021. https://www.britishmuseum.org/collection/term/BIOG217417.

Browne, Clare Woodthorpe. 2003. "Oberkampf, Christophe-Philippe." Grove Art Online. Updated and revised October 22, 2008. https://www .oxfordartonline.com/groveart/view/10.1093/gao/9781884446054.001 .0001/oao-9781884446054-e-7000063134.

Buffalo as an Architectural Museum. n.d. "Fireplace Terms." Accessed August 8, 2019. https://buffaloah.com/a/DCTNRY/fireplace/fireplace.html.

———. n.d. "Rosette." Accessed August 8, 2019. https://buffaloah.com/a /DCTNRY/r/rosette.html.

Cabestan, Jean-Francois. 2012. "Architecture, Textes et Images." Université François-Rabelais. http://architectura.cesr.univ-tours.fr/Traite/Notice /ENSBA_LES223.asp?param=en.

"Campbell, Colen." 2011. In *Chambers Biographical Dictionary*, 9th ed., edited by Liam Rodger and Joan Bakewell. London: Chambers Harrap. https://search.worldcat.org/title/chambers-biographical-dictionary/oclc /839673337.

Campbell, Gordon, ed. 2009. "Gaillon, Château of." In *The Grove Encyclopedia of Northern Renaissance Art*, edited by Gordon Campbell. Oxford: Oxford Univ. Press. https://www.oxfordreference.com/display/10.1093 /acref/9780195334661.001.0001/acref-9780195334661.

Campbell, Gordon. 2008. "Derome Family." Grove Art Online. Accessed January 20, 2021. https://www.oxfordartonline.com/groveart/display/10 .1093/gao/9781884446054.001.0001/oao-9781884446054-e-7002071751.

———. 2014. "Sanderson Family." Grove Art Online. Accessed January 20, 2021. https://www.oxfordartonline.com/groveart/view/10.1093/gao /9781884446054.001.0001/oao-9781884446054-e-7002073811.

Campbell, Patsy. 1995. "Ledoux, Charles-Nicolas." In *The New Oxford Companion to Literature in French*, edited by Peter France. Oxford Univ. Press. https://www.oxfordreference.com/view/10.1093/acref/9780198661252 .001.0001/acref-9780198661252-e-2667.

Canterbury Historical and Archaeological Society. n.d. "Caen Stone." Accessed August 8, 2019. http://www.canterbury-archaeology.org.uk/caen -stone/4592359917.

Castle Ashby. n.d. "History." Accessed August 8, 2019. https://web.archive
.org/web/20101020154714/http:/www.castleashbygardens.co.uk/history
.html.

Certosa di Pavia. n.d. "Monumento." Accessed August 8, 2019. http://www
.certosadipavia.it/monumento/.

Chance, Helena. 2012. "Interior and Garden Design." In *Edith Wharton
in Context*, edited by Laura Rattray, 199–208. Cambridge: Cambridge
Univ. Press.

Château de Cheverny. n.d. "The Château." Accessed August 8, 2019.
https://www.chateau-cheverny.fr/en/discover-the-estate/the-chateau
.html.

Château de Fontainebleau. n.d. "The Petits Appartements." Accessed August
8, 2019. https://www.chateaudefontainebleau.fr/en/explore-the-castle
-and-gardens/fontainebleau-rooms/fontainebleau-kings/?phrase=petits
+apartements#.

Château de Versailles. n.d. "The English Garden." Accessed August 8, 2019.
http://en.chateauversailles.fr/discover/estate/estate-trianon/english
-gardens#the-love-monument.

———. n.d. "The Grand Trianon." Château de Versailles. Accessed April 15,
2020. http://en.chateauversailles.fr/discover/estate/estate-trianon/grand
-trianon#the-empress-apartments.

———. n.d. "L'Appartement de Madame de Pompadour." Accessed May
27, 2019. http://www.chateauversailles.fr/decouvrir/domaine/chateau
/appartements-favorites#l%E2%80%99appartement-de-la-marquise
-de-pompadour.

Château Royal de Blois. n.d. "History and Architecture." Accessed August 8, 2019. https://en.chateaudeblois.fr/2193-history-and-architecture
.htm.

Chevening House. n.d. "Chevening House—A History." Accessed August 8,
2019. http://www.cheveninghouse.com/history.htm.

Chilvers, Ian. 2015. "Pitti Palace." In *The Oxford Dictionary of Art and Artists*, 5th ed., edited by Ian Chilvers. Oxford: Oxford Univ. Press. https://
www.oxfordreference.com/view/10.1093/acref/9780191782763.001.0001
/acref-9780191782763-e-1932.

Chimney Safety Institute of America. 2022. "The Anatomy of Your Fireplace." YouTube, July 7, 2022. https://www.youtube.com/watch?v=qng
WNQoUCPA.

Codman Family Papers (MS001). 1671–1969. Historic New England Collection, Library and Archives. Otis House Museum, Boston, MA.

Coles, William A. 1997. "The Genesis of a Classic." In *The Decoration of Houses by Edith Wharton and Ogden Codman, Jr.: The Revised and Expanded Classical America Edition*, 256–75. New York: W. W. Norton.

Commission Diocésaine d'Art Sacré de Paris. n.d. "Baiser de Paix." Accessed January 20, 2021. https://www.paris.catholique.fr/baiser-de-paix.html.

The Concise Oxford Companion to English Literature. 2013. "Orlando Innamorato." New York: Oxford Univ. Press. https://www.oxfordreference.com/view/10.1093/oi/authority.20110803100254422.

"*The Decoration of Houses*." 1898. *Architect and Building News*, January 22, 1898, 28–29.

Dethan, Georges. 2020. "Jules, Cardinal Mazarin." In *Encyclopedia Britannica*, last updated March 5, 2024. https://www.britannica.com/biography/Cardinal-Jules-Mazarin.

Dictionary.com. s.v. "Guipure." Accessed December 8, 2023. https://www.dictionary.com/browse/guipure.

———. s.v. "Photogravure." Accessed December 8, 2023. https://www.dictionary.com/browse/photogravure.

Domaine National de Chambord. n.d. "The Château." Accessed August 8, 2019. https://www.chambord.org/en/history/the-chateau/.

Dutch Crafters. 2016. "History of the Roll Top Desk." Dutch Crafters, October 24, 2016. https://www.dutchcrafters.com/blog/history-of-roll-top-desk/.

Dwight, Eleanor. 1994. *Edith Wharton: An Extraordinary Life*. New York: Harry N. Abrams.

———. 2007. "Edith Wharton and Ogden Codman: Co-authors, Comrades, and Connoisseurs." *Historic New England Magazine* 8, no. 1 (Summer): 16–21.

Edwards, Clive. 1998. "The Firm of Jackson and Graham." *Furniture History* 34: 238–65.

Ehrlich, Blake et al. 2019. "Rome." In *Encyclopedia Britannica*, last updated March 9, 2024. https://www.britannica.com/place/Rome.

Eliot, George. 1884. "A Minor Prophet." In *The Poems of George Eliot*. Wikisource. Accessed November 26, 2023. https://en.m.wikisource.org/wiki/The_poems_of_George_Eliot_(Crowell,_1884)/A_Minor_Prophet.

Encyclopedia Britannica (EB). 1998a. s.v. "Cortile." Accessed August 8, 2019. https://www.britannica.com/technology/cortile.

———. 1998b. s.v. "Intercolumniation." Accessed August 8, 2019. https://www.britannica.com/technology/intercolumniation.

———. 1998c. s.v. "Melas Carpet." Accessed August 8, 2019. https://www.britannica.com/art/Melas-carpet.

———. 1998d. s.v. "Smyrna Carpet." Accessed August 8, 2019. https://www.britannica.com/art/Smyrna-carpet.

———. 2005. s.v. "Brussels Carpet." Accessed August 8, 2019. https://www.britannica.com/art/Brussels-carpet.

———. 2006. s.v. "Escutcheon." Accessed August 8, 2019. https://www.britannica.com/topic/escutcheon.

———. 2007a. s.v. "Colonna Family." Accessed February 9, 2021. https://www.britannica.com/topic/Colonna-family.

———. 2007b. s.v. "Malatesta Family." Accessed February 9, 2021. https://www.britannica.com/topic/Malatesta-family.

———. 2008. s.v. "Savonnerie Carpet." Accessed August 8, 2019. https://www.britannica.com/art/Savonnerie-carpet.

———. 2010a. s.v. "Perpendicular Style." Accessed August 8, 2019. https://www.britannica.com/art/Perpendicular-style.

———. 2010b. s.v. "Teatro Farnese." Accessed August 8, 2019. https://www.britannica.com/topic/Teatro-Farnese.

———. 2010c. s.v. "Urbino." Accessed August 8, 2019. https://www.britannica.com/place/Urbino.

———. 2011a. s.v. "Chippendale." Accessed August 8, 2019. https://www.britannica.com/topic/Chippendale.

———. 2011b. s.v. "Du Cerceau Family." Accessed August 8, 2019. https://www.britannica.com/topic/du-Cerceau-family.

———. 2011c. s.v. "Minton Ware." Accessed February 10, 2021. https://www.britannica.com/art/Minton-ware#ref285288.

———. 2011d. s.v. "Paneling." Accessed August 8, 2019. https://www.britannica.com/topic/paneling.

———. 2011e. s.v. "Tudor Style." Accessed August 8, 2019. https://www.britannica.com/art/Tudor-style.

———. 2012f. s.v. "Faience." Accessed August 8, 2019. https://www.britannica.com/art/faience.

———. 2012g. s.v. "Gonzaga Dynasty." Accessed February 9, 2021. https://www.britannica.com/topic/Gonzaga-dynasty.

———. 2013a. s.v. "French East India Company." Accessed August 8, 2019. https://www.britannica.com/topic/French-East-India-Company.

———. 2013b. s.v. "Ukiyo-e." Accessed January 26, 2021. https://www.britannica.com/art/ukiyo-e.

———. 2014a. s.v. "Fresco Painting." Accessed August 8, 2019. https://www.britannica.com/art/fresco-painting.

———. 2014b. s.v. "Trompe l'oeil." Accessed August 8, 2019. https://www.britannica.com/art/trompe-loeil.

———. 2015a. s.v. "Statue of Zeus." Accessed February 10, 2021. https://www.britannica.com/topic/Statue-of-Zeus.

———. 2015b. s.v. "Venus de Milo." Accessed January 19, 2021. https://www.britannica.com/topic/Venus-de-Milo.

———. 2016a. s.v. "Arabesque." Accessed August 8, 2019. https://www.britannica.com/art/arabesque-decorative-style.

———. 2016b. s.v. "Gilding." Accessed February 7, 2021. https://www.britannica.com/art/gilding.

———. 2016c. s.v. "Palladian Window." Accessed August 8, 2019. https://www.britannica.com/technology/Palladian-window.

———. 2016d. s.v. "Pendentive." Accessed August 8, 2019. https://www.britannica.com/technology/pendentive.

———. 2016e. s.v. "Pinnacle." Accessed August 8, 2019. https://www.britannica.com/technology/pinnacle.

———. 2016f. s.v. "Rotunda." Accessed August 8, 2019. https://www.britannica.com/technology/rotunda-architecture.

———. 2017a. s.v. "Augustan Age." Accessed August 8, 2019. www.britannica.com/art/Augustan-Age-Latin-literature.

———. 2017b. s.v. "Balustrade." Accessed August 8, 2019. https://www.britannica.com/technology/balustrade.

———. 2017c. s.v. "Fleur-de-lis." Accessed August 8, 2019. https://www.britannica.com/topic/fleur-de-lis.

———. 2017d. s.v. "Palladianism." Accessed August 8, 2019. https://www.britannica.com/art/Palladianism.

———. 2017e. s.v. "Romanesque Architecture." Accessed August 8, 2019. https://www.britannica.com/art/Romanesque-architecture.

———. 2017f. s.v. "Sforza Family." Accessed August 8, 2019. https://www.britannica.com/topic/Sforza-family.

———. 2017g. s.v. "Toile de Jouy." Accessed February 5, 2020. https://www.britannica.com/topic/toile-de-Jouy.

———. 2018a. s.v. "Acanthus." Accessed August 8, 2019. https://www.britannica.com/art/acanthus-ornamental-motif.

———. 2018b. s.v. "Aeneid." Accessed August 8, 2019. https://www.britannica.com/topic/Aeneid.

———. 2018c. s.v. "Albert Memorial." Accessed August 8, 2019. https://www.britannica.com/topic/Albert-Memorial.

———. 2018d. s.v. "Bucranium." Accessed August 8, 2019. https://www.britannica.com/art/bucranium.

———. 2018e. s.v. "Empire Style." Accessed August 8, 2019. https://www.britannica.com/art/Empire-style.

———. 2018f. s.v. "House of Tudor." Accessed August 8, 2019. https://www.britannica.com/topic/House-of-Tudor.

———. 2018g. s.v. "Intarsia." Accessed August 8, 2019. https://www.britannica.com/art/intarsia.

———. 2018h. s.v. "Jeanne Bécu, Countess du Barry." Accessed August 8, 2019. https://www.britannica.com/biography/Jeanne-Becu-comtesse-du-Barry.

———. 2018i. s.v. "Le Morte d'Arthur." Accessed January 19, 2021. https://www.britannica.com/topic/Le-Morte-Darthur.

———. 2018j. s.v. "Majolica." Accessed February 7, 2021. https://www.britannica.com/art/majolica.

———. 2018k. s.v. "Mezzotint." Accessed August 8, 2019. https://www.britannica.com/technology/mezzotint.

———. 2018l. s.v. "Onyx." Accessed February 7, 2021. https://www.britannica.com/science/onyx.

———. 2018m. s.v. "Relief." Accessed August 8, 2019. https://www.britannica.com/art/relief-sculpture.

———. 2018n. s.v. "Rocaille." Accessed August 8, 2019. https://www.britannica.com/art/rocaille.

———. 2018o. s.v. "The Knight's Tale." Accessed January 19, 2021. https://www.britannica.com/topic/The-Knights-Tale.

———. 2018p. s.v. "Vaux-le-Vicomte." Accessed August 8, 2019. https://www.britannica.com/topic/Vaux-le-Vicomte.

———. 2019a. s.v. "Abraham Bosse." Accessed August 8, 2019. https://www
.britannica.com/biography/Abraham-Bosse.

———. 2019b. s.v. "Agostino Di Duccio." Accessed August 8, 2019. https://
www.britannica.com/biography/Agostino-di-Duccio.

———. 2019c. s.v. "Ange-Jacques Gabriel." Accessed August 8, 2019. https://
www.britannica.com/biography/Ange-Jacques-Gabriel.

———. 2019d. s.v. "Annibale Carracci." Accessed August 8, 2019. https://
www.britannica.com/biography/Annibale-Carracci.

———. 2019e. s.v. "Antoine Coypel." Accessed August 8, 2019. https://www
.britannica.com/biography/Antoine-Coypel.

———. 2019f. s.v. "Antoine Watteau." Accessed August 8, 2019. https://www
.britannica.com/biography/Antoine-Watteau.

———. 2019g. s.v. "Augustin Pajou." Accessed August 8, 2019. https://www
.britannica.com/biography/Augustin-Pajou.

———. 2019h. s.v. "Caryatid." Accessed August 8, 2019. https://www
.britannica.com/technology/caryatid.

———. 2019i. s.v. "Catherine di Vivonne, Marquise de Rambouillet." Accessed August 8, 2019. https://www.britannica.com/biography/Catherine
-de-Vivonne-marquise-de-Rambouillet.

———. 2019j. s.v. "Charles Le Brun." Accessed August 8, 2019. https://www
.britannica.com/biography/Charles-Le-Brun.

———. 2019k. s.v. "Domenico Fontana." Accessed August 8, 2019. https://
www.britannica.com/biography/Domenico-Fontana.

———. 2019l. s.v. "Eustache Le Sueur." Accessed August 8, 2019. https://
www.britannica.com/biography/Eustache-Le-Sueur.

———. 2019m. s.v. "Filippo Juvarra." Accessed August 8, 2019. https://www
.britannica.com/biography/Filippo-Juvarra.

———. 2019o. s.v. "Georgian Style." Accessed August 8, 2019. https://www
.britannica.com/art/Georgian-style.

———. 2019p. s.v. "Giovanni Battista Piranesi." Accessed August 8, 2019.
https://www.britannica.com/biography/Giovanni-Battista-Piranesi.

———. 2019q. s.v. "Gothic Architecture." Accessed August 8, 2019. https://
www.britannica.com/art/Gothic-architecture.

———. 2019r. s.v. "Grinling Gibbons." Accessed August 8, 2019. https://
www.britannica.com/biography/Grinling-Gibbons.

———. 2019s. "Jacques-François Blondel." Accessed August 8, 2019. https://
www.britannica.com/biography/Jacques-Francois-Blondel.

———. 2019t. s.v. "Jean Berain, the Elder." Accessed August 8, 2019. https://www.britannica.com/biography/Jean-Berain-the-Elder.

———. 2019u. s.v. "Jean Froissart." Accessed January 19, 2021. https://www.britannica.com/biography/Jean-Froissart.

———. 2019v. s.v. "Jules Hardouin-Mansart." Accessed August 8, 2019. https://www.britannica.com/biography/Jules-Hardouin-Mansart.

———. 2019w. s.v. "Kleinmeister." Accessed August 8, 2019. https://www.britannica.com/topic/Kleinmeister.

———. 2019x. s.v. "Louis XV." https://www.britannica.com/biography/Louis-XV.

———. 2019y. s.v. "Luca della Robbia." Accessed August 8, 2019. https://www.britannica.com/biography/Luca-della-Robbia.

———. 2019z. s.v. "Luca Giordano." Accessed August 8, 2019. https://www.britannica.com/biography/Luca-Giordano.

———. 2019aa. s.v. "Luigi Vanvitelli." Accessed August 8, 2019. https://www.britannica.com/biography/Luigi-Vanvitelli.

———. 2019bb. s.v. "Marcantonio Raimondi." Accessed August 8, 2019. https://www.britannica.com/biography/Marcantonio-Raimondi.

———. 2019cc. s.v. "Marie de Médicis." Accessed August 8, 2019. https://www.britannica.com/biography/Marie-de-Medicis.

———. 2019dd. s.v. "Marie-Antoinette." Accessed August 8, 2019. https://www.britannica.com/biography/Marie-Antoinette-queen-of-France.

———. 2019ee. s.v. "Palazzo del Te." Accessed August 8, 2019. https://www.britannica.com/topic/Palazzo-del-Te.

———. 2019ff. s.v. "Philibert Delorme." Accessed August 8, 2019. https://www.britannica.com/biography/Philibert-Delorme.

———. 2019gg. s.v. "Pre-Raphaelite Brotherhood." Accessed February 9, 2021. https://www.britannica.com/art/Pre-Raphaelite-Brotherhood.

———. 2019hh. s.v. "Robert de Cotte." Accessed August 8, 2019. https://www.britannica.com/biography/Robert-de-Cotte.

———. 2019ii. s.v. "Rococo." https://www.britannica.com/art/Rococo.

———. 2019jj. s.v. "Simon Vouet." Accessed August 8, 2019. https://www.britannica.com/biography/Simon-Vouet.

———. 2019kk. s.v. "Thomas Malory." Accessed January 19, 2021. https://www.britannica.com/biography/Thomas-Malory.

———. 2019ll. s.v. "Thomas Sheraton." Accessed August 8, 2019. https://www.britannica.com/biography/Thomas-Sheraton.

———. 2019mm. s.v. "Valois Dynasty." December 1. https://www.britannica .com/topic/Valois-dynasty.

———. 2019nn. s.v. "Vittore Carpaccio." Accessed February 5, 2021. https:// www.britannica.com/biography/Vittore-Carpaccio.

———. 2020a. s.v. "Albrecht Dürer." Accessed January 26, 2021. https://www .britannica.com/biography/Albrecht-Durer-German-artist/Service-to -Maximilian-I.

———. 2020b. s.v. "Anthony van Dyck." Accessed February 3, 2021. https:// www.britannica.com/biography/Anthony-Van-Dyck.

———. 2020c. s.v. "Antoine-Louis Barye." Accessed February 5, 2020. https://www.britannica.com/biography/Antoine-Louis-Barye.

———. 2020d. s.v. "Antonio Canova." Accessed February 5, 2021. https:// www.britannica.com/biography/Antonio-Canova-marchese-dIschia.

———. 2020e. s.v. "Athena." Accessed February 10, 2021. https://www .britannica.com/topic/Athena-Greek-mythology.

———. 2020f. s.v. "Bartolomé Esteban Murillo." Accessed February 5, 2021. https://www.britannica.com/biography/Bartolome-Esteban-Murillo.

———. 2020g. s.v. "Benozzo Gozzoli." Accessed February 5, 2021. https:// www.britannica.com/biography/Benozzo-Gozzoli.

———. 2020h. s.v. "Benvenuto Cellini." Accessed February 6, 2021. https:// www.britannica.com/biography/Benvenuto-Cellini-Italian-artist.

———. 2020i. s.v. "Don Quixote." Accessed January 26, 2021. https://www .britannica.com/topic/Don-Quixote-novel.

———. 2020j. s.v. "Edwin Landseer." Accessed January 26, 2021. https:// www.britannica.com/biography/Edwin-Landseer.

———. 2020k. s.v. "Giorgio Vasari." Accessed February 10, 2021. https:// www.britannica.com/biography/Giorgio-Vasari.

———. 2020l. s.v. "Jacques-Auguste de Thou." Accessed January 26, 2021. https://www.britannica.com/biography/Jacques-Auguste-de-Thou.

———. 2020m. s.v. "Jean Grolier de Servières, Vicomte d'Aguisy." Accessed February 6, 2021. https://www.britannica.com/biography/Jean-Grolier -de-Servieres-vicomte-dAguisy.

———. 2020n. s.v. "John Addington Symonds." Accessed February 6, 2021. https://www.britannica.com/biography/John-Addington-Symonds.

———. 2020o. s.v. "John Evelyn." Accessed January 26, 2021. https://www .britannica.com/biography/John-Evelyn.

———. 2020p. s.v. "Jules, Cardinal Mazarin." Accessed February 9, 2021. https://www.britannica.com/biography/Cardinal-Jules-Mazarin.

———. 2020q. s.v. "Julius II." Accessed February 9, 2021. https://www.britannica.com/biography/Julius-II.

———. 2020r. s.v. "Meissen Porcelain." Accessed January 10, 2020. https://www.britannica.com/art/Meissen-porcelain.

———. 2020s. s.v. "Parthenon." Accessed January 19, 2021. https://www.britannica.com/topic/Parthenon.

———. 2020t. s.v. "Pinturicchio." Accessed February 5, 2021. https://www.britannica.com/biography/Pinturicchio.

———. 2020u. s.v. "Remiremont." Accessed January 26, 2021. https://www.britannica.com/place/Remiremont.

———. 2020v. s.v. "Renaissance." Accessed January 26, 2021. https://www.britannica.com/event/Renaissance.

———. 2020w. s.v. "Saint George." Accessed January 26, 2020. https://www.britannica.com/biography/Donatello#ref28413.

———. 2020x. s.v. "Sèvres Porcelain." Accessed February 7, 2021. https://www.britannica.com/art/Sevres-porcelain.

———. 2020y. s.v. "William Morris." Accessed February 9, 2021. https://www.britannica.com/biography/William-Morris-British-artist-and-author.

———. 2021a. s.v. "Andrea del Verrocchio." Accessed February 5, 2021. https://www.britannica.com/biography/Andrea-del-Verrocchio.

———. 2021b. s.v. "Erasmus." Accessed January 26, 2021. https://www.britannica.com/biography/Erasmus-Dutch-humanist.

———. 2021c. s.v. "Giovanni Bellini." Accessed February 5, 2020. https://www.britannica.com/biography/Giovanni-Bellini-Italian-painter.

———. 2021d. s.v. "Hans Holbein." Accessed January 26, 2021. https://www.britannica.com/biography/Hans-Holbein-the-Younger.

———. 2021e. s.v. "Jean-Baptiste Pigalle." Accessed January 26, 2021. https://www.britannica.com/biography/Jean-Baptiste-Pigalle.

———. 2021f. s.v. "John Ruskin." Accessed February 9, 2021. https://www.britannica.com/biography/John-Ruskin.

———. 2021g. s.v. "Miguel de Cervantes." Accessed January 19, 2021. https://www.britannica.com/biography/Miguel-de-Cervantes.

———. 2021h. s.v. "Palazzo Medici-Riccardi." Accessed January 23, 2021. https://www.britannica.com/place/Palazzo-Medici-Riccardi.

————. 2021i. s.v. "Pietro Longhi." Accessed February 6, 2021. https://www
.britannica.com/biography/Pietro-Longhi.

————. 2021j. s.v. "Sandro Botticelli." Accessed February 6, 2021. https://
www.britannica.com/biography/Sandro-Botticelli/Secular-patronage
-and-works.

————. 2024a. s.v. "Étienne-François de Choiseul, duke de Choiseul." Accessed April 20, 2024. https://www.britannica.com/biography/Etienne
-Francois-de-Choiseul-duc-de-Choiseul.

————. 2024b. s.v. "François Clouet." Accessed April 20, 2024. https://www
.britannica.com/biography/Francois-Clouet.

————. 2024c. s.v. "Goliath." Accessed April 20, 2024. https://www.britannica
.com/biography/Goliath-biblical-figure.

————. 2024d. s.v. "Sideboard." Accessed April 20, 2024. https://www
.britannica.com/topic/sideboard.

Evans, Anne-Marie. 2012. "Wharton's Writings on Screen," In *Edith Wharton in Context*, edited by Laura Rattray, 167–76. Cambridge: Cambridge
Univ. Press.

Fee, Sarah, ed. *Cloth That Changed the World: The Art and Fashion of Indian
Chintz*. New Haven, CT: Yale Univ. Press, 2020.

Fryer, Judith. 1986. *Felicitous Space: The Imaginative Structures of Edith
Wharton and Willa Cather*. Chapel Hill: Univ. of North Carolina
Press.

Furniture History Society. 2022. "Gillow & Company (1862–1897)." Last
updated December 5, 2022. https://bifmo.furniturehistorysociety.org
/entry/gillow-company-1862-1897.

Gáldy, Andrea M., ed. 2013. *Agnolo Bronzino: Medici Court Artist in Context*.
Newcastle upon Tyne, UK: Cambridge Scholars Publishing. https://
www.cambridgescholars.com/product/978-1-4438-4412-3.

Gere, Charlotte. 1989. *Nineteenth-Century Decoration: The Art of the Interior*.
London: Weidenfeld & Nicolson.

Getty. n.d. "Jean-Michel Moreau le Jeune." Accessed August 8, 2019.
http://www.getty.edu/art/collection/artists/877/jean-michel-moreau-le
-jeune-french-1741-1814/.

Goldman-Price, Irene, ed. 2012. *My Dear Governess: The Letters of Edith
Wharton and Anna Bahlmann*. New Haven, CT: Yale Univ. Press.

————. 2019. *Selected Poems of Edith Wharton*. New York: Scribner.

Goldsmith, Meredith L., and Emily J. Orlando, eds. 2016. *Edith Wharton and Cosmopolitanism*. Gainesville: Univ. Press of Florida.

Goncourt, Edmond Louis Antoine Huot de. 1914. *Madame du Barry: Nineteenth Century Collections Online*: London: J. Long. https://link.gale.com/apps/doc/AUDIGY691121665/NCCO?u=a04fu&sid=NCCO&xid=2b6 9f764&pg=148.

Gondi Palace. n.d. "History and Ownership." Accessed December 8, 2023. https://www.gondi.com/tenute/palazzo-gondi.

Granger Historical Picture Archive. n.d. Image no. 0048430. Accessed August 8, 2019. https://www.granger.com/results.asp?image=0048430& screenwidth=782.

Grier, Katherine. 1988. *Culture and Comfort: Parlor Making and Middle-Class Identity, 1850–1930*. Rochester, NY: Strong Museum.

Grove Encyclopedia of Northern Renaissance Art. 2009. "Shute, John." Oxford Univ. Press. https://www.oxfordreference.com/display/10.1093/acref/978 0195334661.001.0001/acref-9780195334661-e-1704?rskey=ghSJuZ&result =1681.

Hardy, Anne. 2003. "Germ." In *The Oxford Companion to the History of Modern Science*, edited by J. L. Heilbron. Oxford: Oxford Univ. Press. https://www.oxfordreference.com/view/10.1093/acref/9780195112290.001.0001/acref-9780195112290-e-0304.

Harris, Cyril, ed. 2006. "Dutch Tile." In *Dictionary of Architecture and Construction*, 4th ed., edited by Cyril M. Harris. New York: McGraw-Hill.

Herefordshire Past. n.d. "Shobdon Court History." Accessed August 8, 2019. https://herefordshirepast.co.uk/buildings/shobdon-court/.

Hindley, Meredith. 2018. "Edith Wharton in Morocco." *Humanities* 39, no. 3 (Summer): 12–17.

"Hints for Home Decoration." 1898. *Critic*, January 8, 1898.

Holkham Hall. "History." Accessed August 8, 2019. https://web.archive.org/web/20120212231555/http:/www.holkham.co.uk/html/history.html.

Holm, Alvin. 1997. "*The Decoration of Houses* as a Basic Text." In *The Decoration of Houses by Edith Wharton and Ogden Codman, Jr.: The Revised and Expanded Classical America Edition*, 276–79. New York: W. W. Norton.

Hurlingham Club. n.d. "The Estate." Accessed August 8, 2019. https://hurlinghamclub.org.uk/hurlingham-home.

The Hutchinson Unabridged Encyclopedia with Atlas and Weather Guide. 2018. "Borghese Palace." https://search.credoreference.com/articles/Qm9vao FydGljbGU6NTYyNjM3?cid=8903.&aid=98621.

Jayne, Thomas, with Ted Loos. 2018. *Classical Principles for Modern Design: Lessons from Edith Wharton and Ogden Codman's The Decoration of Houses.* New York: Monacelli Press.

Lasansky, D. Medina. 2016. "Beyond the Guidebook: Edith Wharton's Rediscovery of San Vivaldo." In *Edith Wharton and Cosmopolitanism*, edited by Meredith L. Goldsmith, and Emily J. Orlando, 132–65. Gainesville: Univ. Press of Florida.

Landseer, Edwin Henry, Sir. 1844. *Shoeing.* https://www.tate.org.uk/art /artworks/landseer-shoeing-n00606.

Lee, Hermione. 2007. *Edith Wharton.* New York: Alfred A. Knopf.

Lewis, R. W. B., ed. 1968. *The Collected Short Stories of Edith Wharton.* Vol. 1. New York: Charles Scribner's Sons.

———. 1975. *Edith Wharton: A Biography.* New York: Harper & Row.

Lewis, R. W. B., and Nancy Lewis, eds. 1988. *The Letters of Edith Wharton.* New York: Macmillan/Collier.

Lubbock, Percy. 1947. *Portrait of Edith Wharton.* New York: D. Appleton-Century Co.

Macheski, Cecilia. 2012. "Architecture." In *Edith Wharton in Context*, edited by Laura Rattray, 189–98. Cambridge: Cambridge Univ. Press.

MAD Paris. n.d. "Musée des Arts Décoratifs." Accessed August 8, 2019. https://madparis.fr/en/museums/musee-des-arts-decoratifs/.

Madame de Sévigné to Madame de Grignan, February 20, 1671. 1862. *Lettres de Madame de Sévigné, de sa Famille et de ses Amis*, nouvelle éd., tome deuxième. Paris: Hachette.

Magner, Lois N. 2009. *A History of Infectious Diseases and the Microbial World.* Westport, CT: ABC-CLIO.

Mayeux, Henri. 1888. "A Manual of Decorative Composition . . ." Translated by J. Gonino. New York: D. Appleton & Company. https://www.met museum.org/art/collection/search/353799.

Ménard et Desenne, Fils, Libraires. 1826. *Table générales des lois.* Vol. 3, 397. Paris: Ménard et Desenne, Fils, Libraires. Accessed September 30, 2023. https://www.google.com/books/edition/Tables_g%C3%A9n%C3%A9 rales_des_lois_arr%C3%AAt%C3%A9s_d/wUEUAAAAYAAJ?hl=en

&gbpv=1&dq=suppression+de+la+compagnie+des+indes+1794&pg=PA3
97&printsec=frontcover.

Merriam-Webster (M-W). s.v. "Finicky, adj." Accessed August 8, 2019. https://
www.merriam-webster.com/dictionary/finicky.

———. s.v. "Andiron, n." Accessed August 8, 2019. https://www.merriam
-webster.com/dictionary/andiron.

———. s.v. "Bibelot." Accessed February 6, 2021. https://www.merriam
-webster.com/dictionary/bibelot.

———. s.v. "Bituminous, adj." Accessed January 26, 2021. https://www
.merriam-webster.com/dictionary/bituminous.

———. s.v. "Bower, n. (1)." Accessed August 8, 2019. https://www.merriam
-webster.com/dictionary/bower.

———. s.v. "Bric-a-brac." Accessed February 6, 2021. https://www.merriam
-webster.com/dictionary/bric-a-brac.

———. s.v. "Brocatelle." Accessed January 23, 2021. https://www.merriam
-webster.com/dictionary/brocatelle.

———. s.v. "Buckram." Accessed January 21, 2021. https://www.merriam
-webster.com/dictionary/buckram.

———. s.v. "Caisson, n." Accessed August 8, 2019. https://www.merriam
-webster.com/dictionary/caisson.

———. s.v. "Calcimine, n." Accessed August 8, 2019. https://www.merriam
-webster.com/dictionary/calcimine.

———. s.v. "Cheval Glass." Accessed January 24, 2021. https://www
.merriam-webster.com/dictionary/chevalglass.

———. s.v. "Chiffonier." Accessed January 24, 2021. https://www.merriam
-webster.com/dictionary/chiffonier.

———. s.v. "Chimney Breast, n." Accessed August 8, 2019. https://www
.merriam-webster.com/dictionary/chimneybreast.

———. s.v. "Chromo, n." Accessed January 19, 2021. https://www.merriam
-webster.com/dictionary/chromo.

———. s.v. "Chryselephantine, adj." Accessed February 10, 2021. https://
www.merriam-webster.com/dictionary/chryselephantine.

———. s.v. "Cire Perdue, n." Accessed February 10, 2021. https://www
.merriam-webster.com/dictionary/cireperdue.

———. s.v. "Coffer, n." Accessed August 8, 2019. https://www.merriam
-webster.com/dictionary/coffer.

———. s.v. "Commode, n." Accessed February 9, 2021. https://www
.merriam-webster.com/dictionary/commode.

———. s.v. "Corinthian, adj." Accessed January 22, 2021. https://www
.merriam-webster.com/dictionary/Corinthian.

———. s.v. "Courtesan." Accessed January 22, 2021. https://www.merriam
-webster.com/dictionary/courtesan.

———. s.v. "Divan, n. (3)." Accessed January 22, 2021. https://www.merriam
-webster.com/dictionary/divan.

———. s.v. "Draftsman." Accessed January 24, 2021. https://www.merriam
-webster.com/dictionary/draftsman.

———. s.v. "Drugget, n." Accessed August 8, 2019. https://www.merriam
-webster.com/dictionary/drugget.

———. s.v. "Duchesse, n. (1)." Accessed August 8, 2019. https://www
.merriam-webster.com/dictionary/duchesse.

———. s.v. "Embrasure, n." Accessed August 8, 2019. https://www.merriam
-webster.com/dictionary/embrasure.

———. s.v. "Extension Table." Accessed January 23, 2021. https://www
.merriam-webster.com/dictionary/extensiontable.

———. s.v. "Fender, n." Accessed August 8, 2019. https://www.merriam
-webster.com/dictionary/fender.

———. s.v. "Festoon, n." Accessed August 8, 2019. https://www.merriam
-webster.com/dictionary/festoon.

———. s.v. "Furbelow, n." Accessed August 8, 2019. https://www.merriam
-webster.com/dictionary/furbelow.

———. s.v. "Furring, n." Accessed August 8, 2019. https://www.merriam
-webster.com/dictionary/furring.

———. s.v. "Garniture, n." Accessed August 8, 2019. https://www.merriam
-webster.com/dictionary/garniture.

———. s.v. "Gilt, adj." Accessed August 8, 2019. https://www.merriam
-webster.com/dictionary/gilt.

———. s.v. "Gimcrack, n." Accessed August 8, 2019. https://www.merriam
-webster.com/dictionary/gimcrack.

———. s.v. "Guipure, n." Accessed August 8, 2019. https://www.merriam
-webster.com/dictionary/guipure.

———. s.v. "Indienne, n." Accessed January 23, 2021. https://www.merriam
-webster.com/dictionary/indienne.

———. s.v. "Jardiniere, n. (1)." Accessed August 8, 2019. https://www .merriam-webster.com/dictionary/jardiniere.

———. s.v. "Lambrequin, n. (2)." Accessed August 8, 2019. https://www .merriam-webster.com/dictionary/lambrequin.

———. s.v. "Leghorn, n." Accessed January 21, 2021. https://www.merriam -webster.com/dictionary/leghorn.

———. s.v. "Mortise Lock, n." Accessed August 8, 2019. https://www .merriam-webster.com/dictionary/mortiselock.

———. s.v. "Mullion, n." Accessed August 8, 2019. https://www.merriam -webster.com/dictionary/mullion.

———. s.v. "Muniment Room, n." Accessed August 8, 2019. https://www .merriam-webster.com/dictionary/munimentroom.

———. s.v. "Namby-pamby, adj." Accessed February 3, 2021. https://www .merriam-webster.com/dictionary/namby-pamby.

———. s.v. "Objet d'art, n." Accessed February 6, 2021. https://www .merriam-webster.com/dictionary/objetdart.

———. s.v. "Oilcloth, n." Accessed August 8, 2019. https://www.merriam -webster.com/dictionary/oilcloth.

———. s.v. "Old Master, n." Accessed January 26, 2021. https://www .merriam-webster.com/dictionary/oldmaster.

———. s.v. "Ormolu, n." Accessed April 20, 2024. https://www.merriam -webster.com/dictionary/ormolu.

———. s.v. "Overdoor, n." Accessed August 8, 2019. https://www.merriam -webster.com/dictionary/overdoor.

———. s.v. "Pagoda." Accessed January 24, 2021. https://www.merriam -webster.com/dictionary/pagoda.

———. s.v. "Parquetry, n." Accessed August 8, 2019. https://www.merriam -webster.com/dictionary/parquetry.

———. s.v. "Patina, n. (1a)." Accessed February 10, 2021. https://www .merriam-webster.com/dictionary/patina.

———. s.v. "Pedagogy, n." Accessed January 19, 2021. https://www.merriam -webster.com/dictionary/pedagogy.

———. s.v. "Pinchbeck, n. (1)." Accessed August 8, 2019. https://www .merriam-webster.com/dictionary/pinchbeck.

———. s.v. "Plasticator, n." Accessed February 10, 2021. https://www .merriam-webster.com/dictionary/plasticator.

————. s.v. "Portiere, n." Accessed August 8, 2019. https://www.merriam -webster.com/dictionary/portiere.

————. s.v. "Regime, n. (2a)." Accessed January 19, 2021. https://www .merriam-webster.com/dictionary/regime.

————. s.v. "Scagliola, n." Accessed August 8, 2019. https://www.merriam -webster.com/dictionary/scagliola.

————. s.v. "Sinuous, adj." Accessed August 8, 2019. https://www.merriam -webster.com/dictionary/sinuous.

————. s.v. "Still Life." Accessed January 23, 2021. https://www.merriam -webster.com/dictionary/stilllife.

————. s.v. "Stringboard, n." Accessed August 8, 2019. https://www .merriam-webster.com/dictionary/stringboard.

————. s.v. "Surfeit, v." Accessed January 21, 2021. https://www.merriam -webster.com/dictionary/surfeit.

————. s.v. "Terribilita." Accessed January 16, 2021. https://www.merriam -webster.com/dictionary/terribilita.

————. s.v. "Tree Calf." Accessed January 21, 2021. https://www.merriam -webster.com/dictionary/treecalf.

————. s.v. "Trestle." Accessed January 22, 2021. https://www.merriam -webster.com/dictionary/trestle.

————. s.v. "Trestle Table." Accessed January 22, 2021. https://www .merriam-webster.com/dictionary/trestletable.

————. s.v. "Velarium, n." Accessed August 8, 2019. https://www.merriam -webster.com/dictionary/velarium.

————. s.v. "Vitrine, n." Accessed August 8, 2019. https://www.merriam -webster.com/dictionary/vitrine.

Metcalf, Pauline C., ed. 1988. *Ogden Codman and the Decoration of Houses.* Boston: Boston Athenaeum/David R. Godine.

Metropolitan Museum of Art. n.d. "A Complete Body of Architecture . . . In Which Are Interspersed Some Designs of Inigo Jones Never Before Published . . ." Accessed March 5, 2024. https://www.metmuseum.org /art/collection/search/350859.

————. n.d. "Daybed (lit de repos), ca. 1750–75." Accessed August 8, 2019. https://www.metmuseum.org/art/collection/search/194946.

Meubliz. n.d. "Définition d'un salon à l'italienne." Accessed August 8, 2019. https://www.meubliz.com/definition/salon_a_l_italienne/.

Mey, Andree Marie. 1991. "Changing Perceptions of the Bedchamber: A Study of Furniture and Furnishings in Philadelphia County, 1800–1900." Master's thesis, Univ. of Pennsylvania. http://repository.upenn.edu/hp _theses/458.

Middleton, Robert David et al. 2018. "Western Architecture." In *Encyclopedia Britannica*, last updated December 2, 2023. https://www.britannica.com /art/Western-architecture.

Millikin, Sandra. 2019. "Robert Adam." *Encyclopedia Britannica*, last updated February 28, 2024. https://www.britannica.com/biography/Robert -Adam.

Millon, Henry A. et al. 2018. "Colonial." In *Encyclopedia Britannica*, last updated December 2, 2023. https://www.britannica.com/art/Western -architecture.

Mitford, Nancy. n.d. "Jeanne-Antoinette Poisson, Marquise de Pompadour." In *Encyclopedia Britannica*, last updated December 25, 2023. https://www .britannica.com/biography/Jeanne-Antoinette-Poisson-marquise-de -Pompadour.

Murray, Peter J. 2019a. "Giotto." In *Encyclopedia Britannica*, last updated January 4, 2024. https://www.britannica.com/biography/Giotto-di-Bon done.

———. 2019b. "Perugino." In *Encyclopedia Britannica*, last updated January 28, 2024. https://www.britannica.com/biography/Perugino.

Museum of the City of New York. n.d. "Miss Kate Fearing Strong (later Mrs. Arthur Welman." https://collections.mcny.org/C.aspx?VP3=Search Result_VPage&VBID=24UP1GGR4R_X&SMLS=1&RW=1440& RH=708.

Museums of Florence. n.d. "National Museum of Bargello." Accessed December 8, 2023. http://www.museumsinflorence.com/musei/museum_of _bargello.html.

Old English Doors. n.d. "A Short History of Doors in the Victorian Era." Accessed August 8, 2019. http://www.oldenglishdoors.co.uk/latest-news /doors-victorian-era.

Olin-Ammentorp, Julie. 1988. "Edith Wharton's Challenge to Feminist Criticism." *Studies in American Fiction* 16, no. 2 (Autumn): 237–44.

Orlando, Emily J. 2007a. *Edith Wharton and the Visual Arts*. Tuscaloosa: Univ. of Alabama Press.

―――. 2017b. "'Perilous Coquetry': Oscar Wilde's Influence on Edith Wharton and Ogden Codman, Jr." *American Literary Realism* 50, no. 1 (Fall): 25–43.

―――. 2017c. "The 'Queer Shadow' of Ogden Codman in Edith Wharton's 'Summer.'" *Studies in American Naturalism* 12, no. 2 (Winter): 220–43.

―――. 2020. "'One Long Vision of Beauty': Edith Wharton and Italian Visual Culture." *Edith Wharton Review* 36, no. 1: 25–47.

Orlando, Emily J., ed. 2023a. *The Bloomsbury Handbook to Edith Wharton.* London: Bloomsbury Academic.

―――. 2023b. "The Most Unlikable Woman: On Sofia Coppola's Stymied Quest to Bring Undine Spragg to Screen." Literary Hub, November 8, 2023. https://lithub.com/the-most-unlikable-woman-on-sofia-coppolas -stymied-quest-to-bring-undine-spragg-to-screen/.

Overton, Grant. 1923. "Edith Wharton and the Time-Spirit." In *American Nights Entertainment.* New York: Little and Ives.

Owens, Mitchell. 2013. "The Legacy of Edith Wharton's *The Decoration of Houses.*" *Architectural Digest*, February 13, 2013.

Oxford English Dictionary Online (OED). s.v. "Architrave, n." Accessed August 8, 2019. http://www.oed.com/view/Entry/10411?redirectedFrom=archit rave#eid.

―――. s.v. "Black Art, n." Accessed August 8, 2019. http://www.oed.com /view/Entry/19676?redirectedFrom=black+art#eid

―――. s.v. "Brigandage n." Accessed August 8, 2019. http://www.oed.com /view/Entry/23288?redirectedFrom=brigandage#eid

―――. s.v. "Cornice, n." Accessed August 8, 2019. http://www.oed.com /view/Entry/41671?rskey=Z9ewBm&result=1&isAdvanced=false#eid.

―――. s.v. "Moulding/molding, n." Accessed August 8, 2019. https://www .oed.com/dictionary/moulding_n1?tab=factsheet#35723035.

Oxford Reference. s.v. "Orlando Innamorato." Accessed March 5, 2024. https://www.oxfordreference.com/view/10.1093/oi/authority.20110803 100254422.

―――. s.v. "Ulisse Cantagalli (1839–1901)." Accessed August 8, 2019. https://www.oxfordreference.com/view/10.1093/oi/authority.20110803 095546635.

Palazzo Vertemate Franchi. n.d. "Visita a Palazzo: Nuove Disposizioni." Accessed August 8, 2019. http://www.palazzovertemate.it.

Pallucchini, Rodolfo. 2019. "Giovanni Battista Tiepolo." In *Encyclopedia Britannica*, last updated March 1, 2024. https://www.britannica.com /biography/Giovanni-Battista-Tiepolo.

Parrington, Vernon. 2010. "Our Literary Aristocrat." In *Edith Wharton: The Contemporary Reviews*, edited by James W. Tuttleton, Kristin O. Lauer, and Margaret P. Murray, 293–95. Cambridge: Cambridge Univ. Press.

Paul, Robert. 1978. "Clavecin." In *Le Petit Robert, dictionnaire alphabétique et analogique de la langue française*. Paris: Society du Nouveau Littre.

Perkins, Michael. 2014. "The Age of Elegance." *Normal Eye* (blog), July 18, 2014. https://thenormaleye.com/2014/07/28/the-age-of-elegance/.

Powers, Katherine. 2004. "Music-Making Angels in Italian Renaissance Painting: Symbolism and Reality." *Music in Art* 29, no. 1/2: 52–63. http://www.jstor.org/stable/41818751.

Quinlan-McGrath, Mary, and Blosius Palladius. 1990. "Blosius Palladius, 'Suburbanu Augustini Chisii': Introduction, Latin Text and English Translation." *Humanistica Lovaniensia* 39: 93–156. https://www.jstor.org /stable/pdf/23973736.pdf.

Rattray, Laura. 2020. *Edith Wharton and Genre: Beyond Fiction*. London: Palgrave Macmillan.

Rattray, Laura, ed. 2009. *The Unpublished Writings of Edith Wharton: Volume 1, Plays*. London: Routledge.

———. ed. 2012. *Edith Wharton in Context*. Cambridge: Cambridge Univ. Press.

———. ed. 2016. *The Unpublished Writings of Edith Wharton: Volume 2, Novels and Life Writing*. London: Routledge.

Reverso. n.d. "Translation of 'Narghileh' in English." Accessed January 22, 2021. https://context.reverso.net/translation/french-english/narghileh.

———. n.d. "Table à Tréteaux." Accessed January 22, 2021. https://context .reverso.net/translation/french-english/table+%C3%A0+tr%C3%A9 teaux.

Rey, Alain, ed. (1929) 1981. *Le Petit Robert 2*. 5th ed. (Eugène Melchior, vicomte de Vogüé).

Robert, Paul. 1978. *Le Petit Robert*. London: HarperCollins.

Ronin Gallery. n.d. "Eisen (1790–1848)." Accessed August 8, 2019. https://www.roningallery.com/artists/eisen.

Royal Parks. n.d. "The Albert Memorial." Accessed April 17, 2024. https://www.royalparks.org.uk/visit/parks/kensington-gardens/albert -memorial-discover-more.

Ruhmer, Eberhard. 2019. "Albrecht Dürer." In *Encyclopedia Britannica*, last updated February 28, 2024. https://www.britannica.com/biography /Albrecht-Durer-German-artist.

Sash Window Workshop. n.d. "Casement Windows, Sash Windows." Accessed August 8, 2019. http://www.sashwindow.com/images/pdfs/info graphics/timber_window_type_comparison.jpg.

Schmidt, Louise Boisen. 2013. "Château De Choisy." *This Is Versailles* (blog), November 18, 2013. http://thisisversaillesmadame.blogspot.com/2013/11 /chateau-de-choisy.html.

Sheard, Wendy Stedman. 2019. "Andrea Mantegna." In *Encyclopedia Britannica*, last updated February 18, 2024. https://www.britannica.com /biography/Andrea-Mantegna.

Skliar-Piguet, Alexandra. 2003. "Aviler [Daviler; Davillier], Augustin-Charles d'." Grove Art Online. Accessed January 23, 2021. https://www.oxford artonline.com/groveart/view/10.1093/gao/9781884446054.001.0001/oao -9781884446054-e-7000005336.

Southern Methodist University Bridwell Library Special Collections. n.d. "A Forgotten Roger Payne Binding." Accessed January 20, 2021. https:// bridwell.omeka.net/exhibits/show/sixcenturiesbinding/eighteenth/payne.

Summerson, John. 2019. "Inigo Jones." In *Encyclopedia Britannica*, last updated July 11, 2023. https://www.britannica.com/biography/Inigo-Jones.

Sykes, Leslie Clifford. 2020. "Jean de La Fontaine." In *Encyclopedia Britannica*, last updated April 9, 2023. https://www.britannica.com/biography /Jean-de-La-Fontaine.

Taylor, Patrick. 2006. "Rambouillet, Château de." In *The Oxford Companion to the Garden*, edited by Patrick Taylor. Oxford: Oxford Univ. Press. https://www.oxfordreference.com/view/10.1093/acref/9780198662556 .001.0001/acref-9780198662556-e-1390.

Theoi Greek Mythology. n.d. "Komos." Accessed January 23, 2021. https:// www.theoi.com/Georgikos/SatyrosKomos.html.

Totten, Gary. 2012. "Selling Wharton." In *Edith Wharton in Context*, edited by Laura Rattray, 127–36. Cambridge: Cambridge Univ. Press.

Towheed, Shafquat, ed. 2007. *The Correspondence of Edith Wharton and Macmillan, 1901–1930*. London: Palgrave Macmillan.

Trésor de la langue française informatisé (TLFi). s.v. "Cotonnade." Centre Nationale de Ressources Textuelles et Lexicales. Accessed August 21, 2023. https://www.cnrtl.fr/definition/cotonnade.

Triggs, Oscar Lovell. 2009. *The Arts and Crafts Movement*. New York: Parkstone International.

Tuttleton, James W., Kristin O. Lauer, and Margaret P. Murray. 1992. *Edith Wharton: The Contemporary Reviews*. New York: Cambridge Univ. Press.

Vance, William. 1995. "Edith Wharton's Italian Mask: *The Valley of Decision*." In *The Cambridge Companion to Edith Wharton*, edited by Millicent Bell, 169–98. Cambridge: Cambridge Univ. Press.

Villa Valmarana ai Nani. n.d. "The Villa." Accessed November 29, 2023. https://www.villavalmarana.com/en/.

Walsh, Amy L. 2003. "Mariette Family." Grove Art Online. Last updated January 8, 2024. https://www.oxfordartonline.com/groveart/view/10.1093/gao/9781884446054.001.0001/oao-9781884446054-e-7000054348.

Ward, Gerald, ed. 2008. "Vellum." In *The Grove Encyclopedia of Materials and Techniques in Art*. Oxford Univ. Press. https://www.oxfordreference.com/display/10.1093/acref/9780195395365.001.0001/acref-9780195395365-e-2351?rskey=oFhuH8&result=2349.

Watt, Melinda. 2003. "Textile Production in Europe: Silk, 1600–1800." In *Heilbrunn Timeline of Art History*. New York: Metropolitan Museum of Art. https://www.metmuseum.org/toah/hd/txt_s/hd_txt_s.htm.

———. 2011. "Renaissance Velvet Textiles." In *Heilbrunn Timeline of Art History*. New York: Metropolitan Museum of Art. https://www.metmuseum.org/toah/hd/velv/hd_velv.htm.

Web Gallery of Art. n.d. "The Dream of St Ursula." Accessed August 8, 2019. https://www.wga.hu/frames-e.html?/html/c/carpacci/1ursula/2/50dream.html.

———. n.d. "Frescoes in the Villa Valmarana ai Nani in Vicenza (1757)." Accessed August 8, 2019. https://www.wga.hu/html_m/t/tiepolo/gianbatt/6vicenza/index.html.

———. n.d. "Triumphs of Caesar (1485–95)." Accessed August 8, 2019. https://www.wga.hu/html_m/m/mantegna/10/index.html.

Wharton, Edith. 1897. "Education through the Eyes: Mrs. Wharton Addresses the Teachers on Art in the Schoolroom." Speech reprinted in the *Newport Daily News*, October 8, 1897, 8.

———. 1904. *Italian Villas and Their Gardens*. New York: Century Co. doi: https://doi.org/10.5962/bhl.title.119342.

———. 1905. "March in Italy." In *Italian Backgrounds*. New York: Charles Scribner's Sons. https://www.gutenberg.org/files/54932/54932-h/54932-h.htm.

————. 1907. "A Motor-Flight through France (Part II)." *Atlantic*, January 1907.

————. 1916. *The Book of the Homeless (Le Livre des Sans-Foyer)*. New York: Charles Scribner's Sons.

————. 1919. *French Ways and Their Meaning*. New York: D. Appleton & Company.

————. 1934. *A Backward Glance*. New York: Charles Scribner's Sons.

————. 1938. "A Little Girl's New York." *Harper's*, March 1938.

————. 1968. "The Confessional." In *The Collected Short Stories*, vol. 1, edited by R. W. B. Lewis, 314–43. New York: Charles Scribner's Sons.

————. 1973. *The Ghost Stories of Edith Wharton*. New York: Charles Scribner's Sons.

————. 1998. *Italian Backgrounds*. New York: Ecco, 1998.

————. 2001a. *Bunner Sisters*. In *Edith Wharton: Collected Short Stories, 1911–1937*. Edited by Maureen Howard. New York: Library of America.

————. 2001b. "Sanctuary." In *Edith Wharton: Collected Short Stories, 1891–1910*. Edited by Maureen Howard. New York: Library of America.

————. 2003. *The Age of Innocence*. New York: W. W. Norton.

————. 2006. *The Custom of the Country*. Edited by Linda Wagner-Martin. New York: Penguin.

————. 2016. "Life and I." *The Unpublished Writings of Edith Wharton*, vol. 2, edited by Laura Rattray, 185–204. London: Routledge.

————. 2018. *The House of Mirth*. Edited by Elizabeth Ammons. 2nd ed. New York: W. W. Norton.

————. 2019. *Selected Poems of Edith Wharton*. Edited by Irene Goldman-Price. New York: Scribner.

————. n.d. "The Keys of Heaven—Olney Beecher version." Typescript. YCAL MSS 42, box 9, folder 265, Yale Collection of American Literature, Beinecke Rare Book and Manuscript Library, Yale Univ., New Haven, CT.

Wilson, Richard Guy. 1988. "Edith and Ogden: Writing, Decoration, and Architecture." In *Ogden Codman and the Decoration of Houses*, edited by Pauline C. Metcalf, 133–84. Boston: Boston Athenaeum/David R. Godine.

————. 2012. *Edith Wharton at Home: Life at the Mount*. New York: Monacelli Press.

WOOD Magazine. 2018. "Aniline Dyes." March 19, 2019. https://www.wood magazine.com/materials-guide/finishes/aniline-dyes.

Woolf, Virginia. 2008. "Professions for Women." In *Selected Essays*, edited by David Bradshaw, 140–45. Oxford: Oxford Univ. Press.

WordSense Dictionary. s.v. "Femme Galante." Accessed January 22, 2021. https://www.wordsense.eu/femme_galante/.

YourDictionary. s.v. "Finikin." Accessed August 8, 2019. https://www.your dictionary.com/finikin.

Index

Bachelard, Gaston: *The Poetics of Space*, xxix–xxxi

Backward Glance, A (Wharton, E.), xx, xxiv–xxv, xxxvi–xli, xlvi–xlvii, li–lii, lvii

Bahlmann, Anna, xxxix

ball-room, 28, 51, 123, 169, 172–80, 204

balustrade, 22, 140–43, 175, 206

Balzac, Honoré de, xxix

bas-relief, 70, 95, 98–100, 184, 198, 224

bedroom, 25; eighteenth-century, 164, 209, 218; French, 209–11, 215; mediæval, 151, 195, 206; renaissance, 206; state, 151, 173, 206

bedroom suite, 38, 161, 216–18

bedstead, 38, 151, 206–10, 218

benches, 130–31, 146, 179, 196, 203, 217

Benstock, Shari: *No Gifts from Chance: A Biography of Edith Wharton*, xli

Bérain, Jean, 121, 240

Berenson, Bernard, xxv–xxvi

Berenson, Mary, xxvi, xxxi

Bernini, Gian Lorenzo, 135

Berry, Walter, xl, xliii

"Beyond the Guidebook: Edith Wharton's Rediscovery of San Vivaldo" (Lasansky, D. M.), xxvi

bibelots, 233–34, 237–38, 242–45

Blashfield, Edwin H., xlii–xliv

Blomfield, Reginald, xliii–xliv

Blondel, Jacques-François, 74, 92, 98

Bloomsbury Handbook to Edith Wharton, The (Orlando, E. J.), xxii–xxiv

bookbinding, 41, 184–87, 234, 246

Book Buyer, xlii–xliv, xlviii

bookcase, 161, 183, 186–87, 231; French, 185, 188; glazed, 230; moveable, 185, 188–89; plain, xlv, 38

Bookman, xliii

Book of the Homeless, The (*Le Livre des Sans-Foyer*) (Wharton, E.), xx–xxi, xxix–xxxi, xl

books: as ornaments, 38, 144, 154, 161, 184–89, 194

Borghese Palace, 175

Bosse, Abraham, 86, 152

Botticelli, Sandro, 236

boudoir, 152, 215–18, 240–41

Bramante, Donato, 12

Brett, George Platt, xxxix

Brettingham, Matthew, 101

bric-à-brac, 103, 191, 233, 240–42

Bronzino, Agnolo, 229

Brownell, William Crary, xl

Buccaneers, The (Wharton, E.), xxiv

Buckingham House, 245

bureaux à la Kaunitz, 192

Burlingame, Edward L., xl

cabinet-makers, 90, 158–59, 182, 192, 203

cabinets, 15, 36, 118, 156, 159, 240–41

cabinets (small rooms), 183, 195, 236

Campbell, Gordon: *Vitruvius Britannicus*, 169

candles, 157–59, 176, 203–4

Cantagalli, Ulisse, 131, 224

Carpaccio, Vittore, 87, 229; "Dream of St. Ursula," 87

carpet, xlv, 17, 38, 125, 155, 248; color of, 36, 41–42; nailed-down, 123–26, 203, 210; stair-carpet, 127, 147; Turkish/Smyrna, 42. *See also* rugs

Casino del Grotto, 56, 121

Castel Sainte Claire. *See* Sainte Claire du Vieux Château

Edith Wharton: The Contemporary Reviews (eds. Tuttleton, J. W.; Lauer, K. O.; Murray, M.), xlii–xliv

"Education through the Eyes: Mrs. Wharton Addresses the Teachers on Art in the Schoolroom" (Wharton, E.), xlvii, li

Eisen, Keisai, 164

Encyclopedia of Architecture (Gwilt, J.), 132

English Gentleman's House, The (Kerr, R.), 165

Entertainment Weekly, xxiv

Ethan Frome (Wharton, E.), lvii

Evans, Anne-Marie: "Wharton's Writings on Screen," xxxviii

Evelyn, John, 188

Eve, Nicolas, 186

Felicitous Space: The Imaginative Structures of Edith Wharton and Willa Cather (Fryer, J.), xxxvi, xliv

fenders, 105

Fergusson, James: *History of Architecture*, xxv

fire-backs, 100

fire-boards, 106–8

fire irons, 104–5, 108. *See also* andirons

fireplace, 17, 25, 31, 92–95, 98–109

fire-screen, 106, 234

fixed grate, 101–2. *See also* hob-grate

floors: marble, lix, 17, 112, 122–23, 129, 147, 176, 203; mosaic, 112, 123, 147; parquet, 123, 210; stone, 17, 111, 122, 129, 147, 203; wooden, 111, 123–26, 129, 147, 176, 231

France: living in, xxi, xxxiv, xlii, lv–lix

French locksmiths, 71

French Ways and Their Meaning (Wharton, E.), xx, xxv

Froissart, Jean, 223

Fryer, Judith, xxxv–xxxvi, xliv; *Felicitous Space: The Imaginative Structures of Edith Wharton and Willa Cather*, xxxvi, xliv

"Fulness of Life, The" (Wharton, E.), xxxii

furniture: Adam, 24, 114, 118, 160; arrangement of, 31–32, 51, 156–58, 164, 169, 234; Eastlake, lvi; eighteenth-century, xlv, xlix, 24, 158–62; French, 106, 158; gilt, 40, 244; inexpensive, xlv, 36–39; Italian, 160; made-to-carry, 15, 54, 183, 196, 217; Sheraton, 40, 118; ugly, xliv, 34–36, 39, 222–23, 226; well-made, xlv, lxi, 36–39, 42, 51, 230

Gabriel, Ange-Jacques, 73, 114, 142

gala room, 155–60, 168–73, 176–77, 204. *See also* ball-room; gallery; saloon

gallery, 133, 153, 171–73, 199. *See also* musician's gallery

Gardner, Isabella Stewart, xxxv, l

"Genesis of a Classic, The" (Coles, W. A.), xxxvii, xl

Ghost Stories of Edith Wharton, The (Wharton, E.), xxxiv, lv–lvi, lix

Gilded Age, xviii, xlviii–li, lvi, lxii, 247

Gilder, Richard Watson, xli

gilding, 105–6, 179, 244–45

gimcracks, 164

Giordano, Luca, 119

Goldman-Price, Irene (ed.): *My Dear Governess: The Letters of Edith Wharton and Anna Bahlmann*, xxxix–xli; *Selected Poems of Edith Wharton*, lv

Emily J. Orlando is the E. Gerald Corrigan Endowed Chair in the Humanities and Social Sciences and professor of
English at Fairfield University. She is editor of *The Bloomsbury Handbook to Edith
Wharton* (2023) and author of the award-
winning *Edith Wharton and the Visual
Arts*. She co-edited the essay collection
Edith Wharton and Cosmopolitanism and
has published widely on nineteenth- and
twentieth-century literature and culture,
especially Wharton, Nella Larsen, Oscar
Wilde, Elizabeth Siddall, and the Pre-
Raphaelites. She is a past president of the
Edith Wharton Society.

Printed in the USA
CPSIA information can be obtained
at www.ICGtesting.com
CBHW020849180924
14378CB00005BA/12